Ronald Knox's Lectures on Virgil's *Aeneid*

Also available from Bloomsbury

A.E. Housman: Classical Scholar by Christopher Stray and David Butterfield
Marginal Comment: A Memoir Revisited by Sir Kenneth Dover
Scholarship and Controversy: Centenary Essays on the Life and Work of Sir Kenneth Dover edited by Stephen Halliwell and Christopher Stray

Ronald Knox's Lectures on Virgil's *Aeneid*

With Introduction and Critical Essays

Edited by Francesca Bugliani Knox

BLOOMSBURY ACADEMIC
LONDON • NEW YORK • OXFORD • NEW DELHI • SYDNEY

BLOOMSBURY ACADEMIC
Bloomsbury Publishing Plc
50 Bedford Square, London, WC1B 3DP, UK
1385 Broadway, New York, NY 10018, USA
29 Earlsfort Terrace, Dublin 2, Ireland

BLOOMSBURY, BLOOMSBURY ACADEMIC and the Diana logo are trademarks of
Bloomsbury Publishing Plc

First published in Great Britain 2023
Paperback edition published 2025

Copyright Francesca Bugliani Knox & Contributors, 2023

Francesca Bugliani Knox has asserted her right under the Copyright,
Designs and Patents Act, 1988, to be identified as Author of this work.

For legal purposes the Acknowledgements on p. xii constitute an
extension of this copyright page.

Cover design: Terry Woodley
Cover image: John Roddam Spencer Stanhope, The Waters of Lethe by the
Plains of Elysium, 1880. © Painters / Alamy Stock Photo

All rights reserved. No part of this publication may be reproduced or transmitted
in any form or by any means, electronic or mechanical, including photocopying,
recording, or any information storage or retrieval system, without prior permission
in writing from the publishers.

Bloomsbury Publishing Plc does not have any control over, or responsibility for, any
third-party websites referred to or in this book. All internet addresses given
in this book were correct at the time of going to press. The author and publisher
regret any inconvenience caused if addresses have changed or sites have
ceased to exist, but can accept no responsibility for any such changes.

A catalogue record for this book is available from the British Library.

A catalog record for this book is available from the Library of Congress.

ISBN:	HB:	978-1-3501-1828-7
	PB:	978-1-3503-5427-2
	ePDF:	978-1-3501-1829-4
	eBook:	978-1-3501-1830-0

Typeset by RefineCatch Limited, Bungay, Suffolk

To find out more about our authors and books visit www.bloomsbury.com
and sign up for our newsletters.

To R. O. K.

Virgil has, whether deliberately or instinctively, transformed the whole nature of the epic
Ronald Knox

Contents

List of Illustrations ... ix
List of Contributors ... x
Acknowledgements ... xii

Foreword *Charles Martindale* ... 1

Introduction: The Context of Ronald Knox's Lectures on Virgil
  Francesca Bugliani Knox ... 17

Note on the Lecture List (Literae Humaniores) in
  The Oxford University Gazette (18 January 1912) ... 37

Editing Criteria ... 39

Part One Ronald Knox's Lectures on Virgil

1 Virgil's Political Outlook ... 45

2 Virgil's Religious Outlook ... 61

3 Virgil's Romance and Pathos ... 85

4 Virgil's Art and Treatment of His Story ... 97

5 Virgil's Appreciation of Scenery ... 113

6 Virgil's Use of His Sources ... 127

7 Note on the Composition of Book III ... 151

8 Characteristics of Virgil's Style and Versification ... 159

Part Two Critical Essays

9 Ronald Knox's Lectures on Virgil: 'A Wealth of Delicate Tenderness'
   Matthew McGowan ... 179

10 Ronald Knox's Lectures on Virgil: Their Relevance for Scholarly
    Interpretation of the *Aeneid* *Francesco Montarese*   195

11 The Setting of the Lecture Given by Monsignor Ronald Knox
    to the Virgil Society on 31 March 1946 *John Mair*   229

Appendix: J. E. Lowe, Ronald Knox and the Virgil Society
    Lecture Entitled 'The Problem of Dido and Aeneas'
    Francesca Bugliani Knox   241

Index   245

Illustrations

1. Detail from *The Adoration of the Mystic Lamb*, also called *The Ghent Altarpiece*, by Hubert Van Eyck and Jan Van Eyck — 2
2. The Gryphon Club, Trinity College Oxford, 1913 — 23
3. Lecture List (Literae Humaniores) in the *Oxford University Gazette* (18 January 1912) — 38
4. A large Roman galley or quinquereme ready for battle at Actium in 31 BC — 199
5. Detail from *St Francis in the Desert* by Giovanni Bellini, 1480 — 200
6. Detail from *The Agony in the Garden* by Andrea Mantegna, 1457–59 — 201

Contributors

Francesca Bugliani Knox is Honorary Senior Research Associate at UCL. She graduated from Pisa University and has a PhD from the University of London. Her main interest is the connection between literature, theology and spirituality. She has published books and articles on various aspects of English, European and Italian literature from the Renaissance to the present. She is the editor of *Ronald Knox: A Man for All Seasons* (2016).

Matthew McGowan is Associate Professor of Classics at Fordham University in New York City. His research focuses on Latin literature, ancient scholarship and classical reception, and he is the author of *Ovid in Exile* (2009) and co-editor (with Elizabeth Macaulay-Lewis) of *Classical New York: Greece and Rome in Gotham* (2018). He is currently writing a commentary on the *Nux* attributed to Ovid and completing a study of the Classics in early Jesuit education.

John Mair is a retired civil servant who was for some years a part-time student at Birkbeck College, London, where he worked under the supervision of the late Professor Robert Browning. He made a study of the *Institutiones Saecularium Litterarum* of Cassiodorus, and then proceeded to write a doctoral thesis about the Theological Tractates attributed to Boethius. John has published essays and articles in *Festschriften* and in learned journals, and more recently his two books about railways in the Welsh Marches and West Midlands have also been published.

Charles Martindale is Professor of Latin Emeritus at the University of Bristol and is especially known for his work within classical reception studies. He has written widely on the relationship between classical and English literature, and, together with David Hopkins, is general editor of the five-volume *Oxford History of Classical Reception in English Literature*. He is the editor of *Virgil and His Influence* (1984), and *The Cambridge Companion to Virgil* (1997, revised edition co-edited with Fiachra Mac Góráin, 2019). His other interests include translation and aesthetics. He is currently co-editing a volume on Walter Pater as a critic of English literature.

Francesco Montarese teaches Greek and Latin and Classical Civilization at Mander Portman Woodward, London. He has a BA, MA and PhD from the Department of Classics at UCL. His main interests are Lucretius and the reception of Greek philosophy in Latin literature. He has published *Lucretius and His Sources* (2012), an essay 'Lucrèce et Épicure sur la nature', which appeared in the volume *Les préocratiques à Rome*, edited by Carlos Lévy (2018), and a chapter on 'Ronald Knox as Classicist' published in *Ronald Knox: A Man for All Seasons* (2016). Currently he is working on Lucy Hutchinson's translation of Lucretius' *De Rerum Natura*.

Acknowledgements

I should like to thank Lady Magdalen Howard, Executor of the Literary Estate of Ronald Knox and the owner of the copyright in the works of Ronald Knox, for granting permission to reproduce the lectures on Virgil that Ronald Knox gave at Trinity College, Oxford, in 1912. My thanks also to the Earl and Countess of Oxford for their generous hospitality and advice and for their permission to consult the archives at Mells. This volume would not have come about had it not been for the help that I received from Ampleforth Abbey and the access that they granted me to the correspondence between Ronald Knox and Laurence Eyres and to Eyres's transcript of Ronald Knox's lectures. My thanks to the archivist Fr Anselm Cramer, and to the present Abbott, Dom Robert Igo. Fr Nicholas Schofield, Archivist of the Westminster Diocesan Archives kindly helped me consult material relating to Ronald Knox's time at St Edmund's College; to him, too, I owe my knowledge of the 'green box' of unpublished papers on Ronald Knox that the Diocese recently received from the National Catholic Library. Many thanks also to Dr Clare Hopkins, the Archivist at Trinity College, Oxford, for access to the Ronald Knox archives there and for identifying the rooms where the lectures were taught and to whom. The Oxford University Catholic Chaplaincy archives and Jesuit in Britain Archives were also valuable resources for my research.

Members of the Virgil Society, in particular, Carlotta Dionisotti, John Mair and Laurence Kenworthy-Browne encouraged me at the outset to publish the lectures. My thanks to Jill Kraye for her encouragement in the early stages of my endevours. Alice Wright, Lily Mac Mahon and Zoe Osman at Bloomsbury have seen the book through from its inception to its publication. I am most grateful to them.

Thanks are due for permission to reprint the following copyright materials: a) an excerpt from 'Bann Valley Eclogue' from *Electric Light* by Seamus Heaney. Copyright © 2001 by Seamus Heaney. Reprinted by permission of Farrar, Straus and Giroux. All Rights Reserved. b) an excerpt from 'Memorial for the City' by W. H. Auden. Copyright © 1949 by W. H. Auden, renewed. Reprinted by permission of Curtis Brown, Ltd. All rights reserved.

Finally, the person I owe the most is my husband Dilwyn, a great-nephew of Ronald Knox, who has helped me at various stages in the preparation of this book.

Foreword

Charles Martindale

The city of Ghent in Belgium is home to one of the greatest and most famous works of Western art. The Ghent altarpiece, by the brothers Hubert and Jan van Eyck, is a massive polyptych, whose central panel shows the Adoration of the Lamb from the book of Revelation. Among the adoring prophets and patriarchs, close to Isaiah, is a figure with a laurel crown who has been identified as Virgil (see Figure 1). On the outer doors of the altarpiece is a Sibyl, with a scroll containing Latin words adapted from *Aeneid* 6, the book in which Aeneas descends into the Underworld to be shown both Tartarus and the Elysian fields, pagan equivalents of Hell and Heaven. No doubt many of today's visitors to St Bavo's Cathedral in Ghent find the presence of a pagan poet in a Christian scene a puzzling one. It would not have puzzled Ronald Knox, student of the classics turned Catholic priest – indeed he is part of a long and distinguished tradition that in various ways makes connections between Virgil and Christianity.

Why should anyone read Virgil today? Who would not prefer, say, the sexy and anti-establishment Ovid, whose work has seen a remarkable revival of interest in recent decades? The three canonical poems by Virgil, it might be argued, are in genres almost as dead as the dodo.[1] The *Eclogues* is a collection of pastorals, a form of writing that Dr Johnson, in his famous critique of Milton's 'Lycidas', derided as 'easy, vulgar, and therefore disgusting'. The *Georgics* is a didactic work purporting to teach us how to farm, an unpromising subject for many post-Romantic readers of poetry. The *Aeneid* is an epic describing the founding of the Roman Empire and praising Augustus the first Emperor, an autocrat who finally overthrew the Republican system of government established in Rome after the expulsion of the kings. Worse, it is a poem that has been appropriated for some pretty unsavoury causes, including Italian fascism. In Italy the Virgil bimillennial celebrations of 1930 were used to honour Mussolini, who saw himself as Augustus' successor and established a new Italian empire by invading Abyssinia.

Figure 1 Detail from *The Adoration of the Mystic Lamb*, also called *The Ghent Altarpiece*, by Hubert Van Eyck and Jan Van Eyck. Fifteenth-century polyptych altarpiece in St Bavo's Cathedral, Ghent, Belgium.

Why then read Virgil? There are a great many good answers one could give to this question. One of the best would be that anyone who has any interest at all in that entity, or non-entity, which used to be called 'Western civilization', or just 'the West', *has* to take account of Virgil. T. S. Eliot, who wrote two important essays about Virgil, 'What Is a Classic?', the Presidential address to the newly formed Virgil Society in 1944, and 'Virgil and the Christian World', given as a radio talk in 1951, called him 'the classic of all Europe';[2] and it is hard to dissent. In similar vein in 1934 the Austrian writer Theodor Haecker, like Knox a Catholic convert, as well as a leading opponent of Nazism, entitled his once influential book *Virgil, Father of the West*. In particular the *Aeneid*, hailed in advance of its publication by Virgil's younger contemporary, the poet Propertius, as 'something greater than the *Iliad*', displaced all earlier Latin epics (which as a result survive today only in sparse fragments) and became the central text of the school curriculum, just as Homer's *Iliad* had been in the Greek world. And there it remained for more than a millennium and a half, when Latin was the *lingua franca* for the whole of Europe. No poet occupies the same position in the modern world, not even Shakespeare, partly because English does not unite the West in quite the way that Latin did in the Middle Ages and the Renaissance. When Charlemagne, whom some have called the founder of Europe, was crowned Holy Roman Emperor in 800, the transfer of Empire, *translatio imperii*, from the Romans to the Franks was accompanied by the transfer of education, *translatio studii*, the scholarly appropriation of the Roman past, with Virgil as its core text; the two acts of transference, of claimed succession, are closely intertwined.

Poetry matters, quipped the Russian poet Osip Mandelstam, it gets people killed. Many people get killed in the *Aeneid*, and many have been killed in the imperial projects that it helped to underwrite. At the centre of the poem is the famous injunction of Anchises to his son Aeneas and his Roman successors (6.847–53), given thus in Dryden's complete translation of Virgil of 1697:

> Let others better mould the running mass
> Of metals, and inform the breathing brass,
> And soften into flesh a marble face;
> Plead better at the bar, describe the skies,
> And when the stars descend, and when they rise.
> But, Rome, 'tis thine alone, with awful sway,
> To rule mankind, and make the world obey;
> Disposing peace and war thy own majestic way;
> To tame the proud, the fettered slave to free –
> These are imperial arts, and worthy thee.

Imperialism is a crucial part of our history as Europeans, and, if we are to try to understand that history, the *Aeneid* as the great poem of Empire is one essential text. The poem pays tribute to the sufferings of the victims of Empire, like Dido Queen of Carthage, and to the cost paid by the imperialists themselves: the sacrifice of happiness, the loss of home and loved ones – all this is part of the ideology of empire articulated with unique gravity and power by Virgil. And, for all our fine words, we have perhaps not altogether escaped this ideology, nor would we necessarily wish, or be wise, so to do. Both the European Community (formerly the EEC), set up significantly by the Treaty of Rome, and the United Nations with its Security Council charged with maintaining world peace, if necessary by military action, can readily be seen as successors of the Roman Empire. Might we regard, for example, the intervention of the Western powers in a Balkans that had collapsed into tribal violence as an assumption of the duty, enunciated by Anchises in the passage just quoted, 'to add custom to peace, spare those who are humbled, and war down the proud' (*Aen.* 6.852–3)? Whatever one thinks in general of the Roman Empire, the long-lasting *pax Romana* did bring the benefits of peace to many of its inhabitants.[3]

We can likewise ask why today we should read Ronald Knox's previously unpublished lectures on Virgil, delivered in 1912 to students in Oxford, particularly as he himself never prepared them carefully for publication. After all, scholarship has surely moved on since then, and the lectures might seem now merely outdated, with little to teach us. Moreover, they are at that awkward point when they have not yet quite entered 'history' but can occasionally feel quaintly old fashioned, even at times embarrassingly so, like the views of a much-loved elderly relative (as when Knox writes in lecture 2 of 'that fluffy little pink-and-white creature Lavinia', or in lecture 1 that 'Aeneas is to Turnus, what Prospero is to Caliban in the *Tempest*, the White man, and consequently the master of the savage'). One of my predecessors as Professor of Latin at Bristol, Niall Rudd, liked to tell me that the writings of classical scholars normally had a shelf-life of only thirty years, after which they necessarily sunk into oblivion and irrelevance as scholarship advanced. The extraordinary growth of classical reception studies over recent decades has undermined the distinctly Whiggish assumptions in such a view.[4] Of course, we have new data and new discoveries that were unknown to our ancestors, but, like literature itself, scholarship is not on any simple progressive trajectory. There is no classical scholar today who can compete as a textual critic with Joseph Scaliger, Bentley, or Housman; the latest interpretation is not necessarily superior to older ones. We would do better to remember the trenchant couplet from Alexander Pope's *Essay on Criticism* (438–9):

We think our fathers fools, so wise we grow –
Our wiser sons, no doubt, will think *us* so.

From that point of view, it is interesting to find that in his first lecture Knox espouses not only a reception position but a rather extreme version of it:

> That the importance of external history to the understanding of the *Aeneid* lies, not in the history of the world before or during Virgil's life, but in the history of the world since Virgil's death. [. . .] To understand him, you must appreciate not the influence which earlier literature had on Virgil, but the influence which Virgil has had on later literature.[5]

His witty remarks on the spelling of Virgil's name likewise firmly choose reception over origination:

> So the first way to make sure that you understand Virgil is to spell his name wrong. Always spell it with two i's, never with an e. Virgilius is the language of the Ages, and of the Church: Vergilius is a silly piece of pedantry raked up by unsympathetic modern scholars.[6]

Knox even employs presciently a favourite trope of our new receptionists (as previously of T. S. Eliot), the reversal of time's arrow: 'it sounds paradoxical, but it is strictly true that Virgil owes at least as much to Dante as he does to Homer'.[7]

Knox's intimacy with the Western tradition is one advantage he has as an interpreter of Virgil over the narrower sort of classical scholar today. And there is another. Knox was imbued, 'saturated', to use his own word, with the Latin language in a way that is hard to appreciate, let alone replicate today, even among the learned. In that sense he had more in common with earlier ages than with our own, writing to a friend:

> I am now toying with the idea of a new lecture on 'What the Classical Tradition does NOT mean to us,' a general onslaught on the habit of substituting lantern lectures on Syracuse for Latin Verse, and, if I am feeling thoroughly depressed when I write it, a complaint that the classical tradition as an idea in education has already become obsolete, that we are teaching scholarship to specialists, and giving people degrees for knowing how to admire Praxiteles, but no longer attempting to saturate people with the classics, as our grandfathers were saturated with them.[8]

Knox himself started Latin at the age of four, and was reading the *Aeneid* fluently aged six. Latin was to him hardly a foreign language; he was, so to say, at home in it. While it is true that as Anglican Chaplain at Trinity College, Oxford, he taught Classical Mods, he was not quite a classical scholar in the way we might now understand the term (though, as Francesco Montarese has argued, his departures on specific interpretative issues from today's consensus often merit revisiting[9]). But his unusual intimacy with Latin allowed him on many occasions to cut to the quick. Readers of this book will quickly find their own examples. Here are two of mine. First, what *in nuce* makes Virgil's writing so unique, so different from that of other Latin poets? This is Knox's answer, from lecture 8, citing such lines as 'Tendebant manus ripae ulterioris amore' (6.314): 'the whole glory and distinction of which is that there is no word . . . which could not be translated at sight by any private-school-boy, and that the phrases as a whole defy the best efforts of the most competent translators'.[10] Second, the fifth lecture demonstrates persuasively that 'Virgil is the first of the landscape-painters, because he likes landscape for its own sake, and the first of the impressionists, because he is ready to sacrifice the details to give you the effect', a claim once again reinforced by Virgil's reception and his perhaps surprising importance for both garden design and the history of landscape painting.

Knox's deep familiarity with the *Aeneid* is also demonstrated by his choosing to translate parts of it. As the poet-painter Dante Gabriel Rossetti, himself an experienced translator, wisely observed, 'a translation – involving as it does the necessity of settling many points without discussion – remains perhaps the most direct form of commentary'.[11] In the 1920s Oxford's Clarendon Press issued a series of books for teaching use that, rather unusually, combined passages from the original text with passages in translation, and in 1924 Knox contributed a small volume covering *Aeneid* 7–9. For his own verse translations he chose the heroic couplet, as used by Dryden, as in his view the only suitable equivalent for Virgil's hexameter – where many other translators by this date preferred blank verse or longer lines. However, he thought Dryden's own translation – still the best we have in English – too expansive to serve as a crib for a beginner. By contrast, his version kept rather closer to the outlines of Virgil's 'sense'. Knox was obviously not a significant poet, and his version is an exercise in an outmoded poetic idiom, an elegant pastiche if you like. But it is a successful one on its own terms, which reminds the reader that we are dealing with a poem but in a way that would also be rather more useful than Dryden's for someone construing the Latin.[12] Here is Knox's version of the episode in *Aeneid* 7 when Juno opens the Gates of War:

> These stand, inviolate through age-long dread,
> Their hundred brazen bolts securely wed
> To immemorial iron: while he keeps
> Watch o'er their threshold, Janus never sleeps.
> These, if the senate's voice to battle call,
> The consul's self, his vesture Quirinal
> Girt in Gabinian wise, open must fling,
> Their unaccustomed hinges clamouring;

> War he proclaims, for war the people cry,
> And brazen horns utter their harsh reply.
> Resolute in that hour Latinus flees
> From the dread contact of the fateful keys;
> And, called to open duly the grim gates,
> Hides in the darkness from the task he hates.
> Then the Saturnian Queen, from heaven-height
> Descending, thrust apart with unseen might
> The laggard portals; back the hinges swung,
> And back the iron gates of war were flung.[13]

I have already used the word 'appropriation': the absorption of the text into the mind-set and belief system of the reader. Postmodern critics often suggest that all texts are infinitely malleable and thus capable of being appropriated for endlessly diverse, and indeed opposed, positions. No doubt there is a measure of truth in this, as the reception histories of a great many works of literature suggest. Homer's *Iliad*, for example, has been read both as a glorification of war and as an anti-war poem. However, Virgil's poetry has a quite special potency in this regard, which I would argue is a product of what Virgil has made, as well as of the inevitable vagaries and contingencies of reception. An extreme example of the phenomenon is the so-called *sortes Virgilianae*, a practice whose efficacy has been amply confirmed by the historical record. An individual about to make a momentous decision opens Virgil's text at random and alights on a passage that will reveal and shape his or her future. For example, King Charles I consulted a copy of Virgil in the Bodleian library in Oxford, which foretold his defeat by Parliament. This is reading as total appropriation; the text becomes wholly one with the life of the reader. Significantly the only other book that has been regularly used in this way is the Bible. More generally the poems in a curious fashion relate both to the experience of individuals and to what has happened in the West since Virgil's death. Among my favourite insights into the special character of Virgil's art is this from one of Ronald Knox's best loved and most ebullient books, *Let Dons Delight* (1939): 'Virgil – he has the gift, has he not, of summing up in a phrase used at random the aspiration and the tragedy of minds he could never have understood; that is the real poetic genius'.[14] The famous words *sunt lacrimae rerum* (*Aen.* 1.462) in their context where Aeneas views scenes from the Trojan war on the temple gates at Carthage may simply imply something like 'there are people who feel sympathy for Trojan sufferings'. But they have much wider resonances for those with Romantic sensibilities or those who see the world as a vale of tears. In his first lecture Knox notes the extraordinary capacity that passages from the *Aeneid* have for recontextualizations of this kind:

> Virgil [...] writes his memorable lines with reference to a single, definite, and not necessarily very important occasion. 'Timeo Danaos et dona ferentes' is a quite random comment of Laocoon on the Trojan horse: 'Non tali auxilio, nec defensoribus istis/ Tempus eget' is the outcry of Hecuba when she sees a ridiculous old man like Priam putting on his armour to fight against Neoptolemus: 'Facilis descensus Averno' is a perfectly matter-of-fact way of saying that it is easier to get into Tartarus than to get out of it. Yet Daily Mail leaders quote 'Facilis descensus' in connection with national degeneration, and the Spectator pulverizes Tariff Reformers with 'Non tali auxilio', and elderly clergymen write to the Church Times applying 'Timeo Danaos' to Liberal Education Bills.[15]

It is worth noting here how classical and Latinate is Knox's own writing, in its sentence structure and syntax, and with its two tricola.

The appropriation of Virgil that has been most widespread and long-lasting is his appropriation for forms of Christianity. It is a process that begins early. The story went that St Paul visited Virgil's tomb, and declared: 'What would I have made you, if I had found you alive, greatest of poets!' *Anima naturaliter Christiana*, a soul by light of nature Christian, is a phrase of Tertullian, one of the fathers of the Church, which has repeatedly been applied to Virgil. Dante's *Divine Comedy*, the greatest poem of the Middle Ages, can be read as an extended gloss on Tertullian's phrase and as a revision and correction of the *Aeneid*, as Virgil guides Dante through Hell and accompanies him through Purgatory only to vanish at the appearance of Beatrice: 'Virgil had left us bereft of him, Virgil sweetest father, to whom I gave myself for my salvation' (*Purgatorio* 30. 49–51, trans. John D. Sinclair). Virgil is at once the master poet of the Western tradition and a fallible human being whose pessimism Dante implicitly rebukes and who cannot share in the full joys of Paradise. Since late antiquity and the time of Constantine the Great, the fourth so-called Messianic Eclogue, which describes how the birth and maturation of a child will coincide with a return of the Golden Age, had been interpreted as a prophecy of Christ. Dante, whose importance for the understanding of Virgil Knox underlines, makes a memorable scene out of this interpretation; in *Purgatorio* XXII.73 the Latin epic poet Statius explains his double debt to his master: 'through you I became a poet, through you a Christian'– he has already quoted lines from Eclogue 4. Here is Dryden's version of part of Virgil's poem, which gestures towards the Old Testament and Isaiah (which some now think that Virgil himself also alludes to, perhaps by way of the Sibylline Oracles) and towards Christ himself in the phrase 'her infant king':

> The son shall lead the life of gods, and be
> By gods and heroes seen, and gods and heroes see.
> The jarring nations he in peace shall bind,
> And with paternal virtues rule mankind.
> Unbidden earth shall wreathing ivy bring
> And fragrant herbs, the promises of spring,
> As her first offerings to her infant king.
> The goats with strutting dugs shall homeward speed,
> And lowing herds, secure from lions, feed.
> His cradle shall with rising flowers be crowned;
> The serpent's brood shall die; the sacred ground
> Shall weeds and poisonous plants refuse to bear;
> Each common bush shall Syrian roses wear.

Eliot saw the link between Dante and Virgil as central to European civilization, with Virgil as a bridge between pagan and Christian culture. Virgil's 'empire without end' prefigured Augustine's City of God. Eliot did not suppose, any more than had Dante himself, that the historical Virgil was in any way conscious of these things. Rather Virgil's works can be read, as they usually are by scholars, under the aspect of their time, but they can also be read under the aspect of the timeless. As Eliot puts it, 'the Roman Empire which Virgil imagined and for which Aeneas worked out his destiny was not exactly the same as the Roman Empire of the legionaries, the proconsuls and governors, the business men and speculators, the demagogues and generals. It was something greater, but something which exists' – and here note the present tense – 'because Virgil imagined it'.[16] It is in this Eliotic spirit that the Nobel laureate, Seamus Heaney turned to Virgil his 'hedge-schoolmaster' and to Eclogue 4 and 'the child that's due', in his poem 'Bann Valley Eclogue' from *Electric Light* (2001). Here Heaney celebrates the peace process in Northern Ireland, with the sense of a world washed clean, the possibility of a new start. Virgil teaches the poet that the old words have not ended their usefulness, or their power:

> Here are my words you'll have to find a place for:
> *Carmen, ordo, nascitur, saeculum, gens.*
> Their gist in your tongue and province should be clear
> Even at this stage. Poetry, order, the times,
> The nation, wrong and renewal, then an infant birth
> And a flooding away of all the old miasma. (7–12)

Knox's lectures clearly belong to this central tradition in Virgilian interpretation. Virgil is partly being read in the light of the old doctrine of the gradual preparation of the world for the Incarnation, of *praeparatio evangelica*. In his lecture on Virgil's religion, Knox points to Catholic elements in Virgil's thinking, and writes that 'Virgil, whose soul is naturally Catholic, is up to the distinction between mortal and venial sins'.[17] He lays great stress on the religious component in Virgil's conception of *pietas*. An 'inborn liturgical instinct in the Italian mind', strongly embodied in Aeneas 'that trained liturgiologist', with its principle that 'there should be one way of doing things, and one only, for all the world, and that there should be no spiritual contingency, however remote, which could not be met by a fixed and appropriate method of spiritual treatment', fed into 'the ritual of Christendom'.[18] Of one passage (*Aen.* 5.688–9), with its 'thoroughly Jewish' sense of a covenant, he writes that 'we can almost hear the Jew speaking'; and he often cites the Psalms and other Old Testament texts alongside Virgil. And, he also argues, 'Virgil, if he does not reach the idea of Providence, at least rises to that of destiny'.[19] Long ago I was struck by this rather swashbuckling passage from R. M. Ogilvie:

> Virgil is an author who has never appealed to English character; he is too religious, too little Humanist. It's no paradox that Christians from the Middle Ages down to Ronald Knox have turned to him for spiritual comfort, nor is it a paradox that, for the most part, the English editors of Virgil have been either lunatic or incompetent.[20]

Of course, this is a considerable overstatement, since there have been many distinguished English Virgilians, but there is perhaps some truth in it. However, we can flip the judgement: Knox's Catholicism puts him at the centre, not the periphery, of the European classical tradition; and that is something that helps to qualify him as a guide to the *Aeneid*.

Apart from the lectures themselves, the extent to which Knox was saturated with Virgil, and more importantly the way that Virgil is profoundly intertwined in his spiritual life as a Christian, can be illustrated from two other of his works. There is no clear endorsement of the Catholic doctrine of Purgatory in the Bible, hence its rejection by Protestant reformers on the principle of *sola scriptura*. When reflecting on what the experience of Purgatory by souls redeemed but still separated from God might be like in an essay published in *The Tablet* in 1941, 'Virgil and the Future Life', Knox turns, interestingly, not to Dante's *Purgatorio*, but to the sixth book of the *Aeneid*.[21] He ruminates on three highly evocative passages, which in his view are expressive of the *frustration* of souls in Purgatory, including the famous one already quoted describing the unburied dead reaching out in longing for the further bank of the river Styx (where the predominant mood of melancholy is complicated by a sense of hope in the preceding simile about the birds flying to sunny lands):

> my point is that Virgil didn't think of death as cancelling all obligations, reducing you, for better or worse, to the position we describe nowadays as a 'dead end'. No, there was progress still to be achieved, there was lee-way still to be made up, for some of us anyhow, after death.[22]

Of course, Virgil knew nothing of the doctrine, the source is rather, in Knox's characterization of it, in Virgil's dream-world – and frustration, as Knox also remarks, is a particularly common dream experience.

At much greater length Knox drew heavily on Virgil for his account of his conversion from Anglicanism to the Church of Rome – I choose that designation deliberately – which he entitled *A Spiritual Aeneid* (1918). Each chapter of the book is headed by a quotation from the poem, lines and episodes constantly providing parallels to events in Knox's life or spiritual illumination of some kind.[23] Of course, in using Virgil in this way, Knox, as he well knew, was following a tradition of allegorical exegesis of the *Aeneid* that went back through the Renaissance to the Middle Ages and Late Antiquity. For example, in the influential reading of Fulgentius (fifth–sixth century AD), books 1–6 represented different phases in the development of a human soul from childhood to maturity – an approach still reflected in the use of a developmental model in accounts by many modern scholars of the character of Aeneas. In an analogous manner Cristoforo Landino (1424–98), the leading Florentine Neoplatonist and interpreter of Virgil, allegorized the *Aeneid* as a journey to philosophical enlightenment, the *summum bonum*. It is curious in that regard that, while we often talk of a person's odyssey, we do not generally speak, despite Knox's usage, of his or her aeneid.

Over the last couple of centuries Homer appears to have been more generally admired than Virgil, who began to slip from his position as 'the classic of all Europe' and 'Father of the West'. But, like Ronald Knox, I would argue that it is Virgil who speaks most directly to our condition. It is the post-Virgilian, not the Homeric city that we inhabit, and one name for that city has always been Rome. As I write this Foreword, war has again broken out in Europe, as Russian armour sets about the obliteration of Ukraine. It is at such times that Virgil so often assumes a particular resonance. In 1940 Helen Waddell, who did so much to introduce readers to the Latin lyrics of the Middle Ages, turned to Virgil in the face of the threat to civilization posed by Nazism:

It was expedient that Rome should die. For one must die to become a legend: and the Roman legend was the inspiration of Europe. It is a strange thing to remember that in the meridian of her power, she herself looked back to her beginnings in a conquered city and a burning town: and the man who gave her immortality was the hollow-cheeked sad-eyed Virgil of the Hadrumetum mosaic. If all else goes from the schools, let us at least keep the second book of Virgil. I speak of it with passion, for something sent me to it on that September afternoon when the Luftwaffe first broke through the defences of London, and that night it seemed as though London and her river burned. You remember the cry of Aeneas waking in the night, the rush, arming as he went, the hurried question – 'Where's the fighting now?' – and the answer:

> Come is the ending day, Troy's hour is come,
> The ineluctable hour.
> Once were we chosen men,
> And Troy was once, and once a mighty glory
> Of the Trojan race.[24]

That passage ends with Waddell's translation of some of the most moving lines in the poem, a memorable translation in its way, though it cannot match the power and plangency and resonance of the original – no translation into English so far, not even Dryden's, has ever done that for Virgil. *Aeneid* 2 is perhaps the finest account ever given of the end of a city and of a civilization. But the grief is countered by the sense that, in words from T. S. Eliot's *Four Quartets*, 'in my end is my beginning', since a new city will eventually rise, phoenix-like, from ashes of the old. W. H. Auden suggests something similar in his great poem *Memorial for the City*, written amid the ruins of post-war Europe, at the birth pangs of a new age, with a stanza of which I will end:

> The steady eyes of the crow and the camera's candid eye
> See as honestly as they know how, but they lie.
> The crime of life is not time. Even now, in this night
> Among the ruins of the Post-Vergilian City
> Where our past is a chaos of graves and the barbed-wire stretches ahead
> Into our future till it is lost to sight,
> Our grief is not Greek: As we bury our dead
> We know without knowing there is reason for what we bear,
> That our hurt is not a desertion, that we are to pity
> Neither ourselves nor our city;
> Whoever the searchlights catch, whatever the loudspeakers blare,
> We are not to despair.[25]

Notes

1. It is true that the *Eclogues* and *Georgics* are again appealing to classicists as a result of ecocriticism and labour studies; sadly, however, what happens within the discipline of classics today has little impact on the wider culture.
2. It is interesting that many involved in the formation of the Virgil Society were Catholics or High Anglicans; see John Mair's essay in this volume (Chapter 11).
3. For Rome as a precursor of the EU, see Anthony Pagden, *The Pursuit of Empire: A History* (Oxford: Oxford University Press, 2021).
4. A useful survey of the presence of Virgil in the last century is Theodore Ziolkowski, *Virgil and the Moderns* (Princeton, NJ: Princeton University Press, 1993); though Knox is never mentioned, the book gives a broad context for his work on Virgil.
5. See Chapter 1 in this volume, Ronald Knox, 'Virgil's Political Outlook', 46.
6. Ibid., 48.
7. Ibid., 47.
8. Quoted in *Ronald Knox: A Man for All Seasons*, ed. Francesca Bugliani Knox (Toronto: Pontifical Institute of Medieval Studies, 2016), 149.
9. Francesco Montarese, 'Ronald Knox as Classicist', ibid., 147–65; see too Montarese's essay in this volume (Chapter 10).
10. For this reason translations of Virgil give us only a limited sense of what it is like to read the *Aeneid* in the original; see Charles Martindale, 'English Virgil? – From Surrey to Tennyson', in *The Afterlife of Virgil*, ed. Peter Mack and John North (London: Institute of Classical Studies, School of Advanced Study, University of London, 2017), 137–53.
11. D. G. Rossetti, *The Works of Dante Gabriel Rossetti*, ed. W. M. Rossetti (London: Ellis, 1911), 283.
12. See Montarese, 'Ronald Knox as Classicist', 161–3.
13. Virgil, *Aeneid Books VII to IX*, partly in the original and partly in English verse translation. Introduction and translation by Ronald Knox (Oxford: Clarendon Press, 1924), 7. Copies are rare, but there is one in the Bodleian Library.
14. Ronald Knox, *Let Dons Delight* (London: Sheed and Ward, 1939), 197–8. I first encountered this quotation in a fine essay by my friend Stephen Medcalf, another devotee of a Virgil who anticipates Christianity, 'Virgil at the Turn of Time', in *Virgil and His Influence*, ed. Charles Martindale (Bristol: Bristol Classical Press, 1984), 215–44.
15. See Chapter 1 in this volume, Ronald Knox, 'Virgil's Political Outlook', 48.
16. T. S. Eliot, 'Virgil and the Christian World', in *On Poetry and Poets* (London: Faber and Faber, 1957), 130.
17. See Chapter 2 in this volume, Ronald Knox, 'Virgil's Religious Outlook', 77.
18. Ibid., 63.

19 Ibid., 68.
20 Robert M. Ogilvie, *Latin and Greek: A History of the Influence of the Classics on English Life from 1600 to 1918* (London: Routledge and Kegan Paul, 1964), 176.
21 Text in *Ronald Knox*, ed. Bugliani Knox, 349–54, 350.
22 *Aeneid* 6.313–14. The other two passages are 489–93 (the frustrations of the ghostly Greek warriors in trying to cry out); 700–2 (the frustration of Aeneas trying to embrace his father Anchises).
23 For the details, see 'Appendix: Uses of the *Aeneid* in *A Spiritual Aeneid*', compiled by Francesco Montarese, in *Ronald Knox,* ed. Bugliani Knox, 361–70.
24 *More Latin Lyrics from Virgil to Milton*, trans. Helen Waddell (London: Gollancz, 1976), 40 and 43. In the moving introduction (p. 18) Dame Felicitas Corrigan quotes from Waddell's W. P. Ker lecture of 1948, 'Poetry in the Dark Ages', about the end of *Aeneid* 2: 'That is how Virgil saw the beginning of Rome, *Roma Immortalis*, golden Rome: a battered soldier, leading a handful of refugees. This is the pattern of history; and perhaps it is the pattern of eternity, translated into time.'
25 I would like to thank Fiachra Mac Góráin, David Hopkins and Elizabeth Prettejohn for their help and advice.

Bibliography

Bugliani Knox, Francesca (ed.). *Ronald Knox: A Man for All Seasons*. Toronto: Pontifical Institute of Medieval Studies, 2016.

Eliot, T. S. 'Virgil and the Christian World'. In *On Poetry and Poets*. London: Faber and Faber, 1957.

Knox, Ronald. *Let Dons Delight*. London: Sheed and Ward, 1939.

Martindale, Charles. 'English Virgil? – From Surrey to Tennyson'. In *The Afterlife of Virgil*, edited by Peter Mack and John North. [London]: Institute of Classical Studies, School of Advanced Study, University of London, 2017.

Martindale, Charles (ed.). *Virgil and His Influence*. Bristol: Bristol Classical Press, 1984.

Medcalf, Stephen. 'Virgil at the Turn of Time'. In Martindale (ed.), *Virgil and His Influence*, 215–44.

Montarese, Francesco. 'Appendix: Uses of the *Aeneid* in *A Spiritual Aeneid*'. In Bugliani Knox (ed.), *Ronald Knox*, 361–70.

Montarese, Francesco. 'Ronald Knox as Classicist'. In Bugliani Knox (ed.), *Ronald Knox*, 147–65.

Ogilvie, Robert M. *Latin and Greek: A History of the Influence of the Classics on English Life from 1600 to 1918*. London: Routledge and Kegan Paul, 1964.

Pagden, Anthony. *The Pursuit of Empire: A History*. Oxford: Oxford University Press, 2021.

Rossetti, D. G. *The Works of Dante Gabriel Rossetti*, edited by W. M. Rossetti. London: Ellis, 1911.

Virgil. *Aeneid Books VII to IX*. Partly in the original and partly in English verse translation. Introduction and translation by Ronald Knox. Oxford: Clarendon Press, 1924.

Waddell, Helen (trans.). *More Latin Lyrics from Virgil to Milton*. London: Gollancz, 1976.

Ziolkowski, Theodore. *Virgil and the Moderns*. Princeton: Princeton University Press, 1993.

Introduction: The Context of Ronald Knox's Lectures on Virgil*

Francesca Bugliani Knox

Like many of his contemporaries, Ronald Knox began reading and writing ancient Greek and Latin at an early age. When just four years old, he and his brother Wilfred, after losing their mother, went to spend four years, from 1892 to 1896, with their father's younger brother, the vicar of Edmundthorpe at Creeton Rectory, near Grantham. Uncle Lindsey Knox 'crammed into his small nephews, aged six and four, an amazing quantity of Latin and Greek', to such an extent that Ronald was able to write, at the age of eight, a Latin play entitled *Publius et Amilla* – an 'ineffably tedious' drama according to Evelyn Waugh – as a contribution to *Bolliday Bango*, a family magazine devised by his brother Edmund.[1] A little later, letters to his parents from Summer Fields preparatory school written between 1896 and 1900 reveal how proud Ronald was of his results in classics and how keen he was on writing Greek and Latin plays.[2] He and James Montagu Butler were regarded as the two cleverest boys of their generation ever taught in the scholarship class of Summer Fields.[3] *A Century of Summer Fields* (1964) lists several remarkable autograph juvenilia that Ronald wrote when aged between eight and eleven.[4] His interest in languages generally was exceptional for such a young boy.[5]

It was not, then, a surprise when he won the top King's Scholarship to study at Eton from 1906 to 1910. He followed up this feat with another even more impressive one, when, after winning several prestigious school prizes, in 1906 he won the First Scholarship to Balliol College.[6] There, too, he was awarded prizes for Greek and Latin.[7] Among Ronald's numerous contributions to the periodicals of Eton and Balliol were several verse compositions in, or renderings from and into, Greek and Latin.[8] Those written at Eton, including his first published Greek composition OI ENΔEKA, 'The Eleven' (1905), were republished by the Eton College Press in a collection entitled *Signa Severa* (1906).[9] The translation into

Theocritean hexameters of *Pippa Passes* by Robert Browning, which Knox wrote while a student at Balliol, won the Gaisford Prize for Greek verse and was published in 1908 by Blackwell.[10] Two years later, *Remigium alarum*, a poem celebrating Louis Blériot's flight across the channel on 25 July, 1909, won the Chancellor's Prize for Latin Verse and was recited in the Divinity School.[11] By the end of his stay at Balliol, Ronald's remarkable skill at verse composition in Latin and Greek had become widely acclaimed, as was his extraordinary facility at turning English poetry at sight into melodious Greek and Latin.

Knox's work as a classicist has been – it seems fair to say – for the most part overlooked.[12] The Anglo-Catholic and anti-modernist treatises and pamphlets that Knox wrote during his time as Chaplain, Fellow and Lecturer at Trinity College Oxford from 1910 to 1917, for example, have attracted more attention than his scholarly lectures on classical topics. Yet, the latter were no less remarkable. His lectures on Homer's *Iliad* and *Odyssey* were a success.[13] Of the *Iliad* lectures which tackled the Homeric problem, the twenty-three-year-old Ronald wrote to his father: 'The term has fully set in now and the first of the great Homer lectures has been delivered to a fairly large audience, including one fresher at least who was in College with me at Eton (now up at Magdalen)'. With his customary understatement, he added: 'One of the Trinity people is reported to have said it was very profound – I think that is the first time that epithet has been applied to any production of mine.'[14] The lectures on the *Odyssey*, addressing the themes of unity, romance and the common authorship of the *Odyssey* and *Iliad*, were delivered shortly afterwards in 1912, followed by lectures on Virgil's *Aeneid*.[15] In the Michaelmas term of 1914 the few remaining students who had not enlisted in the army or navy were still able to attend Knox's lectures on Virgil in his own rooms in a semi-deserted Oxford. Having left Trinity to take up temporarily the post of classics teacher at Shrewsbury where he remained until December 1916, Knox wrote amusingly in Latin and Greek for the schoolboys and referred to his work with delight.[16] His many contributions to the school journal *The Salopian* were translations into, or verse compositions in, Greek and Latin.

Conversion to Roman Catholicism brought his Trinity Fellowship to an end in September 1917. Knox's teaching of classics, however, continued at St Edmund's College from 1919 to 1922. 'We are glad,' reported *The Edmundian* magazine in 1919, 'to welcome the Rev. Ronald Knox, M.A., who will continue his theological studies while helping the senior boys with their classics.'[17] Besides teaching classics, reading theology and being a prolific preacher, journalist and novelist, Knox composed Latin addresses, plays and congratulatory verses for

The Edmundian.¹⁸ He published Greek iambics and Latin elegiac couplets for *The Dublin Review* and Greek sapphic stanzas and Latin elegiacs for *The London Mercury*, while also planning the publication of a volume collecting together verse compositions that had already appeared in *The Salopian*.¹⁹ On becoming New Testament professor at St Edmund's in 1922, a position that he retained until 1926, he handed over his post of classics teacher to Laurence Eyres – one of the few of his Trinity students who, after surviving the war, had graduated from Oxford.²⁰ He continued, however, to publish translations from English poems into Greek and Latin, original Latin verse compositions, essays on classical topics, articles in schools magazines advocating the study of Greek and Latin at schools and, on the request of the author, a foreword to a textbook of ecclesiastical Latin.²¹

His years as Catholic Chaplain at Oxford, from 1926 and 1939, were largely devoted to works of Catholic apologetics and sermons.²² His interest in classics, though, did not abate. In his unpublished correspondence with Eyres, Knox mentions his lunch time readings of Herodotus, marking of papers and scholarship tutoring.²³ Letters, now held at Ampleforth, from and to Eyres and other correspondents, show that he was well informed about teaching posts in classics that had become available, the examination system and the results of individual students. His return to Oxford also reminded him of his time as Fellow of Trinity College when, as an Anglican, he had lectured on Cicero, Demosthenes, Homer and Virgil. Since he had lent the typescripts of these lectures to Eyres in 1919, Knox now asked Eyres to return the ones that he had given on the *Odyssey*.²⁴ He wished, he wrote, to use them for a talk on 'the *Odyssey* as a Romance' in the presence of Gilbert Murray, Regius Professor of Greek at Oxford, and Shimi Fraser (Simon Fraser, 15th Lord Lovat) during one of Arnold Lunn's tours to Greece at the end of March 1930. For that occasion, he had also 'toyed', as he explained to Eyres, with the idea of another theme, namely, 'What the classical tradition does not mean to us', a lament that the classical tradition as an educational ideal had become obsolete and that scholarly work was now aimed solely at specialists. He regretted there was no attempt anymore to saturate people with the classics in the way that, in his words, 'our grandfathers were saturated with them'.²⁵ Even while busy writing regularly for *The Sunday Dispatch*, *The Times*, *The Universe*, *The Dublin Review*, *The Tablet*, *The Clergy Review* and *The Sunday Times*, he found time to discuss issues of Latin in his letters to Eyres, who had meanwhile taken up a post as classics teacher at Ampleforth.²⁶

As time went by, Knox felt increasingly inclined to put his classical scholarship and mastery of English language at the service of his faith. In an article for *The*

Tablet in 1938, he maintained that the Catholic Douay version relied too much on the Latin of the Vulgate, argued that the English did not sound literary enough and supported the idea of a translation of the New Testament from the Greek in the light of the Vulgate.[27] The following year, on the eve of the Second World War, having received permission from the hierarchy, he left Oxford for Aldenham and started translating the New Testament. Numerous letters to Eyres, to whom Knox turned when faced with difficult points of the translation, reveal the scholarly attention that he devoted to the task. Evelyn Waugh did not mention this interesting part of the Knox–Eyres correspondence in his biography. Indeed he had expressly declined to peruse it. 'Please do not trouble to send me technical discussions of the translation,' Waugh wrote to Eyres, 'Someone else must later write a study of that great work.'[28]

From 1940 to 1957, Knox continued translating and writing on ancient Greek and Roman topics.[29] On 11 June 1957, with only a month or so to live, he gave the Romanes Lecture in the Sheldonian Theatre at Oxford where he had recited the Greek prize poem nearly fifty years earlier in 1908. It was to be his last public appearance. It also happened to be his last word on translation. He died on 24 August, leaving his English translation of *De imitatione Christi* unfinished and his collection of early verse compositions in Greek and Latin unpublished. Thomas Oakley completed the translation of *De imitatione*. Eyres, with Knox's leave, chose and edited the verse compositions, a project they had discussed together for two decades.[30] When Chapman and Hall, after an initial refusal of Eyres's manuscript, eventually published it with the title *In Three Tongues*, Waugh wrote to Eyres: 'Your kind gift of *In Three Tongues* arrived this morning. Thanks most awfully. As you know two of the tongues are lost to me (so far as I ever had them) but shall treasure the book. I hope it finds many more worthy readers.'[31] Unfortunately this did not prove to be the case. It received positive reviews, but the collection did not sell particularly well.[32] Times had changed since H. A. J Munro, Richard Shilletto and R. C. Jebb had successfully published their verse compositions. As Waugh had predicted, very few would buy 'a work largely in dead languages which had not a relation to examinations'.[33]

—•—•—•—•—

Knox's favourite author appears to have been Virgil. By the age of six he could read the *Aeneid* fluently.[34] His father mentioned this to Mrs Gertrude Maclaren, the headmistress at Summer Fields, who promptly accepted Ronald and, at the same time, his eldest brother Dillwyn, then aged ten, whom she had up until that point been reluctant to take on account of his age. A few years later in 1902 he wrote to his mother from Eton: 'I do Extra Books now out of super scribbled school editions of Vergil in a stuffy room on a hard chair instead of a vellum bound Conington in a cool drawing room on a nice cozy sofa, as I would be but for the postponement of the coronation!'[35] Virgil also makes an appearance in two early writings. The first, *A Still More Sporting Adventure* (1911) is a brilliant skit on Miss Moberly and Miss Jourdain's *An Adventure* (1911).[36] It recounts the finding of an imaginary original manuscript dating back to AD 100, containing an account of the encounter of Dido and Aeneas in the grotto and the death of Dido, events that had been 'seen' in a vision and narrated by the Roman matron Clodia and her servant. Beside mocking belief in supernatural occurrences and parodying the prose style of some Edwardian personalities, disguised as ancient Romans, Knox caricatures here, at some points at least, modernist hermeneutics applied to ancient texts. The second writing, a poetical composition made up exclusively of Virgilian phrases and entitled 'The Fifth Georgic: a Cento from Virgil', also dated 1911, is a bravura piece that confirms Knox's remarkable knowledge of Virgil's works.[37]

Virgil became for Knox more than a scholarly focus only after he started lecturing on the *Aeneid* the following year, in 1912, when he discovered that he was, as it were, an 'anima naturaliter virgiliana'. During the last three months leading up to his conversion to Roman Catholicism, he 'carried Virgil about' – still in the 1902 Conington's edition – because, he wrote, 'at an important moment in my life, I half looked to him as a counsellor'. It would be an impossibly delicate task to determine whether Knox's journey of conversion coloured his interpretation of the *Aeneid* or, rather, if his reading the *Aeneid* somehow encouraged and enlightened that journey. Whichever the case, Knox chose the *Aeneid* as a literary, almost allegorical, point of reference when he recounted the story of his conversion in *A Spiritual Aeneid*, published by Longmans and Green in 1918. At the beginning of what he called his 'religious autobiography', he wrote:

> In explanation of the Aeneid-motif which runs through the chapter-headings and parts of the book, I had perhaps better give the key to a somewhat obvious set of symbols. Troy is undisturbed and, in a sense, unreflective religion; in most lives it is overthrown, either to be rebuilt or to be replaced. The Greeks are the doubts which overthrow it. The 'miniature Troy' of Helenus is the effort to reconstruct that religion exactly as it was. Carthage is any false goal that, for a time, seems to claim finality. And Rome is Rome.[38]

Six years later, when still at St Edmund's, once his teaching of classics there had come to an end, he published his own translation, with an introduction, of books VII to IX of the *Aeneid*. He designed it as a textbook for students.[39]

A long time after delivering the Virgil lectures, Knox still considered them valuable. 'Virgil and the Future Life', partly an elaboration on the second Trinity lecture entitled 'Virgil's Religious Outlook', appeared in the *Tablet* in 1941.[40] In February 1946 – when invited to talk to the Virgil Society[41] – Knox expressed a wish to return to one of the topics he had addressed in 1912 and he asked Eyres if he could borrow, 'strictly ad hoc' he promised, the copy that Eyres had typed out and bound.[42] Letters from the unpublished Knox–Eyres correspondence, held in Ampleforth, confirm that Eyres obliged.[43] The lecture was delivered sometime between 25 March and 7 April 1946. The letters do not, however, contain any information about the exact date or title.[44] Neither Waugh in his biography (1959) nor Speaight in his Virgil Society memorial address (1958) mentions the lecture to the Virgil Society.[45] Nor is it to be found in the Virgil Society archives. During my endeavours to find out what became of it, I learned of a lecture in manuscript entitled 'The Problem of Dido and Aeneas' that its current owner, Laurence Kenworthy-Browne, suggested might be what I was looking for.[46] However, an announcement in *The Tablet* confirmed beyond doubt that Knox addressed the Virgil Society on 'Virgil and Romance' – not on the 'Problem of Dido and Aeneas'– on 30 March 1946.[47] The topic of Knox's lecture was the same as that of the third lecture on Virgil that he had delivered at Trinity in 1912.

Given Knox's own regard for his Trinity lectures on Virgil, one may wonder why they were not published during his lifetime, nor indeed posthumously. The reason, I believe, is twofold. First there is the role that Laurence Eyres had in looking after them. On his return from the war in 1919, Eyres, who had attended the lectures at Trinity College in 1912 (see Figure 2), borrowed them from Knox when he resumed his degree at Oxford.[48] Then, ten years later, he transcribed, annotated, indexed and bound them in a volume.[49] From that moment this typescript became the *Hauptexemplar*. It remained under his care and, soon after completing this editorial task, Eyres, now at Ampleforth, where he was teaching classics, had arranged to get the second of the lectures published in the *Ampleforth Journal*.[50] Later, when the secretary of the Virgil Society offered to publish Knox's 1946 address, based on the third lecture, Knox 'resisted the temptation' and immediately sent the transcript of the Virgil lectures back to Eyres, as he had promised.[51]

That Knox had entrusted the only corrected and complete copy to Eyres, who may have had future publication in mind, became evident after Knox's death.⁵² Eyres made clear to Waugh and Speaight that he did not wish to have his name mentioned publicly in relation to the lectures. Waugh, who knew Eyres well and mentioned his name in his biography of Knox, published in 1959, was evasive about their whereabouts: 'Few of his pupils survive. *One* has preserved the text of his Virgil lectures.'⁵³ In order to borrow Eyres's copy to write his memorial lecture to the Virgil Society (1958), Speaight had to promise Eyres that he would not disclose the name of its owner, who, he explained to his audience, was very protective of the lectures and intended to arrange for them to be published.⁵⁴ Yet Eyres did not find the time and energy to publish them. After editing *In Three Tongues* (January 1959), he had become absorbed in the task of transcribing Knox's letters but soon started having problems with his hands, and so found it difficult to work. The death of Waugh – Knox's literary executor with whom Eyres discussed all matters of publication of Knox's works – complicated things

Figure 2 The Gryphon Club, Trinity College Oxford, 1913. Photograph. From the 'Gryphon Club Archives Photograph Albums' in 'Ronald Knox Archives', Trinity College Oxford. It shows Ronald Knox and Laurence Eyres at about the time when Knox delivered the lectures on Virgil. Knox is second from the right in the second row. Laurence Eyres is in the middle of the front row.

further.⁵⁵ As a result, the corrected and complete typescript of the lectures remained, on Eyres's death, at Ampleforth, while the original but uncorrected 1912 version of the lectures which Eyres had borrowed and returned to Knox in 1929 after transcribing them, remained among Knox's papers at Mells, the country house near Bath, where he lived the last ten years of his life.⁵⁶

The second reason why Knox's Virgil lectures were not published posthumously seems to have been commercial.⁵⁷ In 1967, very soon after Eyres died peacefully in his room at Ampleforth on 27 December 1966, Fr Henry Wansbrough OSB, a colleague of his at Ampleforth and admirer of the Virgil lectures, discussed the possibility of their publication with Julian Asquith (son of Katharine Asquith), 2nd Earl of Oxford and Asquith, known as Lord Oxford, who had, by that time, become Knox's literary executor after Waugh's death on 10 April 1966. Wansbrough knew that only a few changes would be necessary to make the Ampleforth typescript ready for publication and recommended mentioning 'Mr Eyres who treasured and annotated so carefully the copy'.⁵⁸ Oxford then wrote to Roger Mynors⁵⁹ to ask if he would like to read Knox's lectures.⁶⁰ Mynors's reply was positive – he would 'love', Mynors wrote, 'to see the lectures'.⁶¹ Since, however, he had not received any update, Wansbrough contacted Oxford again one year later, enquiring about the progress of the project as he was still very keen for the lectures to be published.⁶² Eventually Wansbrough received a letter from Lord Oxford dated 10 November 1970 announcing that Macmillan had agreed to publish them, that Roger Mynors would be delighted to write the introduction and that Harold Macmillan had offered to contribute a foreword.⁶³ In the same letter Oxford asked Wansbrough to either 'send his copy', i.e. Eyres's typescript, or correct the incomplete copy kept at Mells, supplying the Greek quotations and two pages missing from the latter.⁶⁴ Wansbrough chose the second option and acted swiftly.⁶⁵ In December 1970, Oxford thanked him for sending the corrected typescript and informed him that he had sent it off to Macmillan for publication. He would, Oxford added, notify him of any progress.⁶⁶ At this point the correspondence ceases. More letters were exchanged, however, between Lord Oxford and Nicholas Barker, and between the latter and Alan D. Maclean, the Publishing Director for 'General Books' at Macmillan. At first, while Barker was still working for Macmillan, things seemingly moved apace.⁶⁷ Maclean too had been very encouraging. By February 1975, however, the wind changed direction, partly because Mynors had been, Barker wrote, 'well up to Olympic standards for non-delivery'.⁶⁸ But that was not the only reason. It was unlikely now, Maclean wrote to Barker, that Macmillan would be in a position to offer publication since the lectures on their own had no commercial value and Harold Macmillan, who had previously agreed on a much longer historical introduction, had no time, now that he was writing his own memoirs to contribute anything other than a short preface.[69] The poor market viability put an end to Lord Oxford's attempts to find an agreement with Macmillan and see Knox's lectures published.[70] The Trinity lectures on Virgil that Speaight, Mynors, Wansbrough and Barker had longed to see published and that Waugh had described as 'still fresh, witty and original', a 'delightful reading even for a barbarian like myself', languished unpublished for another fifty years – this despite the appreciation of them expressed by contemporaries and, we might add, Knox's fondness for them.[71]

'The problem is the lectures have been left behind by the world.' So Barker had replied when Maclean informed him that Macmillan had decided against publishing Knox's lectures. As if to justify Macmillan's decision, he had added, 'The general reader has no classical background, while the specialist classic reader would consider them superseded.'[72] Perhaps it would be more just to say that Knox's lectures were a casualty of the commercial imperatives of the postwar publishing industry. Now that the lectures have been retrieved from among Eyres's papers held at Ampleforth and are finally being published here, the general reader will have the opportunity to decide for themselves as to their literary qualities and equally the Virgilian specialist, given the burgeoning field of Greek and Latin reception studies nowadays, will have the chance, irrespective of the lectures' scholarly merits, to appreciate them as an interesting addition to the history of Virgil's reception in the twentieth century.

One specific point in particular, I believe, makes them relevant to both audiences today. Like a music conductor sensitively bringing a musical score to life, Knox maintains a fine balance in his lectures on Virgil – or rather, since he mentions his other works only occasionally in his lectures, on the *Aeneid* – between literary skill, academic scholarship and enthusiasm for his topic. What stands out for his readers today is what stood out for his students more than one hundred years ago. Even within the constraints of academic lecturing, he was able to touch on vital points of the *Aeneid* and convey Virgil's 'mind and outlook' as he understood them: the rigorous conception of destiny that animated his theology, his view of the afterlife, his romantic admiration of weakness, the halo of pathos with which he enveloped the death of the young, the artistry of his narrative and his ability to describe the beauty and mystery of natural scenery. It was these qualities that led Speaight to conclude his Knox memorial address to the Virgil Society in 1958: 'Many of us who love our Virgil will now understand him better because Ronald Knox loved and understood him so well.'

Notes

* Abbreviations: AAA = Ampleforth Abbey Archives; KFP = Knox Family Papers; MA = Mells Archives.

1 Penelope Fitzgerald, *The Knox Brothers* (London: Flamingo, 2002; 1st edn: 1977), 28; Evelyn Waugh, *The Life of the Right Reverend Ronald Knox* (London: Chapman and Hall, 1959), 47.

2 'Yesterday I was top for Caesar and for Greek too [...] For Greek I had my place top at first and never went down a single place' (Ronald Knox's letter to his parents, dated 11 November 1896, KFP). 'I have done another scene of my Latin play. Dactylic with 18 lines' (Knox's letter to his parents dated 30 January 1897, KFP). A year later he was completing the Latin play, a comedy in three acts, and writing a Greek tragedy in four acts, entitled Ἡ ψευδη (he added: 'N.B. Please excuse my not putting in accents'); see Knox's letter to his parents dated 3 April 1898, KFP. He also wrote a Greek poem and translated it into English, dated *c.* 1898 (ibid.).

3 Sir James Ramsay Montagu Butler, OBE (1889–1975), a British politician and academic, was Regius Professor of Modern History at the University of Cambridge from 1947 to 1954 and vice-master of Trinity College, Cambridge, from 1954 to 1960. As an undergraduate at Trinity College Cambridge he was a brilliant scholar, winning a number of prizes including the Chancellor's Medal in Classics and the Craven Scholarship, and gaining a double first class in Classics and History.

4 Richard Usborne, *A Century of Summer Fields: An Anthology 1864–1964* (London: Methuen, 1964), 40–2, 54. Usborne (1910–2006) was also educated at Summer Fields.

5 'Dear Mother, you know I was going to do an Italian play, and a French play and perhaps a Spanish one, but now I am going to write a mixed play, in which some people will talk Italian, some English, some Spanish and some French' (Ronald Knox's letter to his mother dated 29 January 1898, KFP).

6 In his last two years at Eton he won the Harvey Verse Prize, the Latin Essay Prize and the Davies Scholarship; see Waugh, *The Life*, 58.

7 At Balliol he was awarded the Hertford (1907) and the Ireland and Craven scholarships (1908), the Gaisford Greek Verse Prize (1908) and the Chancellor's Latin Verse Prize (1910). In 1910 he took a first in Greats (1st class Litt. Hum.); see ibid., 89, 95. While at Balliol Knox read all of Plato's *Republic* in Greek, he tells us in *A Spiritual Aeneid* (London, 1918, 62), in 'a space of nine hours'. Why he took only a 'second' in the first part of the Classics course (Honour Moderations) is unknown. Evelyn Waugh suggests that an overconfident Knox 'did not prepare' as he should have and adds, on the authority of Mr Thomas Higham of Trinity, public orator, that he, Knox, had, in the Theocritus paper, 'betrayed he had never heard of Wilamowitz'; see ibid., 94–5. This is open to doubt. Later Knox cited Wilamowitz on several

occasions in his unpublished lectures on the *Odyssey* (1911), now held in the Mells Archives.
8   While at Eton, Knox contributed to *The Outsider*, *The Eton College Chronicle* (of which he was editor) and *The Supplement*; while at Balliol he contributed to *The Isis*, *The Oxford Review* and *The Oxford Magazine*.
9   R.A.K. [i.e. Ronald Arburthnott Knox], *Signa Severa* (Eton College: Spottiswoode and Co., 1906). 'Fragments of Greek Poets' had already been published unsigned with the title 'Selections (newly discovered) from Greek Poets' in *The Supplement* no. 1 (4 June 1904): 7, and in *The Supplement* no. 2 (21 June 1904): 23–4. The composition in Homeric hexameters ΟΙ ΕΝΔΕΚΑ was first published in *The Eton College Chronicle*, no. 1101 (13 July 1905): 707.
10   Robert Browning, *Pippa Passes III: Evening: Talk by the Way* (Oxford: Blackwell, 1908).
11   Ronald Knox, *Remigium alarum* (Oxford: Blackwell, 1910). His verse composition in Greek, Κύρια Ονόματα, was published in Ronald Knox, *Juxta Salices* (Oxford: Alden and Co., 1910), 8–10.
12   On Ronald Knox as classicist, see Francesco Montarese, 'Ronald Knox as Classicist', in *Ronald Knox: A Man for All Seasons*, ed. Francesca Bugliani Knox (Toronto: Pontifical Institute of Medieval Studies, 2016), 147–65.
13   Starting from Hilary term 1911 Knox was entrusted with tutoring for Honour Mods on Homer, Virgil, Logic and Divinity. A copy of his course on Logic is held in the Mells Archives.
14   Ronald Knox's letter to his father dated 19 October 1911, KFP. Unfortunately, the lectures on the *Iliad* were destroyed . 'I thought when I first opened your letter, that it must be something really serious,' Knox wrote, 'I don't see the least probability of my ever tackling the Homeric problem again, and that old stuff was far too much out of date to be of any use'; see, Knox letter to Eyres dated 12 August 1930, in 'Knox–Eyres correspondence', 98, AAA. To Knox's letter Eyres appended a note confirming that the lectures, which he had borrowed, were destroyed, for reasons unknown, at Stonyhurst while he was teaching classics there.
15   Knox's typescript of his lectures on the *Odyssey* are held in the Mells Archives. Eyres returned it to Knox in March 1930, see n. 24 below.
16   'I write nothing, except full-sense Elegiacs for my form, which amuse me beyond description' (Ronald Knox's letter to Dick Rawstone dated 14 June 1915, KFP).
17   Knox started teaching classics in February 1919; see *The Edmundian* 12, no. 75 (Easter 1919): 234.
18   During his time at St Edmund's, Knox wrote for, among others, *The Evening Standard*, *The Catholic Gazette*, *The Manchester Guardian*, *The Daily News*, *The Catholic Herald*, *The Universe*, *The Morning Post*. He also wrote novels: *Memories of the Future: Being Memories of the Years 1915–1972* (London: Methuen, 1923);

Sanctions. A Frivolity (London: Methuen, 1924); *The Viaduct Murder* (London: Methuen, 1925) and *Other Eyes than Ours* (London: Methuen, 1926). Some of his sermons were published as a collection: *The Beginning and End of Man* (London: The Catholic Truth Society, 1921). His contributions to *The Edmundian* include: *Londinium Defensum, a Play in Three Acts*, in the supplement to the October issue of *The Edmundian* 15, no.1 (October 1925): 1, 5, 10–11; a Latin address for Canon Edward Myers, *The Edmundian* 12, no. 76 (July 1919): 268; a Latin epitaph for Bishop Ward ['Juxta Ossa Eius Ponite Ossa Mea'], *The Edmundian* 12, no. 78 (April 1920): 313; congratulatory verses in Latin addressed to Francis Cardinal Bourne on the occasion of his siver jubilee as a bishop, *The Edmundian* 13, no. 81 (April 1921): [1]–2. For the numerous other Latin verses written for *The Edmundian*, see the bibliography of Knox's works compiled by Patricia Cowan, M.A., accessible online at the website of the 'Ronald Knox Society of North America'. James Chappel gives a list of most significant works written by Knox in: 'Ronald Knox: A Bibliographic Essay', *Theological Librarianship* (an online journal of the American Theological Association), 1, no. 2 (December 2008), 49–53.

19 *The Dublin Review* 168 no. 337 (April 1921): 283; *The London Mercury* 3 no. 18 (April 1921): 600. 'Most of those Salopian things I'd already prepared to publish in the form of a Latin verse book' (Knox's letter to Eyres dated 18 July 1920, in 'Knox-Eyres correspondence', AAA). Not wanting to be thought of as frivolous, Knox never published these early verses during his lifetime. Some of them were posthumously included in Ronald Knox, *In Three Tongues*, ed. Laurence Eyres (London: Chapman and Hall, 1959). Knox was one of the translators who rendered a spurious fifth book of Horace's *Odes* composed in English by C. P. L. Fletcher and Charles Graves and published in English under the title *Q. Horati Flacci Carminum liber quintus*, back into Latin; see the online bibliography of Knox's works compiled by Patricia Cowan mentioned in n. 18 above.

20 Laurence Eyres (1892–1966) remained a lifelong friend of Knox and was also his general executor; see Francesca Bugliani Knox, 'Ronald Knox's Two Recording Angels', in *Ronald Knox*, ed. Bugliani Knox, 75–88.

21 Knox gave a paper on the 'Report on Classical Studies' during the Catholic Headmasters' Conference held at St Edmund's from the 29 May to 1 June 1922, as reported in *The Edmundian* 1922, no. 85 (July 1922): 148. The paper was published in the official Catholic Headmasters' Conference Proceedings. Some of Knox's relevant publications, excluding those mentioned in n. 18 above, are, in chronological order: 'Foreword' to Joyce Egerton Lowe, *Church Latin for Beginners: An Elementary Course of Exercises in Ecclesiastical Latin* (London: Burns Oates and Washbourne, 1923), iv–vi; *Auld Lang Syne* (a broadside in Greek composed at the request of rev. A. B. Purdie, the headmaster of St Edmund's, and published on Purdie's private press, 1923); 'The Classical Touch' (subtitled 'Some Modern Documents in Ancient Dress'),

Morning Post 47, no. 202 (11 September 1923): 4, reprinted as 'Pericles versus Cicero' in Ronald Knox, *In Three Tongues*, 135–9; 'Hymnus in Honorem S. P. N. Edmundi', *The Edmundian* 14, no. 5 (February 1925): 147; a review (written in Latin) of *An Anthology of Medieval Latin* by Stephen Gassier, *The Dublin Review* 176, no. 355 (October 1925): 302–4; *Thesauropolemopompus*, a play in two acts written by R. A. Knox and produced by A. B. Purdie (performed on 1 July 1924), in the supplement of *The Edmundian* (May 1925) and ibid., 107; 'Tractate on Tree Names in Virgil', *The Edmundian* 25, no. 172 (Spring 1959): 100. Knox also translated into Greek and Latin verse thirteen pieces of Maurice Baring's prose; see Maurice Baring, *Translations Ancient and Modern* (London: William Heinemann, 1925).

22 See, for example, *The Belief of Catholics* (London: Ernest Benn, 1927), the only apologetic work that Knox wrote for the general public and *In Soft Garments* (London: Burns and Oates, 1942), a compilation of lectures (apologetics) delivered between 1926 and 1938 to the Catholic undergraduates at Oxford and also the collection of sermons *The Mystery of the Kingdom and other Sermons* (London: Sheed and Ward, 1928).

23 'I have taken to reading serious books at meals [...] and am just starting Herodotus' (Knox's letter dated 22 February 1928, in 'Knox–Eyres correspondence', 82, AAA). Knox tutored, for example, Julian Oxford for a scholarship at Balliol – which Oxford won in December 1934. 'Oxford comes here for a few days at the end of the month to do Latin verses with me. Do you think he ought to do any Greek ones as well?' (Knox's letter dated 9 July 1933, ibid., 111, AAA). Julian Oxford had been a pupil of Eyres at Ampleforth.

24 'Have you got my *Odyssey* lectures?'; 'I would like to have the three last lectures, VII, VIII and IX' (Knox's letters dated, respectively, 26 February and 4 March 1930, ibid., 92, AAA). On receiving the lectures, Knox wrote: 'Thank you most awfully for sending on the lectures. Whenever I come across my old writings I am always struck with the sense, (i) that they are very bad, and (ii) that I could not do it nearly so well now' (Knox's letter dated 13 March 1930, ibid., 94, AAA). The lectures are held in the Mells Archives.

25 Knox relented. In the event, he delivered 'The Greeks at Sea' published posthumously in Ronald Knox, *Literary Distractions* (London: Sheed and Ward, 1958), 1–20.

26 See, for example, Knox's letter to Eyres dated 8 February 1937, in 'Knox–Eyres correspondence', 118, AAA.

27 Ronald Knox, 'The Douay Version', *The Tablet* 171, no. 5119 (1938): 794–5.

28 See Waugh's letter to Eyres dated 29 October 1957, in 'Waugh–Eyres correspondence', AAA.

29 A few examples: 'The Greeks Had a Word for It', *The Tablet* 171, no. 5246 (23 November 1940); 'Virgil and the Future Life', *The Tablet* 178, no. 5303 (27 December 1941): 396–7; 'On the Effect of the Classics on Maurice Baring's Mind', in *Maurice*

Baring: A Postscript by Laura Lovat with Some Letters and Verse (London: Hollis and Carter, 1947), 107–12; 'The Legacy of Greece. The Church and the Classics', *The Tablet* 202, no. 5919 (31 October 1953): 430–1. Translations: *The Westminster Hymnal* (London: Burns Oates and Washbourne, 1940); 'In Memoriam', *The Times* 49, no. 593 (9 July 1943): 7 (a translation in Greek elegiac couplets of Maurice Baring's verses in memory of Lieut. Hugh Trenchard, killed in action March 1943). His last published Latin verse composition was, as far as I know, 'The Rogito' in 'Tribute to Cardinal Griffin', *Westminster Cathedral Chronicle*, Special Number November 1956, 44–5.

30 Knox's letter to Eyres dated 18 July 1920; see n. 19 above.

31 Waugh's letter to Eyres dated 8 October 1959, in 'Waugh–Eyres correspondence', AAA.

32 'Book all jam, with no bread and butter'; see Colin Leach's review of Ronald A. Knox, *In Three Tongues*, edited by L. E. Eyres, *The Classical Review* 10, no. 3 (December 1960): 263.

33 Waugh's letter to Eyres dated 4 July 1958, in 'Waugh–Eyres correspondence', AAA.

34 Fitzgerald, *The Knox Brothers*, 34; Waugh, *The Life*, 45; Terry Tastard, *Ronald Knox and English Catholicism* (Leominster: Gracewing, 2009), 7; Sheridan Gilley, 'Knox, Ronald Aburthnott', *The Oxford Dictionary of National Biography*, 2004.

35 See Knox's undated letter to his mother, *c.* 1902, KFP.

36 Ronald Knox, *A Still More Sporting Adventure* (Oxford: Blackwell, 1911). Patricia Cowan specifies that the idea originated with C. R. L. Fletcher, who asked Knox to expand his, Fletcher's, text. According to Cowan, pages 44–76 are the work exclusively of Knox. For Cowan's bibliography, see n. 18 above.

37 Ronald Knox, 'The Fifth Georgic: A Cento from Virgil', *The Oxford Magazine* 29, no. 24 (21 June 1911): 410–11.

38 Ronald Knox, 'Preface' to *A Spiritual Aeneid* (London: Longmans, Green and Co., 1918). A second edition was published with a preface entitled 'After 33 years' and Knox's own translations of his quotations from Virgil (London: Burns and Oates, 1950). A third, posthumous, edition contained an introduction by Evelyn Waugh (London: Burns and Oates, 1958).

39 Virgil, *Aeneid Books VII to IX*, partly in the original and partly in English verse, with introduction and translation by Ronald Knox (Oxford: Clarendon Press, 1924).

40 See n. 29 above.

41 'The Virgil Society wants me to read a paper' (Knox's letter to Eyres dated 15 February 1946, in 'Knox–Eyres correspondence', 150, AAA). Eyres had facilitated the invitation, 'conspiring', as Knox writes, with W. H. Woollen, the Joint Honorary Secretary of the Virgil Society (Knox's letter dated 8 March 1946, ibid., 151, AAA). Woollen was a Catholic convert clergyman, at the time teaching classics at Campion House, Osterley.

42 'I want to dig up my old lectures. I cannot make out where I have parked all my old Mss... I don't seem to have got them... If the worst comes to the worst, would it be possible to borrow your copy, "strictly ad hoc" and under a vow to return them when I come up for Easter if not earlier?' (Knox's letter to Eyres dated 21 February 1946, ibid., 150, AAA). And two weeks later: 'I cannot for the life of me find out what has become of the blue cardboard box in which my old Trinity lectures are packed away ... do you think you could send me your typed copy, with my faithful promise to cherish and return it? I think the one I want to release is the one about Virgil and Romance. But I can't remember them well enough to be certain' (Knox's letter to Eyres dated 8 March 1946, ibid., 151, AAA).

43 See Knox's letter to Eyres dated 18 March 1946 for receipt of the lectures and his thanks, ibid., 152, AAA.

44 'The Virgil lecture, a congeries of bits and pieces, seemed to me awfully boring but everyone was very nice about it. Kinchin Smith took the chair' (Knox's letter to Eyres dated 7 April 1946, ibid., 153, AAA). F. Kinchin Smith was a classics teacher at Shrewsbury and sometime scholar at Trinity College, Oxford.

45 Waugh died before Eyres had finished transcribing all of Knox's letters and may have not seen or may have overlooked the letters in which the Virgil Society lecture was mentioned. Robert Speaight, the President of the Virgil Society, who usually attended the Virgil Society meetings, was in Paris at the time Knox delivered the lecture. Speaight later gave a memorial lecture for Knox to the Virgil Society. His lecture was published as *A Modern Virgilian: A Memorial Lecture to Monsignor Ronald Knox* (London: Virgil Society, 1959).

46 See the Appendix in this volume: Francesca Bugliani Knox, 'J. E. Lowe, Ronald Knox and the Virgil Society Lecture Entitled "The Problem of Dido and Aeneas"'.

47 'Ronald Knox will address the Virgil Society this afternoon Saturday, March 30th at 3:30 on "Virgil and Romance" at the City Literature Institute, Stukeley Street, W.C. 2'; see *The Tablet* 187 no. 5525 (30 March, 1946): 165.

48 In response to Eyres's request, Knox wrote: 'About the Mods lectures, I'm afraid they are all buried in the general litter of my Oxford effects. The only thing I can suggest is that, if I manage a visit in the autumn, we might try and find out if the papers have been kept in a separate mess, and if so look through them' (Knox's letter dated 23 June 1919, in 'Knox–Eyres correspondence', 6, AAA).

49 See Knox's letter to Eyres dated 11 August 1929, ibid., 87, AAA.

50 Ronald Knox, 'Virgil's Religious Outlook', *The Ampleforth Journal* 25, no. 2 (Spring 1930): 109–29. Knox informed Eyres that he had given his permission to Fr Felix Hardy, the editor of *The Ampleforth Journal*, to publish his lecture (Knox's letter to Eyres dated 8 October 1929, in 'Knox–Eyres correspondence', 88, AAA). In a note appended to Knox's letter, Eyres explains that in 1929 he 'had borrowed and transcribed' the Virgil lectures, had showed the transcript to Felix Hardy, editor of

The Ampleforth Journal, and that Hardy had obtained Knox's leave to print the lecture. Then Eyres sent the original typescript back to Knox and kept 'his' copy (Knox's letter to Eyres dated 15 February 1946, ibid., 150, AAA).

51 Knox's letter dated 8 March 1946, ibid., 152, AAA. Knox returned the bound volume to Eyres on Easter day, 21 April 1946 (Knox's letter to Eyres dated 21 April 1946, ibid., 153, AAA).

52 Knox was under the impression that Eyres had given him a copy of his, Eyres's, transcript but that was not the case; see Knox's letter dated 15 February 1946, ibid., 150, AAA.

53 Waugh, *The Life*, 120.

54 See Speaight's letter to Eyres dated 9 September 1958, in 'Speaight–Eyres correspondence', AAA. The Abbot at Ampleforth, Herbert Byrne, had told Speaight that the lectures edited by Eyres were no longer in the Library and that Eyres possibly had them.

55 'I shall very much like to read Ronald's Virgil lectures. If Speaight sends them to me I will guard them until you are ready to take them back' (Waugh's letter to Eyres dated 19 September 1958, in 'Waugh–Eyres correspondence', AAA). And sometime later: 'Will send Virgil lectures at the end of the week,' Waugh wrote, 'if you will let me keep them so long' (Waugh's letter to Eyres dated 27 October 1958, ibid.).

56 See n. 48 and n. 50 above.

57 A three-year correspondence, from 1967 to 1970, on the possible publication of the Virgil lectures ensued between Wansbrough, Lord Oxford, Roger Mynors and the historian Nicolas J. Barker, then at Macmillan. This correspondence is held partly in the archives at Mells, partly in the archives at Ampleforth. The correspondence between Lord Oxford and Nicholas Barker, and between the latter and Alan D. Maclean, the Publishing Director for 'General Books' at Macmillan, is held in the Mells Archives.

58 Wansbrough's letter to Julian Oxford dated 12 September 1967, in 'Wansbrough–Oxford Correspondence', MA; a copy of the same letter is kept at AAA. Wansbrough refers to Eyres's copy of the lectures as the *Hauptexemplar*.

59 Sir Roger Aubrey Baskerville Mynors FBA (1903–89) was one of Britain's foremost classicists. Educated at Eton College, he read Literae Humaniores at Balliol College, Oxford, and spent the early years of his career as a Fellow of that College. He was Kennedy Professor of Latin at Cambridge from 1944 to 1953 and Corpus Christi Professor of Latin at Oxford from 1953 until his retirement in 1970. His publications on classical subjects include critical editions of Virgil, Catullus and Pliny the Younger.

60 Oxford's letter to Wansbrough dated 29 September 1967, in 'Correspondence between Oxford, Roger Mynors and Nicolas J. Barker', MA.

61 'Do send me Ronnie's lectures,' Mynors had written, 'there is in any case a great shortage of criticism on the *Aeneid* which one can put in the hands of young and old ... I would love to read anything of Ronnie's anyhow, so do send it along' (Mynors's letter to Oxford dated 12 October 1967, ibid.).

62 Wansbrough's letter to Lord Oxford dated 5 April 1969, in 'Wansbrough–Oxford correspondence', MA; a copy of the letter is held also at AAA. Oxford replied that Mynors thought the lectures were worth publishing and that he would do minor editing, but possibly not a foreword because he was very busy (Oxford's letter to Wansbrough dated 16 April 1969, ibid., AAA; a copy of the letter is also held in the Mells Archives).

63 Oxford contacted Nicolas J. Barker, editor for Macmillan. The latter replied saying he had spoken to Harold Macmillan, who sounded very positive (Barker's letter to Oxford dated 2 September 1970, in 'Correspondence between Oxford, Roger Mynors and Nicolas J. Barker', MA). Subsequently, Barker asked for a corrected copy of the lectures, confirming he had reached an agreement with Mynors and Macmillan (Barker's letter to Oxford dated 29 October 1970, ibid.).

64 Oxford specified that in the copy kept at Mells 'none of the Greek quotations has been written in, several of the leaves are bound in the wrong order and one or two are missing' (Oxford's letter to Wansbrough dated 10 November 1970, in 'Wansbrough–Oxford Correspondence', MA; a copy of this letter is kept also at AAA). Presumably this was Knox's carbon copy of the original typescript of 1912, also held at Mells. In fact Oxford later wrote that he found another copy of the typescript at Mells with leaves all in the right order, no missing pages, but still needing the Greek quotations and some corrections (ibid.).

65 'Here is the typescript with references and quotations duly inserted and corrections in punctuation. The other addition would be the index but we will not bother about it until the page proofs come' (Wansbrough's letter to Oxford dated 3 December 1970, in 'Wansbrough–Oxford Correspondence', MA; a copy of the letter is also held at AAA).

66 See Oxford's letter to Wansbrough dated 11 December 1970, ibid., MA.

67 Barker's letters to Lord Oxford dated 29 October 1970 and 7 May 1971, in 'Correspondence between Oxford, Roger Mynors and Nicolas J. Barker', MA.

68 Barker's letter from Oxford University Press dated 4 February 1975 to Richard Garrett Macmillans at Macmillan enquiring on behalf of Oxford if publication was still possible, MA.

69 Maclean's letter to Barker dated 11 February 1975, MA.

70 Barker's letter to Maclean dated 21 February 1975, MA.

71 See Waugh's letter to Eyres dated 2 November 1958, in 'Waugh–Eyres correspondence', AAA.

72 Barker's letter to Maclean dated 21 February 1975, MA.

Bibliography

Archives

Ampleforth Abbey Archives (AAA)
Knox–Eyres correspondence
Waugh–Eyres correspondence (September 1957–March 1964)
Wansbrough–Oxford correspondence
Speaight–Eyres correspondence

Mells Archives (MA)

Lectures on the *Odyssey*
Wansbrough–Oxford correspondence
Correspondence between Oxford, Roger Mynors and Nicolas J. Barker
Patricia Cowan's bibliography of Knox's works

Private Papers in my possession

Knox Family Papers (KFP) (Papers formerly belonging to Patricia Cowan)
Ronald Knox's letters to his parents
Ronald Knox's letters to Dick Rawstone

Printed works

Baring, Maurice. *Translations Ancient and Modern*. London: William Heinemann, 1925.
Browning, Robert. *Pippa passes. III. Evening: Talk by the Way*. Translated into Theocritean hexameters by Ronald A. Knox. Oxford: Blackwell, 1908.
Bugliani Knox, Francesca (ed.). *Ronald Knox: A Man for All Seasons*. Toronto: Pontifical Institute of Medieval Studies, 2016.
Bugliani Knox, Francesca. 'Ronald Knox's Two Recording Angels'. In Bugliani Knox (ed.), *Ronald Knox*, 75–93.
Chappel, James. 'Ronald Knox: A Bibliographic Essay'. *Theological Librarianship* 1, no. 2 (December 2008): 49–53. (An online Journal of the American Theological Association.)
Fitzgerald, Penelope. *The Knox Brothers*. London: Flamingo, 2002.
Fraser, Laura, Baroness Lovat. *Maurice Baring: A Postscript by Laura Lovat with Some Letters and Verse*. London: Hollis and Carter, 1947.
Gilley, Sheridan. 'Knox, Ronald Arbuthnott (1888–1957)'. In *The Oxford Dictionary of National Biography* (version: 26 May 2016).

Knox, Ronald [Aburthnott]. *Auld Lang Syne* [by Robert Burns]. A rendering by Father Knox. [Ware: St. Edmund's College], 1929. Republished in Knox, *In Three Tongues*, 30–1.

Knox, Ronald [Aburthnott]. *The Beginning and End of Man*. London: The Catholic Truth Society, 1921.

Knox, Ronald [Aburthnott]. *The Belief of Catholics*. London: Sheed and Ward, 1939. (1st edn: Fleet Street: Ernst Benn 1927).

Knox, Ronald [Aburthnott]. 'The Classical Touch'. *Morning Post* 47, no. 202 (11 September 1923): 4. Reprinted as 'Pericles Versus Cicero' in Knox, *In Three Tongues*, 135–9.

Knox, Ronald [Aburthnott]. 'The Douay Version'. *The Tablet* 171, no. 5119 (18 June 1938): 794–5.

Knox, Ronald [Aburthnott]. 'The Fifth Georgics: A Cento from Virgil'. *The Oxford Magazine* 29 no. 24 (21 June 1911): 410–11.

Knox, Ronald [Aburthnott]. 'Foreword'. In Lowe, *Church Latin for Beginners. An Elementary Course of Exercises in Ecclesiastical Latin*, iv–vi.

Knox, Ronald [Aburthnott]. 'The Greeks at Sea'. In Ronald Knox, *Literary Distractions*. London: Sheed and Ward, 1958, 1–20.

Knox, Ronald [Aburthnott]. 'The Greeks Had a Word for It'. *The Tablet* 176, no. 5246 (23 November 1940): 408.

Knox, Ronald [Aburthnott]. 'Hymnus in Honorem S. P. N. Edmundi'. *The Edmundian* 14, no. 5 (February 1925): 147.

Knox, Ronald [Aburthnott]. 'In Memoriam'. *The Times* (9 July 1943): 7.

Knox, Ronald [Aburthnott]. *In Soft Garments*. 1st edn. [S.l.]: Burns Oates, 1942.

Knox, Ronald [Aburthnott]. *In Three Tongues*, edited by Laurence Eyres. London: Chapman and Hall, 1959.

Knox, Ronald [Aburthnott]. *Juxta Salices*. Oxford: Allen and Co., 1910.

Knox, Ronald [Aburthnott]. 'The Legacy of Greece. The Church and the Classics'. *The Tablet* 202, no. 5919 (31 October 1953): 430–1.

Knox, Ronald [Aburthnott]. *Londinium Defensum, a Play in Three Acts*. Supplement to the October issue of *The Edmundian* 15 (October 1925).

Knox, Ronald [Aburthnott]. *Memories of the Future: Being Memories of the Years 1915–1972*. London: Methuen, 1923.

Knox, Ronald [Aburthnott]. *The Mystery of the Kingdom*. London: Sheed and Ward, 1928.

Knox, Ronald [Aburthnott]. 'On the Effect of the Classics on Maurice Baring's Mind'. See Laura Fraser, *Maurice Baring: A Postscript by Laura Lovat with Some Letters and Verse*, 107–12.

Knox, Ronald [Aburthnott]. *Other Eyes than Ours*. London: Methuen, 1926.

Knox, Ronald [Aburthnott]. 'Preface'. In *A Spiritual Aeneid*. London: Green and Co., 1918.

Knox, Ronald [Aburthnott]. *Remigium alarum*. Oxford: Blackwell, 1910.

Knox, Ronald [Aburthnott]. Review (written in Latin) of *An Anthology of Medieval Latin* by Stephen Gassier. *Dublin Review* 178, no. 355 (October 1925), 302–4.

Knox, Ronald [Aburthnott]. *Sanctions: A Frivolity*. London: Methuen, 1924.

Knox, Ronald [Aburthnott]. *A Spiritual Aeneid*. London: Green and Co, 1918.

Knox, Ronald [Aburthnott]. *A Still More Sporting Adventure*. Oxford: Blackwell, 1911.

Knox, Ronald [Aburthnott]. *Thesauropolemopompus: A Play in Two Acts by A. B. Purdie and R. A. Knox*. In the supplement to *The Edmundian* of May 1925.

Knox, Ronald [Aburthnott]. 'Tractate on Tree Names in Virgil'. *The Edmundian* 25 no. 172 (Spring 1959): 100.

Knox, Ronald [Aburthnott]. *The Viaduct Murder*. London: Methuen, 1925.

Knox, Ronald [Aburthnott]. 'Virgil and the Future Life'. *The Tablet* 178, no. 5303 (27 December 1941): 396–7.

Knox, Ronald [Aburthnott]. 'Virgil's Religious Outlook'. *Ampleforth Journal* 25, no. 2 (Spring 1930): 109–29.

Knox, Ronald [Aburthnott]. *The Westminster Hymnal*. Rev, edn. London: Burns Oates and Washbourne, 1940.

Leach, Colin. 'Review' of Ronald Knox, *In Three Tongues*, edited by L. E. Eyres. *The Classical Review* 10, no. 3 (December 1960): 263.

Lowe, Joyce Egerton. *Church Latin for Beginners. An Elementary Course of Exercises in Ecclesiastical Latin*. London: Burns Oates and Washbourne, 1923.

Montarese, Francesco. 'Ronald Knox as Classicist'. In Bugliani Knox (ed.), *Ronald Knox*, 147–65.

Speaight, Robert. *A Modern Virgilian. A Memorial Lecture to Monsignor Ronald Knox*. London: Virgil Society, 1959.

Tastard, Terry. *Ronald Knox and English Catholicism*. Leominster: Gracewing, 2009.

Usborne, Richard. *A Century of Summer Fields. An Anthology 1864–1964*. London: Methuen, 1964.

Virgil. *Aeneid Books VII to IX*. Partly in the original and partly in English verse translation. Introduction and translation by Ronald Knox. Oxford: Clarendon Press, 1924.

Waugh, Evelyn. *The Life of the Right Reverend Ronald Knox*. London: Chapman and Hall, 1959.

Note on the Lecture List (Literae Humaniores) in *The Oxford University Gazette* (18 January 1912)

I'm indebted to Dr Clare Hopkins, the Archivist of Trinity College Oxford, author of *Trinity: 450 Years of an Oxford College Community* (Oxford: Oxford University Press, 2005), for the following information:

> Trinity had two lecture rooms at this date, both in the Front Quadrangle. One has now gone – it was a ground floor extension to Kettell Hall (today's staircase 2); the other was on the ground floor of the Northern staircase of the Jackson Building (now staircase 7), which is today in use as the Junior Common Room.
>
> As to which students may have attended Knox's Trinity lectures on the *Aeneid*. These lectures were for students reading for Literae Humaniores [see Figure 3]. The layout of the Lecture List seems odd – if this course was the General Introduction to Virgil, as also given by [Sir] Richard Winn Livingstone (below in the list, from 1933 President of Corpus Christi College) then we could assume it was for undergraduates in their first term following the part one examination – Honour Moderations – which was taken in the fourth term after matriculation. Therefore, the lectures would have been attended by students who matriculated in Michaelmas Term 1910 and took their Finals in Trinity Term 1914. The names of those who achieved Honours are listed in the University Calendar, published annually, which is also available in the Bodleian.
>
> However, the list suggests that some lecture courses were duplicated – e.g. on Horace's Satires I, and Tacitus' Annals I and II. And also in the case of Knox and Livingstone, perhaps. If this is indeed the case, presumably each one was intended for a particular group of Colleges, and I am afraid I do not know how to determine this. It could have been geographical perhaps, for instance, either side of a line drawn south of the Bodleian Library – but that is only a guess.

| 332 | OXFORD UNIVERSITY GAZETTE. | | | January 18, 1912. |

LITERÆ HUMANIORES (continued).
CLASSICAL LANGUAGES AND LITERATURE.

Subject.	Lecturer.	Time.	Place.	Course begins
GREEK BOOKS.				
Euripides, Iphigenia Taurica	Regius Professor of Greek, GILBERT MURRAY, M.A.	T. Th. 12	The Schools	T. Jan. 23
Æschylus, Choephoræ	L. R. FARNELL, M.A., D.Litt.	T. Th. 12	Exeter	T. Jan. 23
Aristophanes, Clouds and Frogs	J. D. BEAZLEY, M.A.	M. W. F. 12	Christ Church	M. Jan. 22
,, Clouds	H. L. HENDERSON, M.A.	T. Th. 12	New College	T. Jan. 23
Demosthenes, Public Orations (with papers)	P. E. MATHESON, M.A.	M. W. F. 10	New College	M. Jan. 22
,, Private Orations	A. W. PICKARD-CAMBRIDGE, M.A.	W. F. 10	Balliol	W. Jan. 24
,, Private Orations	T. W. ALLEN, M.A.	M. W. F. 10	Queen's	M. Jan. 22
,, Private Orations	G. C. RICHARDS, M.A.	T. Th. 10	Oriel	T. Jan. 23
,, Private Orations	E. E. GENNER, M.A.	M. W. F. 10	Jesus	M. Jan. 22
,, Orations, XX–XXIV (with papers)	A. B. POYNTON, M.A.	W. F. 10	University	W. Jan. 24
Pindar, Pythian Odes	L. R. FARNELL, M.A., D.Litt.	M. W. F. 12	Exeter	W. Jan. 24
Plato, Phædo	H. P. RICHARDS, M.A.	M. W. F. 12	Wadham	M. Jan. 22
,, Protagoras and Gorgias	W. PHELPS, M.A.	W. F.	Corpus Christi	W. Jan. 24
Theocritus (continued)	President of Trinity, H. E. D. BLAKISTON, D.D.	T. 12	Trinity	T. Jan. 23
Thucydides, VI (continued) and VII	J. U. POWELL, M.A.	Th. S. 12	St. John's	Th. Jan. 25
,, II	H. L. DRAKE, M.A.	M. W. F. 12	Pembroke	M. Jan. 22
LATIN BOOKS.				
Cicero: Philippics (Reconstruction of the archetype; textual criticism; metrical irregularities)	Reader in Latin, A. C. CLARK, M.A.	To be arranged	Queen's	To be arranged
Cicero: Select Orations	President of Trinity, H. E. D. BLAKISTON, D.D.	T. Th. S. 10	Trinity	T. Jan. 23
,, Selections	A. D. GODLEY, M.A.	T. Th. 10	Magdalen	T. Jan. 23
,, Orations	H. B. COOPER, M.A.	T. Th. S. 10	Keble	T. Jan. 23
,, Select Orations	R. TRUSLOVE, M.A.	M. W. 10	Worcester	M. Jan. 22
,, Verrines	F. W. HALL, M.A.	Th. S. 10	St. John's	Th. Jan. 25
,, Letters (Watson, Pt. II)	G. C. RICHARDS, M.A.	M. W. F. 12	Oriel	M. Jan. 22
Horace: Satires I	A. S. OWEN, M.A.	W. F. 12	Keble	W. Jan. 24
,, Satires I	H. W. GARROD, M.A.	M. W. 12	Merton	M. Jan. 22
Juvenal, Satires I–X	S. G. OWEN, M.A.	T. Th. S. 12	Christ Church	T. Jan. 23
Juvenal	F. W. HALL, M.A.	M. W. 12	St. John's	M. Jan. 22
Tacitus, Histories I, II	C. D. FISHER, M.A.	M. W. F. 12	Christ Church	M. Jan. 22
,, Annals I, II	E. C. MARCHANT, M.A.	T. Th. 12	Lincoln	T. Jan. 23
,, Annals I, II	A. B. POYNTON, M.A.	T. Th. 12	University	T. Jan. 23
Virgil	R. A. KNOX, B.A.	W. F. 10	Trinity	W. Jan. 24
,, (General Introduction)	R. W. LIVINGSTONE, M.A.	T. Th. 9.10	Corpus Christi	T. Jan. 23

Figure 3 Lecture List (Literae Humaniores) in the *Oxford University Gazette* (18 January 1912), p. 332.

Editing Criteria

Ronald Knox's Virgil lectures have come down to us in three versions.

1. The first, kept in the archives at Mells (box: ex/03/2802), is almost certainly the original typescript that Knox used for the Trinity lectures at Trinity College in Trinity Term 1912. It is in loose sheets, incomplete and contains corrections in Knox's handwriting, with summaries on the reverse of most pages. Titles are not typed but handwritten in green ink. The chapters do not follow the order in which Knox gave the lectures. The pages of chapter 8, called here, by whom is not known, 'Style' rather than 'Characteristics of Virgil's Style and Versification', appear after chapter 1; and chapter 2, called here 'Extracts from Virgil Lectures' rather than 'Religious Outlook', is at the end.
2. The second is Laurence Eyres's transcription, corrected, edited and bound in a volume in 1929 when Eyres was still Master at Stonyhurst. He took his transcription with him to Ampleforth, where he started teaching in October 1930.
3. The third, kept at Mells, is a typed transcription of version 2. It was copied out in 1970. It contains all the corrections that Knox had written in by hand in version 1, as well as the corrections that Eyres had included in version 2, but does not contain the summaries that Knox had included in version 1. References to line numbers in the *Aeneid* were added, by whom is not known, in pencil in the margin. Julian Oxford sent this copy to Macmillan.

I have used version 2 as *Hauptexemplar*, checking it against versions 1 and 3. I have taken this procedure for the following reasons:

a) Eyres attended Knox's lectures in 1912 and, after the War, on resuming his degree at Oxford in 1919, he borrowed version 1 from Knox. In 1929, Eyres typed out a copy, version 2. While doing so, he incorporated a few minor changes in consultation with Knox. In a letter dated 21 February 1946, Knox expressed his gratitude to Eyres for having prepared version 2 in such an exemplary fashion.

b) In version 2 Eyres inserted corrections that Knox had added (probably while giving the lectures) to version 1, corrected minor details, added footnotes with full references to passages in the *Aeneid* mentioned by Knox, and included the summaries that he, Knox, had included on the reverse of pages in version 1. He retained the references that Knox had included in the body of the text of version 1.

c) In 1967 Henry Wansbrough OSB, an eminent biblical scholar who had been teaching at Ampleforth since 1966 and was a colleague of Eyres, suggested to Julian Oxford that the lectures be published. Wansbrough prepared version 3, using version 2 to correct version 1, for publication.

The text of the Virgil lectures

In this edition of Knox's lectures I have followed version 2 edited by Eyres. Version 1 does not contain the titles of the lectures in typescript, though a few lectures have titles added in pencil. The titles that I have given are those added by Eyres, who modelled them on the brief descriptions that Knox gave when introducing, at the beginning of the first lecture (see 48–9 below), the lecture course as a whole. Knox added summaries of each paragraph of his lectures on the verso of his typescript. Eyres placed these summaries at the beginning of each paragraph. I have included them as footnotes.

I have retained Knox's punctuation and, almost always, capitalization. I have corrected the few slips in the quotations from Latin and in the line numbering reported by Eyres against the text of Conington's edition of Virgil, *Opera*, 3rd edn, revised, with corrected orthography and additional notes, by Henry Nettleship (London: Whittaker & Co. [1858–71] 1876). I have kept the Latin quotations in double inverted commas, as also the Italian and French. The conclusion to lecture 2, 'Virgil's Religious Outlook', appears only in a loose typescript page now held in the Trinity College archives: OF 22/14 Papers of T. F. Higham (classicist): RA Knox Collection: Knoxiana III.

I have italicized Latin terms, Eyres did not. I have italicized titles of works, Eyres did not. Eyres added footnotes containing references to passages in the *Aeneid*. I have inserted those references in square brackets in the text and added the number of the concluding line in round brackets when necessary. I have added a forward slash to signal, in the text, the beginning of new line in the quotations.

I have not italicized the titles of newspapers.

I have retained italics for emphasis.

I have kept small inconsistencies (B.C. sometimes before and sometimes after the date and 'book 6' as well as 'sixth book').

The references to passages in the *Aeneid* in round brackets are those included by Knox himself. Laurence Eyres added many book and line references by hand in his typescript copy of the lectures. I have included Eyres's references and, very occasionally, book and line references of my own in square brackets.

In quotations from the *Aeneid*, I have retained Knox's punctuation and his capitalization of the first letter of each verse. The English translations in square brackets are mine. The endnote references in Knox's text are also my additions.

Part One

Ronald Knox's Lectures on Virgil

1

Virgil's Political Outlook

§1. The life of Virgil, like that of all great poets, is supremely unimportant. It is enough to know that his life includes the period of the great civil war, – he was born in 70 B.C., before Cicero prosecuted Verres, before Catiline entered on his first conspiracy, before Pompey had won his laurels in the East, before anyone had heard of Caesar. He took the *toga virilis*, as we all know, on the same day on which Lucretius died, in the very year (55 B.C.) which dates the so-called Conference of Lucca, where Caesar, Pompey, and Crassus entered into renewed partnership, and the patriotic voice of Cicero was silenced. He was born at Mantua, brought up at Cremona, educated at Milan. He went to Rome to complete his education in rhetoric, and filled up his leisure time by writing the pseudo-Virgilian poems, *Culex, Ciris, Copa,* and what not. By 40 B.C. he had made the acquaintance of Asinius Pollio, and other less prominent historical figures like Alfenus Varus and Cornelius Gallus, also the poet Horace; and had published the *Eclogues*. It was in the troubles of 41, when Virgil was evicted from his farm in order to provide lands for one of Caesar's veterans, that he was first protected by the Etruscan *eques* Maecenas, who afterwards became his patron. The dating of the *Georgics* is uncertain, but their composition probably occupied the poet between 36 and about 29 B.C. The remaining ten years of his life were left to account for the poem we are to deal with in these lectures. Of his friendship with Horace, who called him "animae dimidium meae" [The half of my soul] and so on, of how he refused to write an epic of the civil war, of how he read the first six books to Augustus and Livia, and they both broke down in the passage of the sixth book when he referred to Marcellus, it is unnecessary to speak. The only two points about his life which are important for our purposes are (1) that he lived to see the pacification of the world and the foundation of the Empire by Augustus after a period of almost unexampled unsettlement in the whole of the known world, after thirty years of practically continuous civil war (59-29 B.C.),

---

§1. "On the life of Virgil, and why it is unimportant."

and (2) that the *Aeneid* itself was published after his death at the command of Augustus by Tucca and the poet Varius, the author himself having strongly expressed the wish that it should be burned, as he had not had sufficient time to put the finishing touches to it before his death in 19 B.C.

§2. But the history of a great poem does not end, it merely begins, with the death of its author. You have to remember, in reading Virgil, not merely the fifty troubled years of his life, but the years, 1930 of them, which have rolled by since his death. To understand him, you must appreciate not the influence which earlier literature had on Virgil, but the influence which Virgil has had on later literature. Virgil is like port, and old port. As you drink it not gulping, but rolling it round the tongue, you are reminded, not of the sunny fields from which the original fruit was gathered, the impression left by champagne, but the long vigil in the cool cellars which it has kept since first it was laid down. Virgil has become a part of history, and you must not read him apart from history. To make another comparison, he is like the Bible, and the book of Psalms in particular. It is idle to speculate what was the meaning in the mind of the author of Psalm 68, "Let God arise, and let his enemies be scattered", because it is for all time *the* Psalm which Cromwell and his men sang as a hymn of triumph on the battlefield of Dunbar. It is all very well to say that the verse "When the company of the spearmen and the multitude of the mighty are scattered abroad among the beasts of the people, so that they humbly bring pieces of silver, and when he hath scattered the people that delight in war" is in the original Hebrew an obscure reference to a hippopotamus in the bulrushes, that may be what the author of the Psalm meant by it, but it is assuredly not what Cromwell meant by it. It may be interesting to speculate what was the particular royal wedding in Palestine, which was celebrated in Psalm 45, but the important thing about it is that in Christendom its phrases have always been taken as applying to the Virgin Mary.

§3. The history of Virgil is hardly less varied or important than that of the Psalms. Quite a long book has been written in Italian on his estimation in the Middle Ages alone.[1] It is not so much the immediate reception, the "Nescio quid

---

[§2.] "That the importance of external history to the understanding of the *Aeneid* lies, not in the history of the world before or during Virgil's life, but in the history of the world since Virgil's death. This illustrated by comparison of port, and of the Bible; more especially the forty-fifth and the sixty-eighth Psalms."

[§3.] "On the effect produced by Virgil on his contemporaries and on later classical writers: on S. Augustine and on Savonarola: on the Middle Ages, and Dante in particular: on the Renaissance and Petrarch: on the classical period and on Voltaire: on the Venerable Bede, Burke, and Bossuet. On the spiritual pride of the nineteenth century: and why Carlyle and Hegel could not understand Virgil. On the mystical interpretation of Virgil, as carried out by the Daily Mail, the Spectator and the Church Times."

majus nascitur Iliade" [Something is coming forth greater than the Iliad] of Propertius, the petty attacks of the *obtrectatores Virgiliani*, who objected fatuously to peculiarities and innovations of style and syntax in his writings. It is not even so much the consideration that Virgil set for all time the type of Roman hexameters, that Lucan tried to reproduce his rhetoric, that Silius, Statius, Valerius Flaccus were mere shadows of him, that Juvenal parodied him and Tacitus based his style on him. It is the Confession of S. Augustine that the thought of Dido "exstinctam, ferroque extrema secutam" [Who had sought her doom with the sword and died] [6.457] affected him more than the peril of his own soul, and that the beauty of Virgil was among the things that made him cling so long to Paganism which could produce such poetry, and on the other hand the statement of Savonarola that the haunting magic of the words

Heu fuge crudelis terras, fuge litus avarum [3.44]

[Ah! Get away from this cruel land, get away from this avaricious shore!]

kept him firm amidst all opposition to his resolution of retiring from the world and becoming a friar. We remember how in the Middle Ages Virgil was held to have been a magician; by some, even to have been born of a virgin; that the *sortes Virgilianae* were as popular as the *sortes Biblicae* as a system of taking omens by opening a book at random, and trusting to the advice contained in the words the eye first lighted on; that S. Paul was supposed to have visited his tomb at Naples, and wept over his premature death:

Quem te, inquit, reddidissem
Si te vivum invenissem
    Poetarum maxime.

[What would I have made you, he said, if I had found you alive, greatest of poets!]

Nor do we forget Dante: it sounds paradoxical, but it is strictly true that Virgil owes at least as much to Dante as he does to Homer. The revival of learning did not cloud Virgil's reputation, as it did those of certain other idols of the Middle Ages, noticeably Aristotle. Petrarch wrote a Latin Epic called *Africa*; Voltaire boldly asserted that if the saying was true "Homer made Virgil", there could be no doubt that Virgil was by far his best work. Burke, like the Venerable Bede, always had a copy handy; Bossuet knew him by heart. It was only the unbearable conceit of the 19th century, that most intolerable form of literary snobbishness which despises all established reputations, and thinks no author good except such as its own appreciations have rescued from obscurity, that clouded the fame of the *Aeneid*. Bede understood Virgil, because Bede took the Christian religion on trust from other people: Hegel did not understand Virgil, because Hegel found it necessary to invent the Christian religion all over again for himself. Burke understood Virgil, because Burke was content to write English: Carlyle did not understand Virgil, because Carlyle insisted on writing Carlylese. Today the recoil has set in, and the world in returning to its old faiths is returning to Virgil. Virgil, like all great authors, writes his memorable lines with reference to a single, definite, and not necessarily very important occasion. "Timeo Danaos et dona ferentes" [I fear the Greeks, more so when they bring gifts] [2.49] is a quite random comment of Laocoon on the Trojan horse: "Non tali auxilio, nec defensoribus istis / Tempus eget" [This hour does not require such help or such defence] [2.521(–522)] is the outcry of Hecuba when she sees a ridiculous old man like Priam putting on his armour to fight against Neoptolemus: "Facilis descensus Averno" [The descent to Avernus is easy] [6.126] is a perfectly matter-of-fact way of saying that it is easier to get into Tartarus than to get out of it. Yet the Daily Mail leaders quote "Facilis descensus" in connexion with national degeneration, and the Spectator pulverizes Tariff Reformers with "Non tali auxilio", and elderly clergymen write to the Church Times applying "Timeo Danaos" to Liberal Education Bills.

§4. So the first way to make sure that you understand Virgil is to spell his name wrong. Always spell it with two i's, never with an e. Virgilius is the language of the Ages, and of the Church: Vergilius is a silly piece of pedantry raked up by unsympathetic modern scholars. All these same qualities which make Virgil attractive to the reader are far from making him an easy subject for the lecturer. You cannot translate Virgil, or comment on him, or annotate him: you can only read him and admire him. The purpose of these lectures is simply to pick out a few of the dominant characteristics of the *Aeneid* which go to make up its greatness and its charm. You will find notes, critical and grammatical and expository, in Conington,[2] if you do not mind their being rather elaborate, or Sidgwick,[3] if you do not mind their being excessively pompous. These lectures will be devoted almost entirely to the appreciation of the *Aeneid*, and that not wholly without a view to the General Paper in Honour Moderations.[4] They will deal, I imagine, with Virgil's outlook, national and political, with his religious outlook and his conception of the future life, with the romance and the pathos of Virgil, with his Art and the treatment of the story, with his use of his sources and

---

[§4.] "On the spelling of the name Virgilius, and what these lectures are going to be about."

models, with the characteristics of his style and his versification – partly with a view to the writing of Hexameter Verse – and also with his appreciation of scenery.

§5. The present lecture will be devoted to a consideration of the political interest of the poem. By the word political I do not mean to imply that Virgil was an independent political thinker. A system of benevolent despotism combined with careful literary patronage does not conduce to independent political thought. I mean that although the whole period of time occupied by the poem does not include any part of the strictly historical age of Rome, and indeed ends long before the city of Rome was built, we are being perpetually reminded by apparently casual allusions throughout the whole course of it that the history of Rome from Romulus to Augustus is present in the author's mind. Anchises, Aeneas and Ascanius contain the germs of all the future greatness of Rome. To take a random instance, in 7.717 the catalogue of the Rutulian troops has occasion to mention Allia, the place where the Romans, then quite a small power, were disastrously defeated by the Gauls under Brennus. The line runs simply

Quosque secans infaustum interluit Allia nomen,

[And those whom Allia, inauspicious name, divides with its stream]

but the words in apposition "infaustum nomen", which suggest to us no more than another beastly allusion to be looked up in the notes, must have made the heart of the Roman reader beat faster as he thought of the battle in which the nascent power of Rome was nearly crushed, as a result of which Rome itself was taken, and the Capitol only saved by the special favour of Heaven. With the same motive the names of the lesser heroes are often connected by an artful etymological device with the names of the families that became best known in later Rome. Mnestheus is the father of the Memmii [5.117], Cloanthus of the Cluentii [5.122–123], Sergestus of the Sergii [5.121], all in boat race in book 5. Clausus the Sabine, though he fights on the wrong side, is nevertheless hailed as the first of the Claudii [7.707–708]. And above all Virgil never loses an opportunity of dwelling on the future by introducing elaborate and singularly accurate prophecies, which he puts in the mouths of convenient seers. From the very first, Apollo guarantees the permanence of the Roman stock in its new soil

---

§5. "On the national tendenz of the *Aeneid*, as illustrated by anticipations of the later history of Rome, by geographical allusion, as in 7.717, by etymological speculation, as in the boat-race in book 5, by prophecies and forecasts, as in 3.97, 3.157, 3.500, and 4.625, and above all in the passages describing Aeneas' shield, the prophecy of Anchises in the Lower World, and the description of the site of Rome, or Pallanteum, in book 8."

[3.97], and the *penates* repeat the lesson of the glory that is to be in 3.157 [-158]. The main passage is of course that in which Anchises is discovered in Elysium marshalling the souls of the great leaders of Rome [6.756–886]. But as if this were not enough, when Vulcan is making a shield for Aeneas, he does not waste the golden opportunity by portraying on it, as he does on the shield of Achilles in the *Iliad*, mere scenes from the daily life of the period, invaluable to the antiquarian of later ages, but comparatively uninteresting to his immediate audience. No, he works in with great care as much of his Livy as time and space will permit [8.626–728]. Here is the suckling of Romulus and Remus, the rape of the Sabine women, the scene where Tullus has Mettius Fufius [or rather Fufetius] torn in pieces by horses, the expulsion of the Tarquins, Horatius swimming the Tiber, Cloelia ditto, Manlius defending the Capitol, the Salii, the Luperci, Catiline, and Cato. And the grand centre-piece of the work is naturally the battle of Actium, Augustus himself, Agrippa, Antony, Cleopatra, and Apollo backing the winner. This brings us down to history contemporary with the time of writing, but except for these broad outlines Virgil prudently abstains from introducing controversial matter, though the wanderings of Aeneas manage to remind us of Caesar's camp at Dyrrhachium and Actium itself by taking him to the Ambraciot gulf and Epirus. Sometimes the poet himself indulges in a mild forecast, as when Aeneas goes to visit Evander, whose city of Pallanteum is by great good luck built on the actual site of the later Rome, so that the poet has an opportunity of pointing out to us the position of the Capitol

> Aurea nunc, olim silvestribus horrida dumis (8.348)
>
> [Golden now, but once wild with forest brambles]

the Carmental gate, the Janiculum, the Argiletum, the Asylum, the Lupercal, and concludes with the pretty remark that they

> ... armenta videbant /Romanoque foro et lautis mugire Carinis (360 [-361]).
>
> [Saw cattle all around, lowing in the Roman Forum and the sumptuous Carinae]

There is something rather uncanny about it all: we are quite accustomed to scenes in poetry where the theatre of past glories is displayed: Byron is full of it: but it is quite another thing to be introduced to a sort of architect's plan of the buildings that are not to be built, we know, for some three generations to come.[5] At other times, Virgil varies his vein of prophecy by crediting his characters, not with divine inspirations indeed, but with very creditable guesses. Thus Dido in 4.625 forecasts the exploits of Hannibal by praying that a warrior of Carthaginian blood may arise to avenge her wrongs on the posterity of Aeneas. And in 3.500 and following in the text the hero himself makes a little complimentary speech to Helenus about how he hopes their respective descendants will be kind to one another, with the object of glorifying some uninteresting little colony founded by Augustus on the Eastern shore of the Adriatic.

§6. The net result of all this insistence on the future gives a peculiar interest to the *Aeneid*, which does not attach, I think, to any other work of fiction, unless we agree with that school of criticism which would apply the name of fiction to the story of Abraham. The key to it is given in the concluding line of book 8, in which Aeneas, having received from his mother the shield made for him by Vulcan, as described above, is said to go on his way

Attollens umero famamque et facta nepotum. [731]

[Raising up high on his shoulder the deeds and fame of his descendants]

The words are symbolic; of course they mean in the first instance simply that Aeneas is going about with a whole Art-gallery on his shoulder. But it is impossible to resist the feeling that Virgil means us to understand more than this, to understand that on the issue of the war to which Aeneas is going, on his own safety and that of Ascanius, who is at this very moment being hard put to it to defend the walls of the camp of which he has been left in charge, hangs the fate of all these interesting people, and the possibility of all these great deeds, this splendid world-power.

§7. And in this, I think, we have the explanation of the prominence given throughout the poem to Ascanius, or, as he is sometimes called, Iulus. Most people in commenting on Virgil seem to be very much attracted by the personal character of Iulus. I confess that to me he seems a rather dull little boy, pretty perhaps and with plenty of go about him, but irritatingly precocious and uninterestingly impeccable. When the Trojan fleet has already been set on fire by the women, at the end of book 5, and is blazing away merrily, what must he do but ride off to the shore, and throw his helmet on the ground and shout "Here am I, your Ascanius"[6] [5.672(–673)] as if that were likely to do any good. Any normally constituted boy of 11 or thereabouts would have been in transports of delight at the spectacle of such a splendid bonfire. And I always think that joke of his about eating tables [7.116] was a badly overestimated one. On the other

---

[§6.] "On the meaning of the last line of the eighth book".
[§7.] "On the meaning of the prominence given to Ascanius, and that Ascanius is in himself rather an uninteresting little boy, and why he is also called Iulus."

hand, the secret of Virgil's own interest in Iulus is quite clearly that he, and not Aeneas himself, is regarded as the founder of the Roman dynasty, rather arbitrarily, since neither of them founded the actual city. No doubt it contributes to the sentiment which enshrines the future of the family that its hopes should be centred in a life so young and so comparatively helpless: also, though Virgil could not very well have given the name Iulus to Aeneas himself as a second name, there was clearly nothing to prevent him applying it to Ascanius, whom he had simply invented himself: and the name formed a convenient bridge between that of Ilus, the eponymous king of Ilium, and the family whose descent the poet was anxious to trace to a Trojan source, that of the Julii [1.268, 288]. It is as if a modern poet, concerned to emphasize the directness of descent which allies our present monarch to the Conqueror, were to attribute to William the First a wholly imaginary son called Guelphiam.

§8. Since he is the repository of the hopes at once of Rome herself and of the family of the Julii, it is easy to see why Virgil made so much of this character in his story. It was not David, but Solomon, who built the house, it was not Aeneas but Iulus who founded the first permanent city of Alba Longa [1.271, 5.597]. So his name is coupled with that of his father when Ilioneus thinks they have both been lost at sea.

> Sin absumpta salus, et te, pater optimeTeucrum,
> Pontus habet Libyae nec spes jam restat Iuli (1.[555–]556).
>
> [If salvation has been taken away, and you, you, noblest father of the Trojans, have drowned in the Libyan gulf, and there is no more hope in Iulus]

And the "spes Iuli" becomes a regular catchword. It is "per spes surgentis Iuli" [By the hope in rising Iulus] that Palinurus adjures Aeneas to take him over with him in Charon's boat [6.364]: it is "per patrios Manes et spes surgentis Iuli" [By the spirit of your father, by your hope in rising Iulus] that Magus in 10.524 entreats him to spare his life. Pater Anchises and Iulus are always associated in this way, the one suggesting the city that has fallen, the other the city that is to be. The combination is most audaciously made in 10.534, where Aeneas, refusing to listen to these representations of Magus, says that the cruelty shown by Turnus in killing Pallas abolished for the moment all the courtesies of war; and adds, by way of authority for the assertion: "Hoc Patris Anchisae Manes, hoc sentit Iulus"

[58.] "On the so-called hopes of Iulus, and the use of the name Iulus in adjurations, as representing the future greatness of Rome, illustrated from 1.[555–]556, 10.524, 6.364, and 4.272[ff.], and explained by comparison of King Solomon.

[Thus deems my father Anchises' spirit, thus Iulus]. One might expect him to take into account what the wishes of his dead father would have been, but that he should allow this almost religious sanctity to the supposed wishes of a mere boy like Ascanius is impossible, unless we understand that Iulus is in a privileged position as the darling of Fate. It is the rights of Iulus, again, that are appealed to by Juppiter when he tells Aeneas to leave Dido and Africa and go on to Italy. If Aeneas himself has forgotten his high destiny, he might at least remember that he has others depending on him:

> Si te nulla movet tantarum gloria rerum
> Nec super ipse tua moliris laude laborem,
> Ascanium surgentem et spes heredis Iuli
> Respice, cui regnum Italiae Romanaque tellus
> debentur. (4.272–276)

[If the glory of such a fortune moves you not, and you do not yourself want to carry the burden for the sake of your own fame, keep in mind rising Ascanius, the promise of Iulus your heir, who is destined to gain the kingdom of Italy and the Roman land.]

Iulus is the important person, Aeneas is merely, it seems, a trustee.

§9. That is exactly the true description of the position of Aeneas: he is a trustee of fate. He has undertaken a contract, so to speak, to build a city, and a city he must build. The words of line 5 set the key for the whole poem, "Multa quoque et bello passus, dum conderet urbem" [Enduring many adversities in war too, until he should lay the foundations of a city]. The speech of Juppiter at any rate realizes the gravity of the issues at stake when Aeneas is suffering shipwreck.

> ... Manent immota tuorum/ Fata tibi, [1.257(–258)]

[Your children's fate remains fixed]

he says, and goes on to give Venus a complete history of Rome, so far as the Julian gens is concerned. If it be true, as the Epistle to the Hebrews tells us, that Levi in a certain sense paid tithes to Melchizedek, being yet in the loins of his ancestor Abraham when Abraham did so, it was equally evident to Virgil that Caesar in a sense conquered the Rutulians, being yet in the loins of his ancestor Aeneas. If

---

§9. "That Aeneas, properly regarded, is a trustee of Fate, valuable not so much in himself as for the line that is to spring from him. This conception illustrated from 1.5 and 1.257, and explained by comparison of Plutarch's *Life of Caesar*, and of the Epistle to the Hebrews. On the obvious parallel between Aeneas and Julius Caesar."

Aeneas had known all that Juppiter knew about the future, he might have said to Palinurus, his helmsman, what Caesar said to the frightened captain of the little boat in which he was having a rather stormy passage between Italy and Dyrrhachium: θάρσει, ὦ ἄνθρωπε, θάρσει, καὶ δέδιθι μηδέν· Καίσαρα φέρεις καὶ τὴν Καίσαρος τύχην συμπλέουσαν: "Be strong, fellow, be strong and fear nothing: Caesar is your passenger, and Caesar's fortunes are your freight". Caesar, like Sulla and Napoleon, had a belief in his star, and we may fancy that some echo of him lingers, despite all the immense difference of their characters, in Aeneas, the favoured of Heaven, the man of fate, the man who prepared the way, like Caesar, not for himself, but for his heir, to found a kingdom.

§10. This resemblance to Caesar has unfortunately followed Aeneas into another department of his conduct, with perhaps less admirable results. I cannot understand why it is that the point to which I am going to allude has received so little notice from Virgil's critics. The point arises in connexion with what must always be regarded as the weak spot in the *Aeneid*, the apparently heartless treatment which Aeneas gives to Dido. I suppose it is the gentleness of Dido's character which has blinded critics to the obvious comparison. Aeneas himself is not made to desert Dido simply because Virgil has got his hero into a hole and doesn't quite see how to get him out of it. Aeneas doesn't desert Dido simply because such good capital can be made out of the situation in the way of declamatory speeches. Aeneas deserts Dido simply because Aeneas is Julius Caesar, and Dido is Cleopatra.

It seems monstrous, an outrage, to compare the two. And yet look at the situation. In either case the man of fate is urgently needed in Italy, Caesar to put down what remain[s] of civil troubles, Aeneas to claim the hand of Lavinia. In either case he is confronted with a fascinating and energetic Queen, who loses her heart to him and determines to win his love. In either case she succeeds; the only question is, how long is it going to last? The call comes, the hero prefers duty to love; and the reason of his decision? In the case of Aeneas, he is moved to obey by the consideration that if he does not, there will be no opportunity for Ascanius to fulfill his glorious destiny, and found the line of Roman Kings. The implication is surely not far to seek. The fact that Caesar tore himself away from the arms of Cleopatra was a fortunate one for this reason if for no other, that but for his return to Rome it might have been impossible for Augustus to fulfill *his* glorious destiny, and found the line of Roman Emperors.

---

§10. "On a further resemblance between Aeneas and Julius Caesar."

§11. Why it is, that the story of Dido fails to give us this impression of a conflict in the breast of the hero between love and duty, there is no need to consider here. We shall have to discuss it later in connexion with Virgil's art and treatment of his plot. It must suffice to say here, that however unenviable, in modern eyes, the part played by Aeneas may appear, there is no doubt at all that Virgil himself regarded him as having chosen the better part, and that if he had remained in Carthage in deference to the feelings of the dusky Queen, he would have appeared in Roman eyes, and especially in Virgil's eyes, as having played the coward: just as Caesar would have done if at the critical moment in B.C. 47 he had failed to go and see and conquer at Zela, and left the world to manage its affairs as best it liked, while he remained in wanton dalliance with an Egyptian princess. In short, he would have been very much in the position in which Antony actually put himself some years later, the scorn and the execration of Europe. Read with this in your mind the directions of Juppiter to Aeneas in 4.227(–230):

> Non illum nobis genetrix pulcherrima talem
> Promisit, Graiumque ideo bis vindicat armis;
> Sed fore, qui gravidam imperiis belloque frementem
> Italiam regeret,

> [His most beautiful mother did not promise us that he would be such a person, nor for this did she twice rescue him from the weapons of the Greeks; but he was meant to be the one who should rule Italy, a land gravid with empire and roaring with war]

And the opening address with which Mercury delivers the message:

> ... Tu nunc Carthaginis altae
> Fundamenta locas pulchramque uxorius urbem
> Exstruis? Heu regni rerumque oblite tuarum! [4.265 (–267)]

> [Are you now laying the foundations of lofty Carthage and, acquiescent to a wife, erecting a fair city. Alas, forgetful of your own fate and kingdom!]

Might not the words have rung like a trumpet-call in the ears of Caesar, or filled the dissolute Antony with vain regrets? And what better compliment could Virgil pay to Augustus than to remind him that he was the heir of a man who in such circumstances had responded to the call of duty, and the conqueror of one who in the same circumstances had ignobly left the call unanswered?

[§11.] "On the issues at stake in the love-problem of book 4."

§12. Virgil is one of those authors who, as we shall see more fully later, are very apt to have a sort of key-word answering to the conceptions which dominate their thought. A careful observation of the small and apparently commonplace words in the *Aeneid* will very often be a clue to the underlying sentiment of the whole. And in this grand conception of the man marked out by destiny, fighting his way through to an issue of world-wide importance, the key-word is a very short and simple one – the word *res* in the plural. You cannot, needless to say, translate it "things". You will very often come across it in combination with the word *regnum*, as in the case just quoted: "Heu regni rerumque oblite tuarum!" [4.267] and elsewhere. Thus Juppiter says of the descendents of Aeneas

> His ego nec metas rerum nec tempora pono
>
> [On their power I set no limits of time or place]

he will set no limits or date to their power (1.278). Juno, too, hoping to thwart the victory of the Trojans, or at least delay its accomplishment, thinks to herself:

> At trahere, atque moram tantis licet addere rebus. [7.315]
>
> [But I can delay and postpone such great accomplishments.]

Evander addresses Aeneas as

> Maxime Teucrorum ductor, quo sospite numquam
> Res equidem Trojae victas aut regna fatebor. [8.(470–)471]
>
> [Greatest leader of the Trojans – for, while you are alive, I will never accept that the power and the kingdom of Troy have been conquered.]

And the very earliest promise made to Aeneas, by the mouth of his dead wife Creusa, tells him, speaking of Italy (2.783[–784])

> Illic res laetae, regnumque, et regia conjux
> Parta tibi.
>
> [There ready for you are a happy life, a kingship and a royal wife.]

Res in the plural means in an ordinary way just fortunes, but in the *Aeneid*, though it is sometimes used in a general, as in the words in 9.188 ("Cernis, quae Rutulos habeat fiducia rerum") [You see what confidence in

---

§12. "On Virgil's habit of referring constantly to these issues by the use of the word *res* in the plural, as in 4.267, 1.278, 7.315, 8.471, 2.783, and in the reference to *Trojana fortuna* in 6.62."

their fortunes possesses the Rutulians], it usually has a suggestion in it of a great future, the prospect of world-power. The unfortunate "res Asiae", the fortunes of Troy, which are spoken of in 3.1, lie behind: the "res Romanae" [The fortunes of Rome] live in the future. There is a very subtle touch in the words of Aeneas to Apollo, when he has at last landed in Italy, and is about to consult the Sibyl:

Hac Trojana tenus fuerit fortuna secuta! [6.62]

[May Troy's fortune only have followed us up to this point!]

We have had enough of the "Trojan fortunes", so proverbially unlucky, henceforth they are to be merged in the *Fortuna Urbis*, the fortune that was never known to fail.

§13. It is this continual orientation, this constant turning towards the dawn, that gives the *Aeneid* at once its atmosphere of optimism, and its sense of grandeur. It is a grand poem, because although its heroes are strictly men with living human characters, our pulses are constantly attuned to the greater issues which beat behind the characters. I do not mean that Virgil preaches, he does not tell us what the issues are, he has only to say Rome, and that was enough, and still may be enough, for his readers. But I think he does reflect in unconscious ways, like most writers of the period, a sense of profound thankfulness for the restoration of order, and the triumph of civilization. The *Iliad* does once compare the wild shouts of the Trojans with the quiet, steady advance of the Greek line; otherwise it gives, so far as I know, no hint of being conscious that the Trojan War is a conflict between civilization and barbarism. But the poets of the Augustan age, who had seen the whole world turned upside down, do appreciate the benefits of order. The lesson of the battle of Actium is to them always that Antony and Cleopatra stood for the wild and untamed East, and in Octavian Western civilization triumphed. "Barbarus" has become a term of reproach. And so Ovid is always complaining of the barbarity of the tribes round Tomi, to which he was exiled: it was not that the barbarians threatened his life, his trouble was that they could not understand his Pentameters. You will find this love of civilization coming out in all sorts of odd corners in the *Aeneid*. Laws and a senate are so much a necessity of life, that you never meet a city

---

§13. "On the underlying idea of the *Aeneid*, which is the idea of Rome: and that Virgil does not feel it necessary to explain or define this idea, as being self-evident: but that he clearly associated it with the march of civilization. On Virgil's love of peace and order, which is the sentiment of all the poets of the period, who represent a reaction from half-a-century of civil war: this illustrated from 1.426, 3.606, 1.263[-264], and the story of Cacus. Contrast between the new civilization of the Trojans and the primitive simplicity of the golden Age, 7.203[-204.]"

in Virgil so young and so newly-founded that its people have not started organizing them. In 1.426 the Tyrians who have emigrated under Dido have only just started building their walls, yet we hear that

> Iura magistratusque legunt, sanctumque senatum.
>
> [They choose laws and magistrates and they also choose a sacred senate.]

The first thing you have to build in any city must, to satisfy the claims of civilization, be the parish pump. And the feeling of disgust at the barbarian races is emphasized in the visit paid by Aeneas' ships to the Cyclops' island. They meet the unfortunate Achaemenides, who has been one of the companions of Ulysses, and has been living in the woods in fear of the cruel monsters ever since. He quite expects them, as enemies and Trojans, to kill him, but

> Si pereo, hominum manibus periisse juvabit. [3.606]
>
> [If I die it will be a blessing to have died at the hands of men.]

homines; not *viri*, brave men as opposed to cowards, but civilized men as opposed to men who are no better than beasts. He wants to die a gentleman's death. And there can be little doubt that the story told by Evander in the 8th book, how Hercules came to Italy, and killed the giant Cacus, a bloodthirsty monster who robbed and terrified the countryside [8.185–275], is in its way a tribute to Augustus: for Hercules is always regarded by the Euhemerist authors of antiquity as the type of civilization triumphant over the successive tasks which are needed before it can purify the world. These are but small indications of the bent of Virgil's mind; what we tend to overlook is the fact that Virgil definitely conceived the people of Latinus, against whom Aeneas fought, as aborigines, and barbarians. If you look at Juppiter's prophecy again (1.263[–264]), you will see that Aeneas when he gets to Italy

> Bellum ingens geret Italia populosque feroces
> Contundet moresque viris et moenia ponet
>
> [Shall wage a great war in Italy, shall crush proud nations and for his people he shall set up city walls and customs]

he is not only to give them walls, but actually to give them manners. We never suspect, from the kindly attitude of dear old Latinus, that his people are living in a state of Arcadian simplicity, yet this is the fact: "Neve ignorate Latinos" [And keep in mind that the Latins], he says (7.202)

Saturni gentem haud vinclo nec legibus aequam,
Sponte sua veterisque dei se more tenentem. [7.203(–204)]

[Are the race of Saturn, righteous not by compulsion or laws but self-controlled of their own initiative and by the custom of their ancient god.]

It is very nice, this Golden Age business, but it has got to vanish before the march of progress under the banners of Aeneas. In Virgil's time civilization was too young to have seen the rise of that disillusioned decadence which aspires to return to simplicity. Aeneas is to Turnus, what Prospero is to Caliban in the *Tempest*, the White man, and consequently the master of the savage. And whether we approve or disapprove, the fact that the *Aeneid* is an epic of civilization lends it grandeur. In the *Iliad*, what does it matter whether Hector falls, or Achilles? It will all be the same fifty years hence. In fact, the moral of the *Iliad* is, that all this waste of life can happen for the sake of a single paltry woman. In the *Aeneid* the moral is just the opposite, that such tremendous issues can hang on one or two very ordinary lives.

§14. That is the grandeur of the *Aeneid*, and its optimism is based on the same facts. We are always quite cheerful about the ultimate result of the war in Italy, because we know that the right cause is going to win in the end. But how do we know which is the right cause? Whence this certainty, that the Trojans are the more deserving side? The answer is, that this conclusion is justified by foreknown results. Their cause is the cause of Rome, and Rome is self-evidently good. Of course this doctrine is arrant imperialism, almost jingoism, but it is the ultimate article of Virgil's creed. Lucretius may have said to himself at the conclusion of the *De Rerum Natura*, "Quod erat Demonstrandum" [This is what needed to be proved]. Virgil, in finishing the *Aeneid* with the triumph of Aeneas, could say with no less confidence, "Quod erat Faciendum" [This is what needed to be done].

Notes

1 Domenico Comparetti, *Virgilio nel medioevo* (Livorno: F. Vigo, 1872).
2 John Conington (1825–69) was Corpus Christi Professor of Latin at the University of Oxford from 1854 till his death.
3 Arthur Sidgwick (1840–1920) was an educationist and classical scholar. He entered Corpus Christi college as a tutor in 1879, became a Fellow of Corpus Christi from

§14. "On the reason why the *Aeneid* is optimistic."

1882 to 1902 and Reader in Greek at Oxford from 1894 to 1906. He was a leading proponent of the admission of women to Oxford University.

4 Honour Moderations, commonly called 'Mods', are a first set of public examinations at Oxford taken during the first part of some undergraduate degree courses.
5 Rome was, in fact, founded over 300 years later.
6 Knox changed 'Iulus' to 'Ascanius' by hand in the carbon copy of his original typescript. Laurence Eyres has 'Iulus'.

2

Virgil's Religious Outlook

§1. Prof. Sellar[1] has a very ingenious paragraph in which he sums up the dominant characteristics of several famous Latin authors by a single word in each case, a favourite word of the author to which it applies. Cicero is the exponent of *humanitas*, Catullus of *lepor*, Horace of *urbanitas*: Lucretius gives the impression of *sanctitas*, Tacitus of the true Roman *gravitas*. It is not difficult to see whither this criticism is tending, when it comes to be applied to Virgil's case. Probably no one who has read any of the *Aeneid* at all would hesitate for a moment in ascribing to it the leitmotif of *pietas*. And this is not merely because the hero is described as "pius" Aeneas. We were told at our private schools never to translate *pius* in this case pious, but always "affectionate" or "dutiful" or some such nonsense. It is absolutely essential to the proper understanding of Virgil that we should forget all we were told about him at our private schools. If you even begin to look at the general usage of the word, you see at once that this sense of "affectionate" is ridiculously narrow, inadequate, and incidental, only fit to be instilled into one's mind at that time of life at which one is not allowed to smoke, or transgress bounds, or use *ut* with the perfect subjunctive in a historic final sequence.

> ... nec te tua plurima, Panthu,
> Labentem pietas nec Apollinis infula texit (2.[429–]430)

> [Neither did your all-round *pietas* nor Apollo's ribbon protect you, Panthus, as you fell]

it was not his affectionate disposition that might have been expected to save the priest of Apollo.

---

[1] "The characteristics of the chief Latin authors summed up in single words chiefly ending in *-tas*. The quality of *pietas* in Virgil, and that the masters at our private schools were wrong in making us translate it "affectionateness". Instances to prove this from 2.429[–30], 3.265[–6,] and 9.493[–4.]

> ... di, talem avertite pestem² [sic]
> Et placidi servate pios: (3.[265–]266)

[Gods, divert this affliction and kindly save the *pii*]

here again the religious sense of *pietas* is clearly uppermost in the poet's mind.

> Figite me, si qua est pietas, in me omnia tela
> Conicite, o Rutuli: (9.493[–494])

[Strike me, Rutulians, if you have any *pietas*, cast all your weapons on me]

had Euryalus' mother any reason to suppose that the enemy had feelings of affection towards Euryalus or herself?

§2. In order to realize the meaning of the word it is necessary to go quite far back into the most primitive Roman religion. It is a religion quite unconnected with the sophisticated anthropomorphic worship, introduced from Greece, which dominates conventional Roman poetry. The world is seen as a place full of mysterious and frequently malignant powers: every place has its genius, every agricultural process its tutelary deity, every action of life, the first cry of the infant, the act of eating or drinking, the act of leaving one's home or returning to it, is regulated and protected by a patron spirit. The woods and mountains are not peopled by jolly satyrs and desperately respectable nymphs, they are full of bogies and goblins. The spirits of the departed are not satisfied with being buried or burnt, they come up every year from their tombs, and have to be placated or exorcized. In a world so full of occult influences, some good, some bad, some merely indifferent, the man who stands most chance of succeeding in life is the man who knows exactly the right forms by which to invoke, to appease, or most frequently to drive away the particular spirit he has to deal with – the medicine man, the man skilled in white magic. It might seem unnatural for a respectable householder to visit the tombs of the dead one night every year, and spit black beans out of his mouth, and shout nine times over his shoulder the spell "Manes exite paterni" [Go out paternal ghosts], but if a man neglects these simple precautions, and is then troubled with ghosts, he has only himself to blame for it: he is as culpable as the modern landlord who refuses to have the drains looked to. Life becomes a preposterous system of taboos, and the further you advance in sanctity of position, the more uncomfortable is the burden of religious obligations

---

§2. "The real meaning of *pietas* determined by a consideration of early Roman religion, and the strong spirit of tabooism contained in it. Illustration of this tabooism, from the uncomfortable life lived by the priest of Juppiter."

you have to meet. It will suffice to instance the case of the unfortunate priest of Juppiter, who: "might not ride, or even touch, a horse, might not touch flour or wheaten bread, might not touch or even name a goat, a dog, raw meat, beans, and ivy, might not walk under a vine, might not see work being done on holy days, might not be uncovered in the open air, might not anoint himself in the open air, might not be for one night away from Rome, might not touch or step over a dead body" (Allen on Plutarch's Roman Questions[3]).

§3. Rome is in fact the birthplace of ceremonial, and it was left for the influence of Rome in the Christian Church to press into the service of a higher cause all that was good in this inborn liturgical instinct of the Italian mind; to vindicate the principle that there should be one way of doing things, and one only, for all the world, and that there should be no spiritual contingency, however remote, which could not be met by a fixed and appropriate method of spiritual treatment. But whereas the ritual of Christendom is, except in the broadest possible outline, admittedly of human invention, the ritual of pagan Rome was a system of magical formulas and sacrifices which the unseen powers demanded as of right; there was constant need of human ingenuity to discover precisely what these demands were, and of human carefulness to see that when discovered they were carried out, that tribute should be paid to whom tribute was due, honour to whom honour, fear to whom fear. You were always fencing with the invisible, always endeavouring to find out the passwords which would secure you safe conduct through this army of impalpable foes.

§4. The man who knows what sins or impurities need expiation, and what *piacula* are appropriate in each different *case* is, radically, the man who is *pius*. In this sense, when we speak of *pius* Aeneas, we mean practically, "Aeneas, that trained liturgiologist". He is the man who, in that horrible phrase invented by the Evangelist Dr. Torrey,[4] always knows how to "get right with God". The priests or poets who have found their way to Elysium in the 6th book are described as "pii vates et Phoebo digna locuti" (6.662), where Conington says "pii = casti" – I do not agree with the comment. I think the true rendering is "Priests, or poets, who were always on the spot and said exactly what Phoebus wanted them to say". Aeneas is usually called *pius* at moments when he appears as doing the right thing.

[3.] "Difference between ancient and modern Roman ritual, that the ancient Roman ritual was not invented by man, but discovered by man, as a series of rites and spells by which alone certain supernatural contingencies could be met."

[4.] "Application of this, that the word *pius* denotes one who is an adept in such white magic. The conception illustrated from the terminology of Torrey and Alexander. This primary meaning of *pius* illustrated from the *Aeneid*, 6.662, 7.5, 6.232, 5.685, 5.26; not a mere metrical necessity, compare 1.699, 5.348. Significant contrast between the attitude of Turnus in 7.415 [ff.], and that of Aeneas in 1.314 [ff.]"

> At pius exsequiis Aeneas rite solutis
>
> [But *pius* Aeneas, having duly performed the funeral rites]

is the description of him when he has to bury his old nurse Caieta (7.5); *pius*, I think, not because he was so affectionate towards the ashes of his nurse, but because he did the whole thing *rite*, decently and in order. It is *pius* Aeneas in book 6, line 232, who raises a mound to the dead Misenus, and puts his arms, his oar, and his trumpet on the top of it. When he finds his ships on fire, he argues, "What we want is some rain, Juppiter is the proper person to apply to for rain", and immediately, with great success, prays to Juppiter (5.685) – here again the favourite epithet is applied. *Pius* Aeneas, the reverent Aeneas, as we might say, is quite equal to the occasion when Palinurus (5.26) finds the wind will not allow him to steer for Italy: "of course", he says, "it has been obvious for a long time that the winds didn't want you to go, it's no good trying to get round the winds. And after all, it's a sort of Providence; what could be more delightful than paying another call on dear old Acestes, who lives quite close?" This is not merely a fanciful emphasizing of the epithet; for it will be found that in most cases when Aeneas is not being noticeably religious he is not *pius* Aeneas, but *pater* Aeneas, as in 1.699 where he is sitting down to dinner with Dido, or 5.348, when he is awarding the prizes at the games. There is no getting round Aeneas; you can't take him off his guard. In 7.415[ff.] the fury Allecto disguises herself as an old priestess, and presents herself to Turnus; he takes her at her face value, is rather rude to her, and gets into dreadful trouble over it. But in 1.314, when Venus goes to meet her son, dressed up as a new woman, Aeneas is on the look-out for something of the kind, and addresses her with infinite tact: "No, I haven't seen any of your sisters about, Miss – let's see, what ought I to call you? You see, your face isn't the face of a mortal, and your voice is more than human – why, you must be a goddess! Diana, perhaps? Or one of the nymphs? Well, whoever you are, please be propitious ..." and so on. That kind of man can never entertain Angels unawares, because he never meets anybody without fully canvassing in his mind the question whether they are Angels or not.

§5. No doubt, the meaning of the word *pius* is extended beyond this purely religious connotation, and is used by Virgil himself to signify loyalty to any natural obligation, to parents for instance or kings quite as much as to gods.

---

[55]. "The use of the word *pius* extended to secular affairs, denoting the fact that a person observes the rules of the game, as in 5.296, or has a sense of the fitness of things, as in 9.493, or is thoughtful for others, as in 1.305."

Anybody is *pius* in so far as he observes the rules of the game; the love of Nisus for Euryalus is called "amore pio pueri" [respectful love for the boy] (5.296) simply to shew that there is nothing inordinate about it. In fact, it comes to mean hardly more than having a sense of the fitness of things. Euryalus' mother appeals to the Rutulians to shoot her, "siqua est pietas" [If you have any *pietas*] (9.493), because it is, as it were, appropriate for his murderers to be her murderers too. And with Aeneas himself it might often be translated just "thoughtful", as in 1.305, where he goes out early in the morning to explore the country and report on it to his companions at breakfast.

§6. But in spite of the root meaning, Virgil has really moralized the epithet. It is not mere scrupulosity, or gratuitous ritualism that *pietas* implies. To Virgil, the carelessness which neglects divine warnings and divine institutions is a criminal carelessness. The real villain of the *Aeneid* is not Turnus, for all his violence and pompousness. It is Mezentius, the "contemptor divum" [Scorner of the gods] [7.648, 8.7]. And in the same way the heroine of the *Aeneid* is not Dido, for all her beauty and pathos; it is that fluffy little pink-and-white creature Lavinia: and this, because Dido went back on the vow of perpetual widowhood which she had made on the death of Sychaeus, without any directions from heaven [4.24(–29), 4.552]. Aeneas on the other hand deserves all he gets from Olympus because he is so painstaking about the whole thing. For instance, when he is stopping in Crete (3.148 [ff.]), the Penates appear to him one night when he is in bed, and direct him as to his further course. A Mezentius would have been grateful for the warning, and turned over to resume his much-needed sleep. Not so Aeneas –

Corripio e stratis corpus tendoque supinas
Ad caelum cum voce manus . . . (3.176–177)

[I hurry out of bed and lift my upturned hands to heaven together with my voice]

he can't even wait till the next morning to express his gratitude. And the extent of his piety is enormous. He kills a good many Rutulians in the *Aeneid* but he kills far more cattle. I had the curiosity to look through the *Aeneid* at the accounts of sacrifice, and count up Aeneas' bag. Besides numerous occasions on which the details are not specified, he manages to dispose of no less than 15 sheep, 13 bullocks, 3 bulls, 3 calves, 3 pigs, 2 lambs, and a cow, not to mention 5 bowls of

---

[§6.] "How Virgil has moralized the purely ritual sense of the word, first, by insisting that it is criminal carelessness not to take trouble about religious observances, as in the cases of Mezentius and Dido. The carefulness of Aeneas instanced from 3.148. Aeneas' sacrificial bag in the course of the *Aeneid*."

wine, 3 of blood, and 3 of milk. Some critic has made a remark to the effect that Aeneas was far more suited to be the founder of a community of contemplative monks than the founder of an Empire. That may be true: but then, it is much easier to found an Empire successfully than to found a successful community of contemplative monks.

§7. And after all, Aeneas got as good as he gave. No hero was ever so signally favoured by Heaven. It was not merely that he had arms made for him by Vulcan [8.441ff.], and was rescued from the sea by Neptune [1.142ff.], and got Juppiter to extinguish his burning ships [5.693ff.], and Venus to supply a special remedy for his wounds [12.411ff.]. He is also emphatically the man of visions: he moves constantly under the guidance of divine revelations. When he is cast up by the storm on the coast of Africa, Venus meets him and explains to him [1.338(ff.)] (incidentally also, of course, to the reader) the precise state of the country and the history of Dido. In his account of his travels, he records a visit of Hector's ghost [2.270ff.], warning him of the doom of Troy, another appearance of Venus cautioning him not to kill Helen [2.589ff.]; a portent which reconciles Anchises to accompanying his flight [2.680ff.]; a visit from the dead Creusa [2.772ff.]; a bit of a start when he tries to pull up a tree, which proves to be Polydorus [3.27(ff.)]; a special oracle, personally delivered, at Delos [3.94ff.]; he is told by the Penates that he must go to Italy [3.154ff.], is given a gloomy picture of his sufferings there by Celaeno the Harpy [3.245ff.], and has his full course mapped out for him by Helenus [3.374ff.]. All this in three books, and the theophanies by no means fall off in the later parts of the poem.

§8. Each fresh revelation evokes fresh piety; each fresh piety evokes a fresh revelation. This is the second way in which Virgil makes a moral advance in his conception of *pietas*. There is only one sense which can be attached to the famous phrase (2.536) used by Priam when he sees his son Polites killed by Neoptolemus:

> Di, si qua est coelo pietas quae talia curet
>
> [Gods, if there is any *pietas* in heaven that cares for such things]

"If there is any piety in Heaven", that is, if there is any corresponding return there for the tribute of *pietas* received from earth. Dido, when deserted by Aeneas,

---

§7. "This carefulness of Aeneas rewarded by singular favours from heaven: a list of some such favours."

§8. Thus, Virgil has moralized the conception of *pietas*, secondly, by making it include an obligation on the part of the gods, corresponding with the obligation on the part of men. Instances of this from 2.536, 4.382, and 5.688. Approach to the meaning of the modern word derived from it, "pity".

recurs to exactly the same idea: Aeneas will inevitably be drowned in his treacherous course to Sicily "si quid pia numina possunt," [4.382] if there is any force in the righteousness of the gods – the gods have rules to observe, duties which they owe to men. And Aeneas, in appealing to Juppiter in a passage already cited, says "si quid pietas antiqua labores /Respicit humanos" [If your *pietas* of old has any regard for human sorrows] [5.688 (–689)], where the idea of justice has almost passed into the fuller conception of our derivative word "pity": we can almost hear the Jew speaking: "Remember, O Lord, thy loving-kindnesses, which have been ever of old" [Ps. 25:6].

§9. But in general the conception is one of justice, rather than of mercy. The gods, too, must have their sense of the fitness of things. There is a sort of pact or covenant between the god and his worshipper which neither side can creditably break. It is thoroughly Jewish: the Trojans, no less than Israel, are a chosen people, with a land of promise: Aeneas, like Abraham or David, have promises they can claim: the Lord hath made a faithful oath unto David, and he shall not shrink from it. This is not the impression one derives from Homer, even in the cases where the resemblance between Homer and Virgil is closest. The sacrifice in Homer is simply a bribe, which the god can take without in any way binding himself, to be influenced by it: ἀλλ' ὅ γε δέκτο μὲν ἱρά [*Iliad* 2.420] [But he accepted the sacrifices], he took the bribe, but did not grant the prayer. Further, although Virgil follows Homer almost slavishly in his representation of the divine agency as it affects human affairs, although the powers of heaven are still at war with one another, although Hercules cannot save Pallas in 10.464, or Diana do more than avenge the death of Camilla in 11.586, there is less sense in Virgil than in Homer of destiny overruling the will of individual gods. Juno is struggling against fate, but the antinomy is softened by the very fact that she is throughout conscious of it. She seeks to delay, rather than to frustrate, the purposes of destiny, to persecute Aeneas, not to kill him. She is sulky, and as she knows she is beaten, is determined not to yield with a good grace.

> Non dabitur regnis, esto, prohibere Latinis,
> Atque immota manet fatis Lavinia conjux;
> At trahere, atque moras tantis licet addere rebus,
> At licet amborum populos exscindere regum. (7.313[–316])

[59.] The conception of a covenant, thus introduced, makes Virgil's conception of Fate a more moral one than Homer's. We find echoes of the despondency of Homer's outlook, as in 10.464, and 11.586, but the contrary principle is vindicated by the attitude of Juno in 7.313 [–316], 10.[622–]623[–624] and 12.147.

[Granted: I am not allowed to keep him from his Latin kingdom and Lavinia remains surely fated to become his bride; but delay and postpone such great accomplishments, that I am allowed to do; indeed, I am allowed to destroy the people of both kings.]

So Juppiter allows her to put off the death of Turnus:

Si mora praesentis leti tempusque caduco
Oratur iuveni meque hoc ita ponere sentis,
Tolle fuga Turnum atque instantibus eripe fatis. (10.[622–]623[–624])

[If what you are praying for is a delay of imminent death and some more time for the young man who is about to fall – if you understand that these are the terms that I set, help Turnus flee and snatch him from looming death.]

and in 12.147[ff.] she herself explains to Juturna, the sister of Turnus, that so long as she *thought* fortune and the fates might allow Latium to triumph, she did her best to defend it, but now she realizes that Turnus has no chance; though it is true that immediately afterwards she urges Juturna, somewhat inconsistently, to save her brother still if there be any way possible. I do not mean of course that in theory Virgil ever gets over the difficulty about the relation of the different gods to fate any more than Homer does, but he somehow manages to keep it in the background by making Juno acknowledge to herself from time to time that her own attitude is not a logical one.

§10. And after all, Virgil's presentation of fate is far more ideal than Homer's. In Homer Zeus simply holds the scales in his hands, and one of them, for no ostensible reason, wins the day. Virgil has imitated this in 12.725, but the general use of the word *fatum* in the *Aeneid* shews that his ordinary conception of it is by no means so childish or colourless. Fate in Homer, if it has any moral determination at all, is uniformly cruel and unpleasant. Virgil, if he does not reach the idea of Providence, at least rises to that of destiny. Juno is thwarted, not because the fates of a Dido or a Turnus are so bad, but because the fates of the Trojans are so uniformly good. Aeneas, we have already seen, is the man of destiny; this fact, combined with the patriotic moral which lies behind it, the moral of the future greatness of Rome, gives an ethical complexion to the divine purposes which Homer's ephemeral champions never dared to claim. Troy was burned in order to satisfy a couple of angry goddesses: Troy rose from her ashes for a much better reason – namely that without this resurrection Rome would

---

§10. "Underlying this theological moral we may trace a political moral: the final cause of the determination of the fates (they are not really indeterminate, in spite of 12.725) is the future destiny of Rome."

never have been built. The methods of Providence are still as inscrutable as ever, but its ultimate motives are now as clear as daylight. Juno is defeated, not simply because she is striving against Juppiter, or against the consensus of Olympian opinion, or even because she is striving against the fates, she is defeated because she is, ultimately, striving against Augustus. The whole thing is a foregone conclusion.

§11. But though Destiny is working out its purposes, there is none the less room for the action of human free-will. The highest duty of man, to put it in theological language, is to find out what are the decrees of fate, and then to correspond to them. This is most forcibly brought out in the case of Dido. She does indeed attempt to find out the divine will by consultation of seers, *but she never for a moment means to follow it*. It is quite futile to understand the famous words of this passage (4.65[-67]), as some have done, to mean that the soothsayers are useless people, because they cannot foresee Dido's tragic end.

> Heu vatum ignarae mentes! Quid vota furentem,
> Quid delubra juvant? Est mollis flamma medullas
> Interea, et tacitum vivit sub pectore vulnus.
>
> [Ah! The blind souls of soothsayers! What good are prayers and shrines to someone who is out of control? All the while the flame keeps eating the tender bone marrow and the silent wound is alive deep in her chest.]

The point is surely this: – if the soothsayers had been really omniscient, they would have known that Dido was not in earnest in consulting the oracle: "tacitum vulnus", the wound of love that is hidden from their eyes, is all the time (to use theological language again) placing a bar against the validity of her sacrifice: Virgil doesn't even take the trouble to tell us whether the oracles were favourable or not, or, for the matter of that, what the question was which she put to them, because it was clear from the start that whatever they said she would go her own way, and take no sort of notice of them. And the tragedy of the situation, which is also the crime of Dido, is that this course of hers is standing in the way of the founding of Rome, of the *Fortuna Urbis*, and she never took the trouble to find out this elementary fact. She is not blamed for falling in love with Aeneas – that was the work of Venus; nor for bringing that passion to what we should consider a guilty consummation in the forest cave –that was the work of Juno: even her desertion of the memory of Sychaeus might have been forgiven her: her crime is, that she has

---

§11. "The function of human free-will is to correspond with the decrees of Fate. Failure to do this instanced from the case of Dido, as is seen by a proper understanding of 4.65[-67]".

not been at pains to identify her own interests with those of the Roman Empire that is to be.

§12. Indeed, to Virgil's *pietas*, the very fact of struggling against fate is not a noble thing, but a very blasphemous and irreverent thing. "Desine fata deum flecti sperare precando" [Stop hoping that by praying you may alter the fate set by the gods] is quite sufficient answer to Palinurus when he expects to get ferried over the Styx as a member of Aeneas' suite (6.376); and Juppiter himself is shocked when Cybele wants him to make the Trojan fleet, which was built in her own woods, invulnerable against the attacks of the Rutulians:

> O genetrix, quo fata vocas? aut quid petis istis?
> Mortaline manu factae immortale carinae
> Fas habeant? (9.94)

> [What are you asking fate to do, Mother? What are you asking for these ships of yours? Should keels built by mortal hands have a right to become immortal?]

He can't understand her attitude: that sort of thing simply isn't done. We all know the famous description of Cato in Lucan's *Pharsalia*: "Victrix causa deis placuit, sed victa Catoni" [The victorious cause pleased the gods, but the vanquished cause pleased Cato] and most of us admire the quality it conveys. Now, that line, so far as diction goes, is one that Virgil might have been proud of; but the sentiment is one that would have seemed to him pure nonsense. Cato might possibly, through invincible ignorance, have failed to realize which side the Gods were fighting on, and indeed, presumably on this understanding, he may have been included in the picture of Elysium on Aeneas' shield ("Secretosque pios: his dantem iura Catonem", 8.670) [And set apart are the *pii*; and Cato giving them laws], though it seems highly probable that here the elder Cato is meant, and the patriot of Utica is simply passed over in silence. But the suggestion that Cato, being a good man, saw what the will of the fates was, *and then deliberately set himself against it*, is hopelessly un-Virgilian; it would put Cato in the same category as Mezentius.

§13. It is a point not to be left unnoticed, that *pietas*, the duty of punctual performance of dues to the gods, and careful ascertaining of their will, by no means obscures in Virgil's mind the purely moral, not distinctively religious duties of man. The verb *mereor*, with its corresponding adjective *dignus*, is quite

---

§12. "Further instances of the impiety, according to Virgil's creed, of trying to thwart the purposes of Fate, from 6.376, and 9.94[–96]. Difference of attitude between Virgil and Lucan."

§13. "*Pietas*, in the sense of ceremonial accuracy, is not the sole moral conception of the *Aeneid*, but is corrected by a frequent insistence of the doctrine of merit, which may be illustrated from 7.[304–]307, 12.[851–]852, and 6.664."

one of the key-words of the *Aeneid*. Thus in 7.[304–]307 Juno, complaining that the other goddesses have been allowed to wreak their vengeance on their enemies, while she is not allowed to persecute Aeneas, says

> ... Mars perdere gentem
> Immanem Lapithum valuit; concessit in iras
> Ipse deum antiquam genitor Calydona Dianae,
> Quod scelus aut Lapithas tantum, aut Calydona *merentem*?

> [Mars had the strength to destroy the giant Lapith race; and the Father of the gods himself gave old Calydon up to Diana's rage, and yet what great crime had the Lapiths or Calydon committed to deserve such fate?]

The anger of the gods is thus not based on a mere caprice: their victims are people who have incurred some kind of moral guilt. Just as in 12.[851–]852 Juppiter

> ... letum horrificum morbosque deum Rex
> Molitur, meritas aut bello territat urbes,

> [The king of the gods lets loose horrible deaths and diseases or terrifies with war cities which have deserved them]

only the cities which have *merited* his vengeance by their sins. And he even carries us into the more attractive sphere of positive merit, of righteousness claiming a reward, in a single golden line (6.664), where he places among those who have reached Elysium

> Quique sui memores aliquos fecere merendo.

> [Those who have made other people remember them by behaving in a deserving manner.]

Look through the whole of the *Iliad*, and you will never find the word ἄξιος used in any but the purely commercial sense of "fetching so much".

§14. This leads us on to the consideration of Virgil's greatest and best-known achievement in the department of religion – the account of a future life in the 6th book. A great deal of unnecessary difficulty has been felt by various critics about this part of the poem – unnecessary, because we have here that most valuable of all commentaries, the commentary of another great poet freely and without

---

§14. "Virgil's conception of a future life, and the value of Dante's *Divina Commedia* as a commentary on it. This includes most of the sixth book."

apology imitating his predecessor. If you cannot understand the fitness of things in Virgil's scheme, you have only to turn up the *Divina Commedia* and see how a kindred spirit dealt, *mutatis mutandis*, with precisely the same problems.

§15. The anteroom of hell [6.273ff.] is occupied by all the supernatural agencies, some mythological, some merely personified, which cause distress to mankind, furies and Gorgons and harpies, Death and Cares and War and Disease and Lethargy and so on: all the things which there was no room for anywhere else, since they did not naturally belong to earth, clearly would be out of place in heaven, and yet could not be supposed to have deserved the punishments of hell. It is purely a matter of convenience to locate them here, on the hither side of Acheron: Dante, having no use for such classical conceptions, assigned this region

> ... a quel cattivo coro
> Degli Angeli, che non furon ribelli
> Né fur fedeli a Dio, [Inf. III, 37–39]

> [To that evil choir
> Of Angels, who have not rebellious been,
> Nor faithful were to God]

the angels who refused to take either one side or the other when Michael fought against the Dragon, and with them the souls of men

> Che visser sanza 'nfamia, e sanza lodo, [III, 36]

> [Who lived without infamy or praise]

the mugwumps,[5] in fact, the Tomlinsons,[6] who could not make up their mind between light and darkness, and therefore cannot enter either Hell or Purgatory, but are none the less very justly punished.

§16. On the further side of Acheron the first region arrived at is that of Limbo (line 426ff.), reserved for those spirits who never had the opportunity of shewing what use they would have made of their lives; primarily, therefore, infants

---

[§15.] "Approach to the infernal regions (6.273–294). This is occupied in Virgil by various mythological lumber, and personified abstractions, for which there was no room anywhere else. In Dante, this position is assigned to the mugwumps."

[§16.] "The first division of the lower world, which is limbo, the place of babies who died in infancy, and those who, being condemned on earth by unjust judgment, never had the chance they deserved of shewing how their characters would have developed. Conington is here in error, because he thinks that the duty of Minos was to judge the souls when they got to limbo, whereas it is clear that they are sent to limbo only because the verdict of Minos has been given "not proven". This occupies lines 426–433 of Book 6."

> Quos dulcis vitae expertes et ab ubere raptos
> Abstulit atra dies et funere mersit acerbo. [428–429]
>
> [Those whom the day of doom swept off, torn away from the breast, and having had no taste of sweet life, plunged in bitter death.]

But not only infants; it includes also those who were condemned by false judgement – why these? Surely because of the fact that their death was unmerited, that they were unjustly deprived of part of their time of probation on earth through no fault of their own. This claim is set against a certain amount of demerit on their part. If they had been given the space of life the fates were prepared to allot them, no one can be sure they would not have repented, so they cannot be assigned either rewards or punishments. And here the commentators find a difficulty, for Virgil adds

> Nec vero hae sine sorte datae, sine judice sedes:
> Quaesitor Minos urnam movet; ille silentum
> Consiliumque vocat, vitasque et crimina discit. [6.431–433]
>
> [But they were not assigned their places without lots, without juries. Minos, the president of the Court, shakes the lots in the urn; it is he who summons the council of the dead and enquires about the misdeed in their lives.]

"We are ready to ask", says Conington, "whether it is not the business of the tribunal of the other world to rectify the inequality of earthly judgments; and lest the thought should not occur to us, Virgil himself suggests it by telling us that the cases of these misjudged sufferers are reheard below. The natural conclusion would be that, after this rehearing, the spirits, now truly judged, are sent to Tartarus or Elysium; but of this no word is said, and we are left to suppose that they remain in the dubious limbo where we first find them." Now, this criticism is all hopelessly beside the mark. What Virgil says is not that when they get to limbo, they are thereupon judged, it is the judgment of Minos which *sends* them to limbo. At least, Virgil's language must be strangely un-Virgilian if he does not mean us to understand by the words "Nec vero hae sine sorte datae sedes", "This sphere is not assigned to them at random, without proper investigation." That is to say, they are first judged by Minos, and he weighs their previous life: if they were exceptionally good or exceptionally bad, we must suppose that he would send them off to Hell or Heaven, as the case might be; but if they have been on the whole wicked, and yet have not been allowed, through human injustice, to give proof of the direction in which their characters would ultimately have developed, it is no discredit to Minos that he cannot make up his mind either way, since there is literally no evidence to be had on the subject. So he sends them to limbo. Dante does not follow his Master in this distinction, because he is anxious to reserve limbo for the souls who have died without receiving Baptism.

§17. The next circle [6.434–476] is occupied by those who have committed suicide: this being, we must imagine, their only serious crime. These, therefore, are punished in a peculiarly appropriate way:

> ... quam vellent aethere in alto
> Nunc et pauperiem et duros perferre labores! [6. 436(–437)]
>
> [How willing would they be now to endure poverty and hard toils in the upper world!]

They are not subjected to the actual *poena sensus*, the torments of hell, but they are continually oppressed by the thought of what they have lost – in a word, they are the victims of the *poena damni*. In Dante, this *poena damni* affects equally all the souls in limbo; it is "duol sanza martiri" [Inf. IV, 28], regret without torment, they live "sanza speme in disio", continually aspiring to heaven with an aspiration that can never be satisfied. "Nec procul hinc" [Not far from here] [6.440] – we can never be quite certain whether Virgil implies in such phrases a transition to a further region, or merely to a different part of the same region; he makes no sharp distinctions – "nec procul hinc" we come upon the plains called *Lugentes campi*, where dwell the souls of those who have died of love. There is clearly no guilt implied, so far as this fact goes: but we can see from several of the instances given – Eriphyle, Phaedra, and Pasiphae [6.445, (447)] – that they are people who have sinned, but that their love is accounted a palliation of their offence: as in French law, the crime *de la passion* is preferentially treated in the Underworld. It might surprise us to find Laodamia [6.447] in such company, but we must remember that she falls under the old condemnation of trying to go beyond the fates, in expecting her husband to be restored to her. The crime of Dido, explained above, relegates her to a similar punishment [6.450]. If we are inclined to regard this condemnation as unnecessarily severe, we must remember that Virgil is very lenient compared with his predecessors in the same field, when he allows anybody to get into Elysium at all: Homer consigns Achilles himself to the *poena*

---

§17. "The limbo of excusable suicides, and of those who, though otherwise blameworthy, are sent to limbo instead of hell because they have died of love. These people suffer the *poena damni*, since they did not get to Elysium, but not the *poena sensus*, which is inflicted on the souls in Hell. Failure of Conington to appreciate these theological distinctions." (6.343–476) *damni*. Again Conington fails to take the point. "Is it intended that the Mourning fields should contain all who have suffered by human vengeance?" he says. "Eriphyle is there, would Virgil have ventured to introduce Clytemnestra?" Of course he wouldn't, but then, nothing whatever of the kind is intended. The people who have got to the Mourning fields have got there not in virtue of the fact that they suffered by human vengeance; Virgil never says so: it is not even true that they all *have*, or how did Dido get there? They are people who have died for love. Clytemnestra could not palliate the crime of a murdered husband by saying she was overcome by passion: the whole thing was planned and executed in cold blood, and I have no doubt that Virgil pictured her in hell, among those who are described as "ob adulterium caesi" [Slain for adultery] [6.612].

§18. The last division [6.477–547] of this part is given to those who were *bello clari*, a fresh shock to the tender conscience of Conington. He cannot understand why the people who were simply *bello clari* should be in limbo, while those who have the further claim "Martiaque ob patriam pugnando vulnera passi" [Those who bore wounds for their country's sake in the course of battle] [6.660] find a special place in Elysium. He points out that the Trojans such as Deiphobus whom Aeneas meets in the lower region are capable of being described as having died for their country, and therefore ought to have attained heaven. But this is to argue without the doctrine of intention: patriotism can be accounted meritorious only in so far as it is entirely "ob patriam" that the wounds have been suffered, and for no motive of private interest or lust of battle. There is force in that *ob*: they have been hurt not merely in the course of fighting for their country, but as a direct result of fighting for their country. The sense becomes clearer if we take "ob patriam" not with "pugnando" but with "passi": "Those who bore wounds for their country's sake in the course of battle." I do not mean that Virgil was necessarily conscious in his own mind of making such a fine distinction; but I do think he had these two separate aspects of the case in mind at the separate times of writing. What is meant here must simply be that heroism in war is accounted for righteousness to certain otherwise rather shady characters, and they thereby escape actual hell. The assumption that all Trojans are white and all Greeks are black is an assumption which Conington makes here, Virgil nowhere.

---

§18. "Limbo of those who have been excused from a heavier punishment, in consideration of the fact that they have fought with a pure intention for their native country. Conington's failure to understand this passage due to his want of understanding of the doctrine of intention (6.477–547)."

§19. It is, I think, a great instance of Virgil's artistic prudence that he realized that there were horrors which even his skill could not make vivid to the reader, and consequently only allows Aeneas to learn the torments of Hell [6.548–627] by hearsay from the Sibyl, instead of witnessing them in person. First and foremost among the crimes which are eternally punished is impiety; the other offences [6.608ff.] detailed are – hatred of brothers, beating of parents, defrauding of clients, miserliness, or rather selfishness, (for the *gravamen* is that the *miser* does not lay aside any of his wealth for his friends), adultery caught in *flagrante delicto*, following "impia arma", and cheating of masters by slaves. The "impia arma" are not, I think, necessarily "unpatriotic", but simply, in accordance with the principle laid down above as to *pietas*, arms unblessed by heaven, the deliberate espousal of the wrong cause. In any case, the sins are all in a sense sins against *pietas*, since they are all, as Conington points out, violations of contract, whether the contract be family, social, marital, or national.

The merits which win heaven [6.637–665] are by comparison few. Its inhabitants are the patriots and the "pii vates", whether priests or poets – these two classes we have had occasion to deal with already – also

> Inventas aut qui vitam excoluere per artes,
> Quique sui memores aliquos fecere merendo. [6.663–664]
>
> [Those who have improved human life by the skills they have discovered and who by behaving in a deserving manner left a memory of themselves.]

It is Virgil as the poet of civilization who includes the inventors of the useful arts, it is Virgil as the prophet of righteousness who includes the wearers of the crown of merit.

§20. So far all would seem to be fairly clear and well-ordered, it is when we meet Anchises that the most widely felt difficulty of Virgil's eschatology presents itself to us. In his account of hell he has been more or less Homeric, though he has extended the scope of the *poena sensus*, and at the same time allowed the comparatively innocent shades a place of rest and peace, if not of light and refreshment. In his view of Heaven, influenced by the Orphic or Eleusinian doctrines, he has made a distinct advance on Homer, by throwing it open to all

---

§19. "The demerits which deserve Hell, and the merits which win Heaven (6.548–665)."

§20. "Virgil's views on Purgatory (6.724–751). A comparison of them with those of the Prayer-book, and with those of Plato. Plato's good souls go through 1000 years of happiness, while the bad ones go through 1000 years of pain, and they are both ready to revert to human bodies. Virgil has followed Plato in introducing the doctrine of metempsychosis, or transmigration of souls, but his bad people go straight to hell for ever, while his good people do not get to Elysium till they have undergone a period of penal suffering, to wipe out their lesser or venial sins."

people with certain moral qualifications: Menelaus in the *Odyssey*, you will remember, only goes to Elysium because he is the husband of Helen and has through her become the son-in-law of Zeus. But when he tackles the question of Purgatory [6.724–751] Virgil declares himself frankly and unreservedly Platonic. He embraces the doctrine of transmigration: souls by their very nature contain a spark of the divine fire: when they have left the earthly life, they need purification:

> Non tamen omne malum miseris nec funditus omnes
> Corporeae excedunt pestes, penitusque necesse est
> Multa diu concreta modis inolescere miris.
> ...
> Donec longa dies perfecto temporis orbe
> Concretam exemit labem, purumque reliquit
> Aetherium sensum atque aurai simplicis ignem. [6. 736–738, 745–747]

> [The wretches however are not altogether freed from all evil and afflictions of the body; and many taints, long ingrained, must become deeply rooted in them in wondrous ways . . . until the circle of time is completed and the long passage of days has removed ingrained corruption and left a pure ethereal sense of rarified fire.]

It is almost the language of the Prayer-book: "That whatsoever defilements it may have contracted in the midst of this miserable and naughty world, through the lusts of the flesh, or the wiles of Satan, being purged and done away, it may be presented pure and without spot."[7] It is noticeable however that in two respects Virgil has modified the Platonic system. Plato had instituted a sharp distinction between the good souls and the bad: sheep and goats are separated all in a moment after death, and the good immediately enjoy a journey of a thousand years in great comfort, while the bad are subjected to a corresponding thousand-year pilgrimage in the midst of torments, both companies meeting again at the end for their reincarnation. Virgil, whose soul is naturally Catholic, is up to the distinction between mortal and venial sins: those who die in mortal sin go straight to hell, while everybody else – we might suppose, however good – has to go through some form of punishment, variously graded; then, and not till then, these few chosen souls reach Elysium. The second modification here becomes necessary. The good spirits in Plato have enjoyed their good things all through the thousand years' journey, they have already had their heaven, and are ready to pass over Lethe and enter on a new course of earthly existence as soon as they are wanted. But Virgil's good spirits, when they have gone through their purgatory, have their Elysium afterwards, as Ilus and Assaracus [6.650] and Orpheus [6.645] appear to be doing when Aeneas sees them. In a word, the soul according to Plato has a thousand years either of happiness or of misery, at the end of which it returns to a mortal body, while the soul according to Virgil has *in any case* a certain number of years of penal suffering, in proportion to its deserts, and then has *in any case* a certain number of years in Elysium before reincarnation.

§21. But all this time there is a difficulty staring us in the face – the great difficulty of the whole book. Let us examine closely the account of Purgatory in lines 739 and following.

> Ergo exercentur poenis veterumque malorum
> Supplicia expendunt: aliae panduntur inanes
> Suspensae ad ventos, aliis sub gurgite vasto
> Infectum eluitur scelus aut exuritur igni:
> Quisquis suos patimur Manes; exinde per amplum
> Mittimur Elysium, et pauci laeta arva tenemus;
> Donec longa dies, perfecto temporis orbe,
> Concretam exemit labem, purumque reliquit
> Aetherium sensum atque aurai simplicis ignem.

> [So they are made to go through punishments, and make reparation for old crimes. Some are hung and stretched out to hollow winds, others have their dirty offence washed away under whirling floods or cleansed out by fire: we all have our own burden; then we are sent, few in numbers, to wide Elysium, to possess the happy fields; until the circle of time is completed and the long passage of days has removed ingrained corruption and left a pure ethereal sense of rarified fire.]

It is lines 743 and 744 which cause the problem. It does not much matter how we translate the first words, beautiful as they are: whether each of us is said to bear the burden attaching to his own ghost, or disembodied spirit, or whether Manes means our own death, that is, the lower or corporeal element of our nature which needs to be purged away. The point is, how are we to account for the sequence of the lines? It looks, I mean, as if we first of all had purgatory, and then, few in number (or perhaps, a few out of our number) were sent to Elysium, and there, in Elysium, went through some further and higher process of purification which

---

[§21.] "The great difficulty of the passage from 739 onwards, in which Virgil appears to assert that the souls first undergo Purgatory, then get to Elysium, and while in Elysium continue in some way the process of purification, which we should expect to be completed in Purgatory."

took away our stains gradually, and then returned to the body. But surely all classical precedent, as well as reason itself, demands that the purification should be completed *before we ever get to Elysium*. You can atone for your sins, wipe off your temporal debt, either on earth or in Purgatory, but surely you cannot be expected to be still wiping it off in Heaven!

§22. I cannot understand how so many editors have been content to leave this glaring enormity unexplained. Conington did so, believing that Virgil never put the finishing touches to this passage, and he assumes quite gratuitously that Purgatory lasts a thousand years, and then this strange probationary Elysium another thousand years on top of it. But there is no word about the duration of purgatory, if Conington's way of printing the passage be adopted: we are told simply that there will be a purgatory, and then a thousand years in heaven. But let that pass, what is to be said of the main crux? Some bold editors have taken the two offending lines (743 and 744) and transshipped them bodily to a later position, after line 747. This simplifies matters: for the process of purgation described in lines 745–747 is thus made part of the account of Purgatory, and we are left with a thousand years in which to enjoy ourselves in Elysium with no bother about a continued probation going on all the time. But it is a rather heroic measure textually, inasmuch as it is quite unsupported by any manuscript reading. The suggestion of Henry[8] seems to me entirely convincing, that the two lines are a parenthesis, a figure of speech of which Virgil is particularly fond. "Donec longa dies" will thus follow in sense, though not in the mere order of lines, the words "aut exuritur igni", and apply all right to Purgatory, while "Quisque suos patimur . . ." will simply be an explanatory bracket. The sense will run: "So they are all punished for their old misdeeds, some by wind, some by fire, some by water (you see, each of us has to bear his own allotted burden, and not till we have borne it – "exinde" – can we arrive, few in number, at Elysium) we are all punished, I say, till the lapse of a long period of time has left the soul pure and ethereal once more." This is perfect sense, and quite characteristic Virgil. It is worth noticing that the sudden transition from the 3rd person in "expendunt" to the 1st person in "patimur", and then back to the 3rd again "revisant" (750) is extremely awkward with the ordinary way of taking the lines, while it is quite natural if the verbs in the first person are merely the verbs of a parenthetic and logically independent clause.

[§22.] "The great difficulty entirely solved by the simple expedient of bracketing lines 743 and 744, not as a later insertion, but as a parenthesis. The words in the parenthesis, which have their verbs in the first person plural, are an anticipation of what follows after what is described in lines 745–747."

§23. I think we can go further, and claim that the use of the first person is meant to shew that the process described by these first person verbs, or at any rate by "mittimur" and "tenemus", is not true of all souls that go through Purgatory, but only of a chosen few ("pauci"). And the thousand years represent the whole time between death and rebirth, Purgatory and heaven alike. You've only a thousand years to spend over the whole thing, and therefore the sooner you escape from Purgatory the better. The man who has been very good may get his purgation done say in a couple of years and then has 998 years in which to kick his heels in Elysium. The bad man, who has only just escaped going to hell once for all, may have to do 998 years in Purgatory, and return to the world after only two years of blessedness. Or again it is even possible to take a still more elaborate view. If the phrase about going to Elysium is a parenthesis, the subsequent remarks about drinking Lethe and going back to life do not necessarily apply to the people in the parenthesis: it is conceivable that if you manage to get through the expiation of your crimes in a space of time less than 1000 years you go to Elysium *forever*, whereas if the thousand years are up and you are still in Purgatory you will have to go back again to earth. But I think this explanation is less satisfactory. You see, the souls which are about to be born, presumably therefore to be reborn, into the world are represented in a later passage (756ff.) as including people like Numa and Romulus, who must be reincarnations of an age quite long before. No, these souls are already out of purgatory, yet they have to wait several generations before they are to come to life again: therefore they will have to wait in Elysium: therefore *it is possible* to get out of Purgatory before the 1000 years are accomplished, and yet be destined ultimately to resume mortal existence. In fact, though there may have been exceptions, it seems the normal thing that a soul should return to earth exactly 1000 years after death, irrespective of how its time beyond the grave had been divided between Purgatory and Heaven. Conington could not understand how Anchises had been let out of Purgatory so early; but the answer is simple enough: Anchises had lived a pious and religious life, so his purgatory was merely nominal – a single year, to be exact – and he turned up at once in Elysium, prepared to meet his son when he could

---

§23. "Consequences of this reading of the passage. The souls do not, as Conington appears to think, have 1000 years in purgatory, and then 1000 years in Elysium; Virgil never suggests that they do; they have 1000 years to be spent partly in purgatory and partly in Elysium, or more Elysium and less purgatory, according as it has [or rather "they have"] been bad or good during life. It is not certain what may have been supposed to happen in exceptional cases, nor whether Anchises was a special case, but the ordinary soul cannot have been meant to go to Elysium forever, if it once escaped purgatory before 1000 years were up, as we may see from the position of the descendants of Anchises; it must have been meant to put in x years in purgatory, and 1000 – x years in Elysium, and then as of necessity to return to the earth."

come down to interview him. He is more or less in the position of the Blessed Saints, already enjoying the Vision, already in *statu patriae*.

§24. Conington was also puzzled by the inconsistency, as he regarded it, between the existence of an abode of permanently doomed spirits, who never get on beyond where they are – "sedet aeternumque sedebit/ Infelix Theseus" [Doomed Theseus sits and will forever sit (in Tartarus)] [6.617(–618)] – and the doctrine of Purgatory and reincarnation which the poet takes over from Plato. "According to this doctrine", he says, "Dido and Deiphobus, Salmoneus and the Lapithae, ought to have undergone a prolonged purification, with a prospect of resigning their identity and becoming other personages in other ages." Now, in the first place it is not true that the Platonic doctrine of transmigration of souls involves a return to mortal life for *everybody*, however bad or good. In the tenth book of the *Republic*, Er the son of Armenius, who has the vision which describes the events of a future life, is standing at the mouth of the pit from which those who have finished their purgatory come out and meet their friends who have been enjoying the pilgrimage of 1000 years' happiness. He hears one of these say to another, "Isn't it about time that Ardiaeus came up? He must be about through", and the other replies "οὐχ ἥκει, οὐδ'ἂν ἥξει δεῦρο"[615d], "He has not come, nor will he be likely to come here". Even Plato condemned some people to eternal punishment; even Plato would not have allowed a reincarnation of Salmoneus and the Lapithae. All that Virgil has done is to extend Plato's principle as laid down in the case of Ardiaeus, who was a very wicked man and had eaten, if I remember right, most of his children: Virgil makes reincarnation the exception instead of the rule, granted only to the pick of the lot. The ordinary wicked person – and most people are wicked – goes to hell, unless there are extenuating circumstances, as in the cases mentioned above of unhappy lovers, suicides, and so on, who go to Limbo. When a person has deliberately thrown away her life, like Dido, she can't expect to have a nice new one given her. And as for the infants, they didn't matter much since they could not be supposed to have much feeling of regret for a life whose pleasures they had never been able to experience.

---

§24. "Further difficulties raised by Conington. Is there not an inconsistency between the old idea of Hades, as a place in which people live to all eternity, and the Platonic doctrine of a reincarnation, preceded by a purgatory in the world below? Instances of people permanently detained – Theseus, Dido, Deiphobus, Salmoneus, and the Lapithae. Eternal punishment shewn not to be inconsistent with the idea of a purgatory and even a reincarnation in certain cases, proved on the testimony of Plato himself, in the matter of Ardiaeus the tyrant. This principle recognized by Plato in connexion with the utterly wicked is simply extended by Virgil to the less serious offenders whom he sends to Limbo."

§25. So much for Conington's difficulties. They disappear if you bracket lines 743 and 744 in your copy of the *Aeneid*, and what you have left is a consistent, a reasonable, and if you except the Platonic doctrine of transmigration, a comparatively modern view of the future life. And there are two points at least, not yet mentioned, in which Virgil's account is quite startlingly Christian. One is the Sibyl's account of how a Fury with a whip extorts confessions of all the souls in Tartarus of all the crimes

> Quae quis apud superos, furto laetatus inani
> Distulit in seram commissa piacula mortem. (6.568[–569])

> [Whenever anyone in the world above, having rejoiced in vain deceit, has delayed the necessary expiation until death's late hour.]

It is not everywhere that you can find a heathen poet expounding the disastrous consequences of dying with unconfessed mortal sin on your conscience. It is not merely unconfessed crimes, it is unconfessed *piacula*, sins which demand some sort of ceremonial purification. The other point is an unnoticed touch in the account of Elysium. Anchises on meeting Aeneas, congratulates him on his filial obedience in coming down to the shades, and says:

> Quas ego te terras et quanta per aequora vectum
> Accipio! Quantis jactatum, nate, periclis!
> Quam metui, ne quid Libyae tibi regna nocerent! (692[–694])

> [How far by land and sea you have come to visit me! And how much hardship you have suffered, my son! How I feared that the realm of Libya might harm you!]

In a word, Anchises, living the life of a beatified Saint, has actually witnessed the sufferings of his son in the meantime, and sympathized with them. I know of no other case in the classics, where knowledge of what is going on in the world is attributed to the departed, even to those who have attained Elysium.

I think anybody who will read Virgil's *Aeneid* bearing in mind this conception of *pietas*, and noticing how constantly this idea recurs in the poem, will feel that Virgil has, whether deliberately or instinctively, transformed the whole nature of the epic. Homer was his master in the heroic vein, Apollonius Rhodius, perhaps, in the romantic; Virgil himself has taken a step further and

---

[§25.] "Particular instances of the modern nature of Virgil's conception of the Four Last Things, from 6.568 [–569] and 6.692 [–694]."

written the first religious epic. He is not content to think of man as the plaything of those capricious creatures, the Homeric gods, nor yet as the sport of a blind, purposeless influence called Fate. In Virgil, the gods too have laws which bind them; they owe to man a *pietas*, a fidelity, which bids them keep covenant with their chosen servants. And man on his side has a corresponding duty of *pietas*. It is his duty to inquire, as best he may, the mind of Heaven, and to conform himself to its purposes. The *Aeneid* does not set out, *ex professo*, to justify the ways of God to man. But it assumes, throughout, the existence of a moral purpose in history.

Meanwhile, how to account for the inequalities of human conditions and human fortunes? Virgil, following Plato in the main, gives what answer he gives in the famous description of the Lower World which occupies book VI. Just as he takes over from the Greek poets the machinery of Olympus, so he takes over from them the machinery of Hades. But he moralizes it beyond recognition in the process; his Tartarus stands between the Hades of Homer and the Inferno of Dante, and really he is closer here to his successor than to his predecessor. He is not only content to register a series of rewards and punishments; he must investigate how those rewards, how those punishments were deserved; what gradation there is in them, what hope of amelioration.

Notes

1 Professor William Young Sellar (1825–90) was a Scottish classical scholar.
2 Version 2 (Ampleforth) has 'pestem' (as in 3.620) instead of 'casum' (as in 3.265).
3 G. C. Allen, *Roman Problems from and after Plutarch's Roman Questions* (London: Beckers and Son, 1904), 8–9. Allen reports Frazer's passage from the *Golden Bough* and adds his own summary. Knox simplifies it slightly.
4 Reuben Archer Torrey (1856–1928) was an American evangelist, pastor, educator, and writer.
5 'Mugwump' was slang in Knox's day for a person who remained self-satisfiedly non-committal.
6 I have been unable to identify whom Ronald Knox alludes to.
7 'A Commendatory Prayer for a Sick Person at the point of Departure' in *The Book of Common Prayer*.
8 James Henry (1708–1876) was an Irish classical scholar and poet.

3

Virgil's Romance and Pathos

§1. I have tried to shew, in speaking of the political presuppositions of Virgil, and also of his religious outlook, that his work is dominated by a strong sense of destiny, ultimately, the destiny of the Roman people. Fate is no longer a blind engine, cruel, relentless, and unmeaning, but a purposeful agency, to which it is man's duty to accommodate himself even to the detriment of his own petty aims and immediate interests. It might have been supposed that a writer swayed by such considerations would find it impossible to adopt anything but a rather hard and ascetic attitude towards the life and death of this or that individual character: that a single character in the story would appear to him nothing more or less than a single pawn in the great game. What are a thousand hardships, what are the deaths of a thousand friends or kinsmen to Aeneas, the man of Fate, "dum conderet urbem", so long as he can fulfil the divine purpose which is his mission? Surely the moral of the poem will be quite simple and straightforward. Aeneas is the strong man; the strong man is bound to win, and the weakest must go to the wall.

§2. It is the greatest triumph of Virgil's art, it is the chief secret of Virgil's pathos, it is the highest claim which Virgil has, to be considered the first romantic poet the world has seen, that this is precisely the way in which Virgil does not commend Aeneas to our admiration and our sympathies. One of the easiest differences by which to distinguish romantic from classical literature, is that the sympathies of romantic literature are always on the side of the underdog. You can trace it right back to the fairy stories. If any of you have read that very delightful book *The Golden Age* by Mr. Kenneth Grahame, you will remember his admirable description of the effect produced on children who have been

---

§1. "Virgil's belief in destiny, as treated in the last two lectures, might well be expected to have blunted his sense of romance, and dried up the springs of his pathos."

§2. "But this is not so. Virgil at once pathetic and romantic. Sympathy for the weak and the conquered side the most important element distinguishing romantic from classical literature: this instanced from *The Golden Age*, and the stories of Cinderella and Prince Charming."

brought up to appreciate the romantic fairy story of the nations of northern Europe, when they were first introduced to Greek and Roman mythology. "We missed the pleasant alliance of the animal, the fox who spread the bushiest of tails to convey us to the enchanted castle, the frog in the well, the raven who croaked advice from the tree; and – to Harold especially – it seemed entirely wrong that the hero should ever be other than the youngest brother of three. This belief in the special fortune that ever awaited the younger brother, as such . . . had been of baleful effect on Harold, producing a certain self-conceit and perkiness that called for physical correction." This is by no means a trifling point: the youngest brother of the romance succeeds uniformly where the other two have failed, simply because he is the youngest brother, the weakest, the naturally defenseless brother. The democratic sentiment rallies round him; it is the reversal of the natural order, the revenge for all the slights and bullyings he has endured from the rest of his family in his youth, that gives the triumph of the youngest brother its piquancy and charm. It is just because we have known Cinderella as a grubby little girl sitting and crying in the fender that we are genuinely pleased to see her sitting in a six-horsed carriage, wearing glass slippers. It is just because Prince Charming, or whatever his name is, has always been the family drudge and the family dunce, and can't even get his father to give him a proper sword, that we are profoundly glad when it is Prince Charming, and neither of the elder brothers, who kills the Dragon or whatever it is, and goes off with the princess. And we instinctively back David against Goliath, not so much because we want Goliath beaten, as because David was taken from among the sheepfolds, when all his handsome and conceited brothers had been rejected by Samuel with the words "Neither hath the Lord chosen this" [1Sam. 16:9]. It is a romantic feeling, because romance demands a reversal of the obvious: it is a democratic feeling, because we always like the worst man to win: it is a Christian feeling, because the Lord chooses the weak things of the world to confound the wise.

§3. Virgil possessed the romantic instinct – instinct, I say, because I do not think he deliberately and purposely forsook the Homeric outlook, which in the *Iliad* at any rate is always inclined to back the winner, and has no sympathy for the weaker side, though it is free to pity the weaker side. But Virgil can be seen

---

§3. "This romantic, and democratic, and Christian sympathy for weakness strongly marked in Virgil. Instances of it from the episode of Nisus and Euryalus (9.176–449), by comparison of it with the episode of Dolon in the *Iliad*, and also from that of Entellus and Dares in 5.362–484, by comparison of the boxing in the 23rd *Iliad*, and by the story of Polydeuces and Amycus in Theocritus and Apollonius of Rhodes."

even in his imitations of Homer to have romanticized his version of the story. Look at the tenth book of the *Iliad*, and you will see how Dolon goes out on the Trojan side, and Odysseus and Diomede on the Greek. Odysseus and Diomede murder Rhesus and his men in their beds, and then they meet Dolon; Dolon runs away, and they catch him, delude him into giving them information by treacherous promises of safety, and then butcher him. Throughout the whole incident the author of the *Iliad*, or rather, the author of the tenth book of the *Iliad*, has no word of sympathy for Dolon, or of condemnation for the Greek heroes. Now look at book 9 of the *Aeneid*. Nisus and Euryalus [9.176–449] go out just like Odysseus and Diomede, and murder large numbers of the sleeping Rutulians. So far, we may admire Nisus and Euryalus, but we do not love them, and Virgil feels that. Nisus and Euryalus are no longer Odysseus and Diomede; they are put into the position of Dolon instead; they are caught, and outnumbered, and mercilessly slain: Volcens is the villain, and the man who cannot shed a tear over Nisus and Euryalus had better give up reading Virgil altogether, and take Pass Mods.[1] There is another instance, less prominent, but no less significant, in which Virgil has reversed Homer's method of treatment, and this time has actually represented the weaker side not merely as deserving our sympathy, but as ultimately triumphant. In the 23rd book of the *Iliad*, Homer portrays a boxing-match as part of the funeral games of Patroclus: Epeus comes forward at once and claims the prize – a bull – as his, in the absence of other champions. Euryalus – another Euryalus – comes out to meet him, and now we, being moderns, and brought up on romantic literature, expect that the boaster is to pay the penalty for his presumption. But not a bit of it: Epeus beats his adversary into a cocked hat: Euryalus is simply nowhere. We can trace the progress of this scene in later poets, as literature tends to become more and more romantic. In Theocritus, the greatest of the Alexandrians, Polydeuces boxes with Amycus: Amycus is here the boaster, the truculent aggressor, but Polydeuces, who beats him, preserves, to say the least of it, a very "We don't want to fight but by Jingo if we do" sort of attitude throughout. Precisely the same incident is recorded by Apollonius Rhodius, and here Polydeuces is represented in an even more favourable light; he is quiet and good-tempered about the whole thing. The germ of the romantic treatment is there, but the fact remains that Polydeuces is Polydeuces, the unconquerable, and the reader has not for a moment the smallest doubt as to the issue. In Virgil [5.362–484], the boaster is a Trojan of the name of Dares, who claims the bull in very much the same way as Epeus in the *Iliad*. At first there are no rival competitors; then an elderly Sicilian, Entellus, is persuaded to come forward. This Entellus has, it is true, a very helpful pair of boxing-gloves, with lead let into them, but on a question being raised as to the rules he gracefully consents to fight without the gloves. Now surely the boaster has every chance. Entellus has done some boxing in younger days, but he is out of training, and old enough to be Dares' grandfather. It is as if Nestor had taken up the challenge of Epeus; he doesn't seem to stand as much chance even as the old blacksmith in Rodney Stone. He is knocked over in the first round. But in the end he wins very handsomely. The triumph of weakness is complete.

§4. And it is not only in these minor incidents that Virgil shews the romantic spirit. It pervades the whole story. Aeneas is not, it is true, a younger son, but he is the representative of a beaten side. We like Aeneas, not because he is great, but because he feels small. We like him because he is an exile, not because he is a warrior. We like him because he has been badly treated by the fates, not because they are in the end going to treat him well. It is not merely that the fortunes of the Greek and Trojan heroes are reversed since we saw them in the *Iliad*. It is that the characters of the hero and the villain are reversed. When the Sibyl in her prophecy says of Turnus "alius Latio iam partus Achilles" [A second Achilles is already born in Latium] [6.89], she has laid hold of a very important point. It is Turnus, not Aeneas, who has succeeded to the character of Achilles. The hero of Homer is the strong man, Achilles: Hector, the pious man, is doomed to defeat; in the *Aeneid*, Turnus is the strong man, and he is going to get beaten by the pious man. Turnus has in the fighting the place of Hector, but his violence, his fiery eloquence, his egotism are those of Achilles. It is noticeable that Turnus is always mentioning his own name, as if he were pleased with it, and expected everyone else to be frightened at it. When he is carried away in the bark, he appeals to the winds to send him back to the battle in the words:

> In rupes, in saxa – volens vos Turnus adoro –
> Ferte ratem. (10.677–678)
>
> [I, Turnus, implore you with all my heart to drive my ship onto the rocks, onto the cliffs.]

"Volens vos Turnus adoro" – here am I, Turnus, no less, actually asking a favour from insignificant deities like you. In his speech in the council he says of Aeneas:

[§4.] "Application of this to the story in general. Our sympathy for Aeneas due to the fact that Trojans are the beaten side. Contrast of this with the *Iliad*: Turnus, though in his fate the counterpart of Hector, in his character the counterpart of Achilles. The egoism of Turnus illustrated from 10.677[–678], 11.440[–442], 12.11, 12.74, 12.97, and 12.645. Drances, the opponent of Turnus and counterpart of Thersites, not caricatured by Virgil as Thersites was caricatured by Homer."

> ... Vobis animam hanc soceroque Latino
> Turnus ego, haud ulli veterum virtute secundus,
> Devovi. (11.440–442)
>
> [I, Turnus, second to none of my forefathers in bravery, have offered up my life to you and to Latinus, the father of my bride.]

He, Turnus, a match for any of the older heroes. "Nulla mora in Turno" (12.11) [Turnus keeps no man waiting], is his acceptance of the challenge to single combat, and he cements it with "neque enim Turno mora libera mortis", "A Turnus is not free to put off the date of death" (12.74). Even his spear he cannot address without pointing out to it that whereas it was once the property of Actor, "Te Turni nunc dextra gerit", "You're in the hands of Turnus now" (12.97). To the last, in his farewell to Juturna, the egoism still persists: "Terga dabo" he says, "et Turnum fugientem haec terra videbit?" [Shall I turn my back? Will this land see Turnus on the run?] (12.645). This way of talking, which might be rather fine if used only once, irritates us when it begins to become a mannerism; he is almost like the people who have that dreadful habit of talking about themselves as "Yours truly". It is one of the subtle influences which make us instinctively dislike Turnus, otherwise rather a noble character, and reconcile us easily to his final defeat and death. You see his haughtiness best if you read the debate between him and Drances in the council, which occupies lines 301–444 in the eleventh book. Drances is precisely the same character, up to a point, as Thersites in the *Iliad*: Thersites is the demagogue who wants to go back home to Greece, and Drances is the demagogue who wants to make peace with the Trojan invader; Thersites is badly knocked about by Odysseus, Drances is violently, though not physically, attacked by Turnus. But whereas Homer is clearly all against Thersites, Virgil, in spite of the fine speech he puts into the mouth of Turnus, makes it plain to us that all the time Drances was in the right. Thersites is a bald, bandy-legged, thin-headed, low-down little cad: Drances is a wise councilor who has been profoundly impressed by the bearing and attitude of Aeneas. Again, Virgil has shewn himself romantic enough to be a democrat. Again we see strength rushing to its ruin.

§5. All through the early books, Virgil is steadily winning our sympathy for the Trojan cause by a subtle yet constant insistence on the hardships of the exiles. He knows quite well that if the reader has any romance in his system, that cause in order to be an attractive cause must be a lost one. It is a triumphant cause in

---

§5. "Virgil's steady insistence on the dignity of a lost cause, illustrated from Mr. G.K. Chesterton and King Charles I. Instances of this from 1.198[–199] and 1.437."

the end, but it must be a lost cause from the start. Mr. G.K. Chesterton, who probably understands the secret of romance better than most people living, has done something the same in his poem "The Ballad of the White Horse." He has found in King Alfred a hero who really did have all the odds against him, whom you can pity before you begin to admire him. After all, the characters in history who have commanded the most pathetic devotion, so far at any rate as their memories were concerned are not the successes but the failures. Cromwell may have done much more for England than King Charles I, but he was never worshipped as Englishmen have worshipped and still do worship the memory of the Royal Martyr. It was common among the Highlanders to speak of Charles Stuart as Prince Charlie, but the wildest of his supporters never dreamt of referring to George the Third as King Georgie. And so we are continually being reminded in the *Aeneid* that Troy is a lost cause. In all the buoyant hopefulness of the Trojans there is a continual undercurrent of regret. When they are shipwrecked the only way to cheer them up is to address them as "O passi graviora"

> O socii, neque enim ignari sumus ante malorum,
> O passi graviora, dabit deus his quoque finem. (1.198–199)
>
> [O comrades, this is not the first time we have known misfortune, you who have suffered worse in the past, god will make sure that this too comes to an end.]

And there is no more diabolical stroke of Art in the whole of Virgil's poetry than the way in which he makes Aeneas approach Carthage and see its wall, the walls of a new city, in process of construction (1.437)

> O fortunati, quorum jam moenia surgunt.
>
> [How fortunate are those whose walls are already rising.]

The sight carries his mind in a single moment at once backwards and forwards: happy the people whose walls are rising, instead of falling, like the walls of Troy, and happy are the people whose walls are rising *now*, instead of waiting, who knows how long, before they can be built, like the walls of Rome.

§6. This pathos of homesickness is conveyed to us chiefly, I think, in the deliberate preference for the word *fuit* in all the earlier part of the poem. You cannot say of Troy merely *erat* so and so, you must always say *fuit* so and so, it was

---

§6. "Deliberate use of the word *fuit* in the *Aeneid*, to arouse our sympathy for the lost cause of Troy. Instances of this from 1.534, 1.[544–]545, 2.6, 2.325[–326], 2.[426–]427, 3.[10–]11, 3.[15–]16, 3.498[–499], 6.62, 10.[42–]43, 10.[59–]60.

and it has ceased to be. There is a gloomy finality about the perfect tense which recalls the picture of Cicero announcing the execution of Catiline's accomplices in the single word "vixerunt", "they have lived their life: all is over." "We are going to Italy" says Ilioneus; "hic cursus fuit", it was, but it was not to be (1.534). "Our King *was* Aeneas", "erat" Aeneas, he goes on in lines 544–545, "than whom there *used to be* none more righteous, none more brave", "nec pietate fuit" – there used to be none, in those old days when Troy was a city. And so Aeneas constantly when he is describing his adventures to Dido: "Et quorum pars magna fui" [And I played an important role in these things] (2.6), "Fuimus Troes, fuit Ilium et ingens /Gloria Teucrorum" [We Trojans exist no more, Ilium has come to an end, and so has the great glory of the Teucrians] (2.325[–326]), "Ripheus, iustissimus unus/ Qui fuit in Teucris et servantissimus aequi" [Ripheus, the one who was the most righteous and the greatest lover of justice amongst the Trojans](2.[426–]427), "portusque relinquo/ Et campos ubi Troja fuit" [I leave behind the harbours and the plains where once stood the city of Troy] (3.[10–]11), "hospitium antiquum Troiae sociique penates/ dum fortuna fuit" [While things were going well, this people had a long standing tie of hospitality with Troy and shared household gods] (3.15–16), and as he leaves Helenus in his newly founded city in Epirus, he prays "melioribus, opto,/ Auspiciis, et quae fuerit minus obvia Grais" (3.498[–499]), "may it *prove to have been* less unlucky than the original Troy." And even later on, when they have reached Italy and hopes are brighter, they can never quite forget what they have lost: "Hac Troiana tenus fuerit fortuna secuta." Let the ill fortune of Troy be a thing of the past even as Troy herself is (6.62). And Venus' complaints to Juppiter have the same weary echo:

> Nil super imperio moveor; speravimus ista,
> Dum Fortuna fuit. (10. 42–43)

[I care no more for empire, we had that hope for as long as fortune lasted.]

And again:

> Non satius, cineres patriae insedisse supremos
> Atque solum, quo Troja fuit? (10.59–60)

[Would it not have been better to have settled on the dead ashes of their country, on the soil where Troy once stood?]

The Trojans can fulfil the directions of the Epistle to the Hebrews in desiring a better country, but they cannot ever for long fail to be mindful of that country from whence they came out.

§7. It may not be of the *esse*, but it certainly of the *bene esse* of a romance that it should have a happy ending. A tragedy may end sadly, or it may simply leave us wondering which was right and which was wrong: if it is a good tragedy, it should be able to persuade us that, things having gone so far, that was the most satisfactory end you could have had; but all the same it is, regarded in itself, a sad ending. But it is almost essential to the true fairy story that they should all live happily ever afterwards; it is true of most of the Northern European fairy stories, and in one case, that of Shakespeare, [that] the word romance is habitually used in the classification of a large number of works, to denote those which neither end unhappily enough to deserve the name of tragedy, nor contain enough humorous element to pass for comedies. The *Tempest*, the *Winter's Tale*, perhaps some of the earlier ones such as the *Merchant of Venice*, are romances in this sense. It is the broadest distinction between the *Iliad* and the *Odyssey* that the *Iliad* is tragedy – because the death of Hector no more compensates for the loss of Patroclus than the deaths of Regan and Goneril in *King Lear* atone for the broken heart of Cordelia: whereas the *Odyssey* is a romance, and the misfortunes and discomforts of Odysseus in the course of it only serve to lead up to the comfortable feeling of having all scores paid off, which we get at the end of it. Romance is generally speaking optimistic, because if it represents the triumph of evil, that triumph is sure to be only temporary, and gives the hero an excuse for a well-earned rest in the last chapter. It is the feeling of a hot bath after a hard game of football.

§8. But though romance is thus optimistic, it by no means follows that it does not leave room for a great deal of pathos. The incidents which go to make up a romance may in themselves be utter tragedies. Rome was worth building, even at the cost of the lives of a Dido, a Nisus, an Euryalus, and a Pallas, but what a cost! This explains the curious fact that Virgil is at once the most romantic and the most tragic of ancient writers. His pathos is one of his most obvious qualities, and fully deserves the now hackneyed criticism of Tennyson, "Thou majestic in the sadness at the doubtful doom of human kind". One might have expected Lucretius, who violently disbelieved in a future life, would have more sense of the bitterness of death than the poet of the 6th *Aeneid*. But the fact remains that whereas Lucretius never gets beyond a sort of irritable surprise that anybody

---

[§7.] "A romance, although it should properly differ from a tragedy by having a happy ending, leaves plenty of room for incidental pathos in the course of the story. The *Iliad* as tragedy compared with the *Odyssey* as romance."

[§8.] "Strong element of pathos in the *Aeneid*, illustrated by hackneyed quotation from Tennyson. This pathos deals with the shortness of human life, and the consequent waste involved in war, as instanced by 10.758[–759], 10.861[–862], 11.49 [–52], 11.182 [–183], 6.882[–883]."

should be so unreasonable as to object to dying, Virgil's tenderness for the mourner has become a byword. It is the mere fact of mortality which seems to Virgil an inexplicable tragedy. This is most clearly brought out in 10.758[–759] where

> Di Jovis in tectis iram miserantur inanem
> Amborum...
>
> [In Jupiter's palace the gods pitied the useless rage of both sides]

that is, of the Trojans and the Rutulians alike,

> ... et tantos mortalibus esse labores.
>
> [(and grieved) that mortals should endure such great suffering.]

Mortals have so little time to spend in the enjoyment of life, it is a wonder they care to waste it in the pursuit of empty quarrels; there are already so many influences at work to shorten life, that it seems monstrous to endanger it any more than is absolutely necessary. This same impression of the briefness of mortality is the ground of what is perhaps the most beautiful line in Virgil. Mezentius (10.861[–862]) has been wounded in the battle, and has retired, when news is brought to him of the death of his son Lausus. Returning to the fight to die there, he addresses his horse Rhaebus:

> Rhaebe, diu, res si qua diu mortalibus ulla est,
> Viximus.
>
> [We have lived long, Rhaebus, if anything at all lasts long for mortals.]

Life as a rule is all too short, there is no such thing as *diu* in mortal experience, but now the broken man, who has seen his people revolt from him and cast him out, and has heard that his son has given up life in defence of such an unworthy father, now the bitterness of death is past; he has lived too long already. There is hardly a sentiment in the whole range of the mourner's sorrow on which Virgil has not touched. The famous lines of *In Memoriam*

> O father, wheresoe'er thou be
> That pledgest now thy gallant son,
> A shot, ere half thy draught be done
> Hath stilled the life that beat from thee[2]

have hardly added anything to the speculations of Aeneas as to what the feelings of Evander will be when he hears of the death of Pallas (11.49[–52]):

Et nunc ille quidem spe multum captus inani,
Fors et vota facit, cumulataque altaria donis;
Nos iuvenem exanimum et nil jam caelestibus ullis
Debentem vano maesti comitamur honore.

[Even now, much taken in by vain hope, he is perhaps offering vows and heaping altars with gifts; but we accompany with tears and useless honours a young warrior who is dead and now owes nothing to any of the gods.]

The death of the young hero so affects the poet's mind that the world itself seems all out of joint. It is common enough for Virgil to speak of "mortalibus aegris" [e.g. 2.268, 10.274, 12.850] as a sort of Homeric epithet; this means little beyond the fact that in the sweat of our brow we eat bread. But it is only, I think, in the opening of the passage immediately following on the death of Pallas that he permits himself the phrase

Aurora interea *miseris* mortalibus almam
Extulerat lucem (11.182-183)

[Meanwhile Aurora had brought forth her bountiful light for afflicted mortals]

Here it seems that life is not really worth living when such sorrows are ready to befall us. Even Anchises himself, blessed with the full knowledge of the *comprehensores* who have won their way to heaven, cannot resist the famous tribute of tears to the yet unborn Marcellus, "Heu, miserande puer, si qua fata aspera rumpas,/ tu Marcellus eris". [Oh young boy, deserving to be pitied! If only you may break the harsh laws of fate, You will be a Marcellus.] [6.882-883]

§9. Possibly it was the remembrance of Marcellus' death, the impression which it left on the Emperor himself, and doubtless on the whole Roman world at the time, that made Virgil so peculiarly sensitive to the tragedy of early death, so peculiarly prone to dwell on its sadness. This is not a characteristic of the *Iliad*; we are accustomed to think of Sarpedon and Patroclus as young, but I do not know that there is any suggestion in the original that Sarpedon is to be considered younger than the other victims of the Trojan war, and certainly it is definitely stated in the case of Patroclus that he was older than Achilles. But the *Aeneid* is full of it. In the fall of Troy we have the death of Coroebus [2.424(–426)] who has

---

[59.] "Suggestion as to a possible reason for this emphasis on the briefness of mortality, that the death of the young Marcellus made a great impression on contemporary Rome. This emphasis illustrated from the case of Coroebus, Polites, Polydorus, Icarus, Nisus, Euryalus, Camilla, Lausus, Pallas, and others, (2.424[–426], 2.526(ff.), 3.499(ff.), 6.[30–]31, 6.307[–308], 9.444[–445], 9. 433[–434], 11.587, 7.[649–]650, 10.489)."

not yet got over his calf love for Cassandra, and that of Polites [2.526(ff.)], the youngest of the sons of Priam. Almost immediately after, we hear of the murder of young Polydorus [3.49ff.] by the treacherous Thracian king Polymestor. Among the shades whom Aeneas sees waiting on the banks of Acheron, quite a disproportionate amount of space in the category devoted to the

> ... pueri innuptaeque puellae
> Impositique rogis juvenes ante ora parentum. [6.307–308]

> [Boys, unmarried girls and young men placed on the pyre before their parents' eyes.]

We have in the sixth book, too, the pathetic story of Daedalus, trying to portray the fall of his son Icarus (6.[30–]31). And in the Rutulian war the only death-scenes, except those of Mezentius and Turnus, on which any particular emphasis is laid are those of Nisus [9.444–445], who is a youth, and Euryalus [9.433–434], who is no more than a boy; the virgin Camilla, who is expressly said to fall by an *untimely* fate (11.587), Lausus, most beautiful of all the host except Laurentian Turnus (7.[649–]650), and Pallas who is slain in his first battle [10.489].

The pathos, then, and the romance of Virgil are not mutually destructive. Just as he makes us feel that the winning cause is the cause of destiny, and nevertheless can indulge himself in the luxury of a hero who claims our sympathy by his misfortunes; so Virgil is romantic enough to make us feel that in the end there will be no wrong unavenged, no wrong uncompensated, and nevertheless is always touching our feelings with the tenderest pathos at what is to him the saddest of all sights – that of a beautiful life brought to an unmerited and untimely close.

Notes

1 'Pass Mods', short for Pass Moderations, that is Moderations (for which, see 60 above) consisting of fewer test papers than Honour Moderations. No class qualifications were awarded.
2 Alfred Lord Tennyson, *In Memoriam*, Section VI, 9–12.

4

Virgil's Art and Treatment of His Story

§1. I think it must be obvious to you from what has already been said, as well as from your previous reading, however cursory, of the *Aeneid* itself, that Virgil is not one of those ancient authors in whom we admire the simplicity and naivete of natural spontaneous poetry. He did not live, as Homer lived, in an age when poetry was almost the natural vehicle for the expression of thought, when the simplest way of saying a thing was necessarily the best way of saying it, when everything was heroic, and matter for heroic poems, because it had never occurred to anybody to regard anything as commonplace. When it comes to a drawing of distinctions between art and nature, Virgil is obviously and inevitably an artist. The question at present to be discussed is whether he was a good or a bad artist.

§2. Any such discussion must necessarily begin with an apologetic. It is one of the highest tributes to Virgil's art, that we immediately notice it whenever he sins against modern canons of taste. The great instance is his treatment of the story of Dido. If a Statius, or a Silius, or a Valerius, even an Ovid, had made his hero desert his heroine in the fourth book of his epic, and leave her to commit suicide, with no sign of hesitation and very few signs of compunction, we should, I think, have hardly noticed it. And the fact that in Virgil's case we instinctively take exception to this and demand some explanation of it, is a great testimony to the fact that, after all, we do regard Virgil as a supreme artist, and feel that he would not have treated his characters so without some reason.

§3. There are two broad differences between our own day, or at any rate our own outlook, and Virgil's, which are very largely responsible for the outraged

---

[§1.] "Virgil's genius is not one which we admire for its naif and primitive simplicity, like that of Homer or Caedmon, but a genius distinctly allied to Art, like that of Sophocles or Shakespeare."

[§2.] "Proof of the universal recognition of Virgil's greatness as an artist, from the fact that we notice it at once when Virgil appears to make an artistic blunder, and principally in the case of the desertion of Dido."

[§3.] "Our moral objection to Aeneas' part in the story, such as might be supposed to be advanced by a retired colonel, that Aeneas ought to have stopped in Carthage and made an honest woman of Dido."

feelings with which a modern reader shuts up the fourth book of the *Aeneid*. There is a difference of moral principle, and a difference of artistic taste. We will take the difference of moral principle first. If Virgil had simply made Dido conceive a passion *malheureuse* for Aeneas, which he never requited or encouraged, we could hardly have blamed him. But when he not only reciprocates the passion of Dido, but actually brings their love to the consummation so delicately described in lines 4.165–168 – when this has once happened, modern standards of ethics, however rough, demand that the lover should stay where he is, in despite of all the thunders of an angry heaven, and offer marriage. It was his duty, as the saying goes, to make an honest woman of her.

§4. Now in saying that this view of the case simply never occurred to Virgil, I am not saying for a moment that the standard of theoretical morals was, in the time of Augustus, particularly low. Theoretical standards of morality unfortunately seldom involve equally high standards in practice, and there is no doubt that the desperate efforts made by Augustus to restore the purity of ancient Roman home life did affect to a certain extent the tone of contemporary literature. It is not every age in history that would have condemned the *Ars Amatoria*. Still less would I suggest that Virgil had anything but a singularly pure mind, a mind that shrank from plainspokenness, and yet never condescended to suggestive innuendo. With the exception of a few passages in the *Eclogues*, there is nothing in Virgil that is unsuited to the drawing-room, or even the nursery. But in this respect, like Horace, he was tied down by his models. If Virgil imitated Homer so elaborately in other respects, it is hardly to be wondered at that he assumed as a background of his poem more or less Homeric standards of morality. Ulysses, the prototype of Aeneas so far as his travels were concerned, had notoriously a wife in every port. Nobody ever expects him to stop and make an honest goddess of Calypso, nor even regards him as having acted disloyally towards Penelope. Whether Virgil was right in assuming this Homeric standard, there is no need for us to discuss; what is quite certain is that he did assume it.

§5. For, if you come to look at his language, you will never find it suggested that Dido had any right to demand, or even to expect, marriage. Rather, I think

---

§4. "This is not to be explained as merely a difference between the ethical standards of Virgil's time and our own, or between Virgil's morality and that of the colonel, but simply by the fact that Virgil was faithful to his models, and principally to Homer."

§5. "Indeed, Dido is actually blamed for thinking that she had any matrimonial rights over Aeneas (4.172) after what was, in spite of 4.193, probably a simple indiscretion. Even this single indiscretion is not made much of by Virgil, as may be seen from the solitary reference in 4.327."

you will find that Dido is held up to our censure for the way in which she tries to cement the alliance. In line 172 we read:

> Conjugium vocat; hoc praetexit nomine culpam.
>
> [She calls it marriage using the word to disguise her love entanglement.]

Culpa is of course the regular word in the Augustan poets for a love entanglement. What was to Aeneas, and should have been to Dido, nothing more than a stray indiscretion, brought about by the circumstances of their meeting in the wood, she insists on calling by the solemn name of *conjugium*, a marriage with full religious rites. I think it is doubtful if the indiscretion was even repeated, for the statement of Rumour, in line 193[-194],

> Nunc hiemem inter se luxu, quam longa, fovere
> Regnorum immemores, turpique cupidine captos,
>
> [Now they indulge themselves the whole winter in luxury, forgetful of their realms, seized by shameful lust]

is discredited by the warning a few lines higher up that she

> ... pariter facta atque infecta canebat. [4.190]
>
> [Reported in song truth and untruths in equal measure.]

Virgil characteristically tries to forget the incident itself. The possibility of Dido's having a child by Aeneas is never contemplated, except in line 327[-329] where the nature of the sentence – an unfulfilled condition – makes the allusion as delicate as possible. In Ovid's *Heroides*, Dido, like most of the other mournful ladies, appeals with painful emphasis to the contingency of an heir. And indeed it is clear from the first that the love of Dido is not of the kind that could content itself with a few days or even a few years of pleasure, she wants Aeneas to have and to hold, and she is desperately anxious to make him compromise himself so far that it will be impossible for him to draw back. But I repeat, so far as the morals of the epic go, Aeneas is under no positive duty to stay with the woman who has consented to be his mistress.

§6. And if the standards of morals in literature have changed since the days of Augustus, the standards of art have changed too. It is practically impossible for us nowadays to go back on so many centuries of romantic tradition; we forget how

---

§6. "A second, and artistic objection, such as might be brought forward by an aesthetic young gentleman, that Aeneas would have been right to brave the anger of the gods for the sake of a woman. This would be quite out of keeping with Virgil's thought, as already delineated."

largely, in all probability, Virgil himself is responsible for the existence of that tradition. I have heard of a young man, who, being much pestered by Roman controversialists who wanted him to change his religion, invented a quite imaginary young lady in the case, who would be much distressed by such a course of action on his part. When asked, "Would you let yourself be damned for the sake of a woman?" he immediately replied, "Of course: any gentleman would." His attitude, right or wrong, is so familiar nowadays, that it is very difficult to pull ourselves up and ask "Why on earth should one?" – a question which would immediately leap to the lips of an ancient Greek or Roman, brought up in times when chivalry simply did not exist. More especially if I have been right in saying that in Virgil's eyes the position of Aeneas was one in which he was called upon to choose between carrying out a heaven-sent mission, or failing in that mission, that the whole picture is profoundly influenced by reminiscences of Caesar and Cleopatra, that, finally, the very *pietas* of Aeneas was exactly the attitude which inevitably would react on such circumstances in the less romantic, but from a certain point of view more heroic way, then I think it is hard to blame the poet for his hero's faithlessness. Aeneas has the defects of his qualities, if we like to regard it in that light; no more.

§7. But, it will be urged at once, if that is so, why did Virgil put himself at such pains to represent to us, in long-drawn agony, the sufferings of the deserted woman? Why does he leave Aeneas a mere mute, a plaything in Dido's hands, and then in the hands of Juppiter? Why does he make such lame apologies, or, if he cannot apologize for himself, why does not the poet attempt to make excuses for his action? Would it not have been possible, for example, to represent Dido as a scheming minx, who simply ran after the Trojan superman; could not Virgil have afforded to be a little more Shavian[1]? Or, failing that, could he not have made Dido play the Cleopatra more to the life; could she not have sent out immediately, at the first whisper of desertion, soldiers to intercept his flight, so that he could have cut his way through them and emerged with credit? Does not the sympathy which the author shews for the lady really throw out the balance of the whole book, and make a cad of Aeneas in order to make a heroine of Dido?

§8. The real answer to these objections, which at first sight have great weight, is that up to about line 361 this is actually what Virgil is trying to do. Dido is, till

---

[§7.] "A third objection, arising out of this, such as might be brought forward by a don: that for the sake of the plot, if the hero was to desert his mistress, that mistress ought not to have been represented in so favourable a light; she should have been either more of an advertiser or more of a virago."

[§8.] "Answer to this: that up to line 361 Dido is represented as an advertising creature, as may be seen from lines 74–79. She is represented as being unreasonable in not accepting what sound to us very poor excuses, (lines 333[–361]), as may be seen from the calm assertion in line 554[–555]."

then, a scheming minx. The attitude ascribed to her in lines 74–79, running about with Aeneas, shewing off her wealth, breaking down in the middle of her sentences, continually having him to dinner, and making the long-suffering raconteur repeat the whole of books 2 and 3 over and over again for her benefit, must have seemed to Virgil's public conduct as shameless as that of the most man-hunting of Mr. Bernard Shaw's heroines. Classical mythology had no place for the lady who was advertising for a husband, except the peculiar and distressing case of Phaedra. "My dear", you can imagine an old Roman matron saying to her daughter, on reading the *Aeneid*, "my dear, that may be the way they manage things in Carthage, but in my day such conduct would have been considered most forward and improper. Why, I assure you that when I married your dear father, I had never seen him before, much less spoken to him." And further, the excuses made by Aeneas in lines 333 onwards are, in the eyes of Virgil's contemporaries, perfectly valid excuses: he is quite conscious that she has deserved well of him, he says, and he won't forget it; if the fates would allow him to stay on in Carthage, he could imagine nothing jollier, but unfortunately they won't; she has got her city all right, why can't she let him get his? and so on. To us it all sounds intolerably frigid; they are the sort of arguments a man would employ in explaining matters to his hostess when determined to cut short a boring weekend. But to the Roman mind it is all perfectly sensible, perfectly reasonable. The plea, which, borrowing the words of a famous modern poem, we might express as

> Can't get away to marry you to-day,
> My fates won't let me,[2]

that plea is one to which no reasonable woman could possibly take exception. And even when, immediately after one of Dido's finest rhetorical outbursts, Virgil calmly goes on to inform us:

> Aeneas celsa in puppi, jam certus eundi,
> Carpebat somnos rebus jam rite paratis, (554[–555])
>
> [With everything ready for sailing, Aeneas, now determined to leave, was taking his rest on the high stern]

I do not think he is poking fun at the man who can quietly wind up his watch and go to sleep when a woman is crying her heart out for him. I do not think he foresaw that in the 20th century Englishmen would call his hero a fish, and English ladies a perfect pig.

§9. But when he got to that fateful line 361, his art broke down before an enormous temptation. Symmetry, classical precedent, the whitewashing of his hero, all demanded that Dido should either bow to fate, like Calypso, or lose our sympathy by cutting up rough and trying to murder Aeneas. But either at the last moment he lost his heart to Dido, or else the mere opportunity for a "situation" in the technical dramatic sense was too strong for him. Technically, it is a blemish to make us sorry for Dido at the cost of making us hate Aeneas. But Virgil is not the only great artist who found himself in a position where he had to sacrifice plot in the interests of situation. Sophocles did it, in the *Philoctetes*; Meredith did it, in *Diana of the Crossways*. Somebody, I forget whether it was Gibbon or Macaulay or who, said he rose from reading *Paradise Lost* with the feeling that Satan was a very fine fellow.[3] It would have shocked Milton to hear this criticism; it would have shocked Virgil quite as much to hear that you regarded Dido as the heroine of the *Aeneid*. In either case the dramatic instinct was too strong for the poet, and made him make the best of what he really believed to be a thoroughly bad cause. Virgil could not resist the allurement of that closing scene, those final declamations. He is like that sculptor in Plato, who, arguing on Post-impressionist grounds that purple is the most decorative of all colours, insisted on making the eyes of his statue purple. He lost the effect of the whole work for the sake of a few purple patches.

§10. And what purple patches they are! At first, (305–330) Dido is merely reproachful, the appeal is *ad misericordiam*; she urges the madness of attempting to set sail in winter, complains that she has sacrificed her reputation for him; tries to rouse his jealousy by the mention of Iarbas. When he has made his reply, she looks him up and down

> Huc illuc volvens oculos, totumque pererrat
> Luminibus tacitis [4.363–364]

[Rolling her eyes from side to side, and examines the whole man in silence]

and bursts into a storm of scornful denunciation, calling him a monster, gibing at his excuses, pouring ridicule on his appeal to Heaven, hoping that he will be drowned on his passage, that she may hear of it among the shades [4.365–387].

---

§9. "From lie 362 onwards, Virgil's dramatic instinct was too strong for his sense of artistic propriety, and he was thus led to make a heroine of one whom he had determined to regard as a weak and rash woman. Instances where other great artists have blackened their good characters (Sophocles and Meredith) or whitewashed their bad characters (Milton)."

§10. "Synopsis of Dido's outbursts against Aeneas: (1) an appeal to pity, (2) a storm of ridicule, (3) a suggestion of motives of prudence, (4) a last hope of thwarting his purpose by violence or guile, (5) a fierce execration."

Here she faints, and is carried from his presence, never to see him again [4.391 (-392)]. But in a last despairing effort she sends Anna with a message, no longer claiming the right to his hand, but imploring him to stay till the spring, to give her some respite [4.416-436]. On his refusal, she meditates suicide, and half in pretence, half in earnest, has recourse to the old magical spells for recovering a faithless lover which Virgil had learned from Theocritus [4.504-521]. Then she reviews her situation; can she salve her broken heart by offering herself to the Libyan suitors she has so often refused? Can she go as a stowaway on Aeneas' ship? Shall she lead out a fleet against them and compel them to return? No, death is the only hope now [4.534-552]. Next morning she finds they have set sail [4.587]. For a moment she seriously entertains the idea of stopping them by force, then checks herself when she remembers that such an attempt if made at all should have been made earlier. Rather she ought to have treated them as enemies from the first, as soon as they landed. This reminds her again of the ingratitude of it all, and she curses the faithless one, praying that if ever he reach Italy, he may not gain his kingdom without bloodshed and foreign assistance, and in any case may not live long to enjoy it, and that Carthage may some day find a leader to avenge her on Rome [4.590-640]. Then, after a few more broken sentences, in which she dwells for a moment with pride on the glory she has achieved, she falls on the dagger [4.651-662]. It is difficult not to feel, that if Virgil had been more interested in the character of Aeneas, and less in that of Dido, what we should have gained in unity of plot would not nearly have compensated us for the loss of such passages as these.

§11. There is one other scene in the *Aeneid*, where Virgil manages to outrage our feelings, without apparently being conscious that he is doing anything of the kind. This time, it is not so much romantic feelings as our sporting instinct that he has offended. In book 5, in the account of the running at the sports [5.315 ff.], two of the competitors are Nisus and Euryalus, the David and Jonathan of the *Aeneid*. Nisus is leading, the runner-up being one Salius; Euryalus is third. Suddenly Nisus slips and falls but the poet adds:

Non tamen Euryali, non ille oblitus amorum,
Nam sese opposuit Salio, per lubrica surgens,
Ille autem spissa jacuit revolutus arena.
Emicat Euryalus et munere victor amici
Prima tenet . . . (lines 334[-338])

§11. "An allegation of fault of taste against Virgil in the matter of running (5.334[-338]). Question whether Nisus really did trip up Salius deliberately."

[He had not forgotten Euryalus nor the love he had for him; so, arising through the sodden ground he put himself in the way of Salius, and the latter, rolling over, fell prostrate on the clotted sand. Euryalus rushes past and, thanks to his friend, takes first place and wins . . .]

and so on. It hardly accords with modern ideas of racing, that our hero should deliberately trip up the second runner: we feel for Salius, when a few lines later he complains to the bystanders,

Ereptumque dolo reddi sibi poscit honorem, [5.342]

[And demands that the honour, which had been taken away from him by cheating, should be given back to him]

and marvel at the cynical insolence of Nisus, when he claims a consolation prize on the ground that he would have won himself,

Ni me, quae Salium, fortuna inimica tulisset. [5.356]

[Had not the bad luck that brought down Salius, brought me down too.]

Now of course it is entirely possible that Virgil may not have been alive to the fact that he was not representing his heroes in a very amiable light at this point, and in that case I think he can be justly accused, if not of an error in art, at least of an error in taste. But there does seem to be a possible explanation of the difficulty which has not been generally observed. We make sure that Nisus tripped up Salius deliberately for two reasons; first because his getting in the way is represented as an act of homage to his friend who is running third, and partly because Salius later claims compensation on the ground that he has been fouled. On the other hand, Nisus quite cheerfully talks of having lost the race through bad luck, the same bad luck which had overtaken Salius, being tripped up. I suggest it with much hesitation, but is it not possible that Nisus did trip Salius only accidentally, "sese opposuit per lubrica surgens", he got in his way in the process of rising from the slippery ground where he had fallen? And that it was only a playful touch on Virgil's part, to say that in this action he was good friend to Euryalus, just as we might say playfully that a referee was a good friend to one side in a football match, if he had happened to be knocked over at some critical moment, when the other side were claiming an offside? In that case, it would be easy to explain Salius' accusation of foul play as genuinely made, but undeservedly, whereas Nisus would have a perfect right to say that he and Salius had both suffered from misadventure.

§12. Whatever be the true explanation of the incident, it is quite certain that Virgil imputes no blame to Nisus in this connexion, and we may observe here a prominent instance of Virgil's great triumph of artistic skill in making us interested in his characters on very short notice. It is easy to underestimate the immense difficulty under which Virgil laboured, of making his characters real. Homer had practically no need of any such arts, for the characters which formed his stock-in-trade were doubtless characters with which his readers were already familiar, or at least their individualities could be assumed without apology, for it was an understood thing that all the great contemporary heroes of Greek mythology were present at the siege of Troy: each part of Greece which was of any prominence at the time claimed to have been represented there by its local contingent, so that you just said "Ajax" or "Diomede", and everybody understood what you meant. Further, as is common in all fairy stories, most of these heroes had each his own special characteristic, in which he excelled all the rest, except of course Achilles, the paragon of all virtues. One Ajax was the strong man, another the sprinter, Teucer was the crack shot, Nestor the sage counselor, Odysseus the man of sound common sense, and whenever you, as a bard of the Homeric age, introduced one of these characters, everyone knew what to expect of them, just as in the medieval ballads everyone knew what to expect of Robin Hood or Little John. Now consider the case of Virgil. He was working with very few characters who were already familiar to his readers: Aeneas himself was not a particularly exciting person in the *Iliad*: Dido was a rather unreal figure from Carthaginian legend, renowned chiefly for the famous Semitic trick by which she secured land for the building of her city. That was all. There was just a chance of introducing one or two of the old lot in a minor capacity, but death had been at work with these so busily, that practically only Helenus remained on the Trojan side, and Diomede on the Greek. What did Virgil's hearers know or care, to start with, about Ilioneus, and Achates, and Palinurus, and Misenus, and all that lot? How was he to get them interested in these people, all in the space of 12 books?

§13. The fact that in reading Virgil – if you are reading him as literature at all – you are interested in them, is due to Virgil's remarkable power of dashing off lightning vignettes, his unrivalled impressionist skill. Sometimes the whole effect

---

§12. "Artistic cleverness of this passage, as an introduction to Nisus and Euryalus, two characters who are to become prominent later. Difficulty of Virgil in such cases, due to the fact that he was not on the whole working over a mythological ground where all the characters would already be known as household words to his readers."

§13. "Instances of Virgil's skill in getting over this difficulty, from 1.510, and 2.426[-427]."

is secured by a single adjective. Take Ripheus, for example, who is killed in lines 426–427 of book 2.

> ... Cadit et Ripheus, justissimus unus
> Qui fuit in Teucris, et servantissimus aequi.

> [Ripheus also fell, the one who was the most righteous and the greatest lover of justice amongst the Trojans.]

You have never heard of Ripheus before, you are never to meet him again, and yet that brief character-sketch makes him live for a moment – he was such a straightforward fellow; never did a dirty thing – and it is hard not to feel a sense of regret as you read it, that you never recognized the man's merits till it was too late. And then in the storm in book 1, line 222, you find Aeneas lamenting his companions whom he has lost sight of in the storm, a mere string of names, ending up with "fortemque Gyan fortemque Cloanthum". The pair are still strangers to you, but there is something vivid about the phrase – good old Gyas, good old Cloanthus – that make you sorry for them, and it is a brilliant stroke when Aeneas, finding that they have not been drowned after all, but cast up on a different part of the coast, comes upon Cloanthus with just that same epithet (line 510):

> Anthea Sergestumque videt, fortemque Cloanthum,

> [Sees approaching Antheus, Sergestus and brave Cloanthus]

and in line 612 reveals himself to them, and shakes hands with them all round:

> Post alios fortemque Gyan, fortemque Cloanthum.

> [Then others, brave Gyas and brave Cloanthus.]

Good old Gyas, good old Cloanthus, safe after all! You can almost hear him saying it.

There are some characters, destined for a more prominent part in the action, who need a more elaborate introduction. This is the case with Nisus and Euryalus, whose midnight expedition is one of the chief incidents of book 9. I think here is a case in which Virgil definitely does improve on his model. Homer has an account of funeral games, from which much of the 5th *Aeneid* is imitated, but it is all in the last book but one of the *Iliad*, and, I cannot tell why, it does not excite one very much to see these heroes engaged in chariot-races and boxing and so on, when you are accustomed to see them breaking through the ranks of Troy. But Virgil deliberately puts his funeral games quite early in the story, so that you have a chance of making the acquaintance of his characters first of all, when they are, so to speak, in mufti. We have begun to take a personal and human interest in this pair of friends long before we arrive at the point where their tragedy begins. We, who have laughed with them in the 5th book, find it all the easier, for that very reason, to weep for them in the 9th.

§14. So it is that even on the Italian side the principal actors, though we do not begin to come in contact with them till the poem is already half-way through, have yet a wonderfully distinct personality. Camilla is, I admit, something of a stock figure, but this can hardly be said of the kindly-disposed and singularly ineffectual king Latinus, the egoist Turnus, the blasphemer Mezentius, his unfortunate son, Lausus

> ... dignus patriis qui laetior esset
> Imperiis, et cui pater haud Mezentius esset, [7.653(–654)]

> [A worthy boy who would have been happier under the guidance of a true father,
> a father other than Mezentius]

and Drances, the cool councillor, the Italian statesman of all ages. If you want to see at its highest the familiarity and ease with which Virgil moves among people whom he has only invented just a minute ago, look at the account of the killing of the tame doe by Ascanius, which was the signal for the first outbreak of war. It belonged to the sons of Tyrrhus, the royal forester, and we are suddenly told that their sister Silvia (as if we had known her all her life) used to wash it and comb it out, and put flowers round its horns [7.487–489]. When it is wounded,

> Silvia prima soror, palmis percussa lacertos,
> Auxilium vocat, et duros conclamat agrestes, [7.503–504]

> [First Silvia, the sister, beating her own arms with her hands (in grief), calls for
> help and summons the rough country people]

and then she disappears from the *Aeneid* forever. Who is Silvia? What is she, that all our swains should come up and make such a fuss about her beastly doe? There is no answer to the question, she is just Silvia, sister of the sons of Tyrrhus – we are not even told whether her age was 5, or 20, or five-and-forty. Yet who has not got the picture of a simple forest girl, moaning for her lost pet, and going round to make all her young admirers promise to avenge its death on these Trojan pirates; all unknowing that the dead creature is to be the *casus belli*, which

---

§14. "Our introduction to the characters on the Italian side, with especial reference to Silvia in 7.475ff."

will set Turnus at war with Aeneas, and ultimately lay the foundations of a world-empire?

§15. Virgil is also a master – though here the art is so well concealed that the casual reader of the *Aeneid* never observes it – of the art of giving plausible reasons for the necessities of his plot. Why were the Trojans ever such fools as to take a great wooden horse within their walls? We have all of us felt before now that it did not require the genius of a Holmes to suspect some treachery in this incident; read it in Virgil, and you will see how carefully the minds of the Trojans are worked on. Cassandra points out the danger [2.246–247], but then it was notorious that no one ever did believe Cassandra: that was what she was there for. Laocoon saw through it [2.40–53], but when the baffled fury of Juno punished him for his perspicacity, the Trojans simply misinterpreted it as a warning against speaking ill of the divine object [2.199–233]. But the crowning touch is the story of Sinon, the Greek traitor who has been left behind to inveigle the Trojans into accepting the fatal gift. He pretends to be a deserter, and gives them a full account [2.108–194] of the discussion which is supposed to have led the Greeks to the decision of going away. It was the anger of Athene, he says, who is so annoyed by the stealing of the Palladium, that she refuses to help the Greek cause any longer. At the advice of Calchas, they left the horse behind as a sort of expiation of their offence. But then it remains to be explained, why the horse need have been so uncomfortably large. Ah, that, says Sinon, was for fear the Trojans should lug it inside the walls, and thereby win themselves good luck. Sinon is the Meldon of antiquity:[4] in a single breath he has explained the awkward fact of the enormous size of the horse, and made everybody in the city desperately anxious to have the thing inside the walls.

Take another case of a difficult development in the plot. Aeneas had to be driven ashore on the Syrtes; but how could any mariner be so unskilful as to get driven out of his course all that way, when he was merely trying to get across from Epirus to the heel of Italy? Virgil accounts for it all: Aeneas is warned not to land in Italy, because there have been Greeks settling down there lately: "Cuncta malis habitantur moenia Graiis" [All the cities are inhabited by evil Greeks], says Helenus in 3.398. But why shouldn't he go round Italy the natural way, through the straits of Messina? Instantly mythology is called to the rescue: he can't go through them, because they are Scylla and Charybdis. So, "praestat Trinacrii metas lustrare Pachyni" [Better is it to round Cape Pachynus in Sicily]

---

§15. "Virgil's skill in giving plausible explanations of unconvincing complications in his lot, illustrated from the story of Sinon in book 2, from Aeneas' travels to Africa, and from 5.730ff."

[3.429], he tries to go right round the end of Sicily, and is instantly caught by a North wind, which of course drives him in the required direction. Again, how does it come about that the Trojans intermarried with the Latins – Virgil wanted to represent it as a mixed stock – when they had brought a lot of womenfolk away with them from Troy? The answer is given in book 5, about line 730 [or rather in 5.750–771], where it is explained that all the people who had got tired of wandering, and most of those who were no use in the war, were left behind at Eryx in Sicily, where Aeneas founded a colony for them.

§16. Virgil is also particularly rich in, and particularly skilful at managing, what is known as situation. Instances of this are so common and so obvious that it is hardly necessary to do more than refer to some of the better known ones. There is the scene in book 1, with its purely gratuitous magical element, where Aeneas arrives at Dido's court at exactly the same moment [1.509] as the other half of the shipwrecked party, each supposing the other to be drowned, – Aeneas himself being invisible by his mother's precautions – when at last he can contain himself no longer, and is suddenly revealed to the eyes of the court, who are just talking about his supposed death, with that splendid: "Coram, quem quaeritis, adsum" [I, whom you seek, am here before your eyes] [1.595]: or again, the scene a little earlier in the same book, where he comes upon a Carthaginian sculpture representing the fighting round Troy, his own figure among others [1.488]. There is the scene where Andromache weeps over Ascanius, because he reminds her of the lost Astyanax (3.489). There is the scene in book 9 already alluded to, where Nisus, hidden in the wood, sees Euryalus about to be slain, and bursts out crying:

> Me, me, adsum qui feci, in me convertite ferrum,
> O Rutuli! [9.427(–428)]

> [Here, here I am, the one who did it. It's against me that you must turn your weapons]

You could name a score of "situations" in which Virgil shews the dramatist he might have been, if the genius of the native tongue had ever found a natural outlet in the drama. What dramatist has such a situation as that in the sixth book, where Aeneas in Hades meets Deiphobus, the horror of his mutilated limbs still marking him in death, and the hero, as if overlooking the fact that the piteous object is trying to hide himself for shame, accosts him in the old formula of happier years:

[§16.] "Virgil as a master of situation. Illustrated from 1.595, 3.489, 9.427 [–428], 6.500."

Deiphobe armipotens, genus alto a sanguine Teucrum [6.500]

[Oh Deiphobus, mighty warrior, descended from the noble blood of the Trojans]

§17. Even his lesser incidents are sometimes sketched in with the minutest care. I mean such incidents as the fight in the wood, with the uncouth rustics coming up to the fray, armed as best they may be with clubs and stakes, and old Tyrrhus himself mightily pleased – "spirans immane" [Breathing savagely] [7.510] – to have got hold of an axe [7.505–510]: or the Arcadians under Pallas swarming up the glen in 10.362ff., or the taking up of the dead, and throwing on pyres the well-known armour of lost friends

> ... munera nota
> Ipsorum clipeos, et non felicia tela. (11.195[-196])

[Their familiar possessions, their shields and doomed weapons.]

Keep these passages, and such as these, in mind, and then remember that imbecile criticism of Coleridge: "Take away from Virgil his diction and his metre, what have you left?" and you will wonder how it is that one man of genius could possibly be so blind to the merits of another as to indulge in comments of that sort. And if Virgil's art does sometimes overshoot itself, and become unnecessarily elaborate, as in the fanciful description in 1.174ff. of the simple process of lighting a fire, or the very matter-of-fact recipe for the manufacture of a thunderbolt in 8.429–432, we may at least remember that the best of poets have the defects of their qualities, and that a moment's comparison of him with Apollonius Rhodius or Milton will leave us in no doubt which is the greatest Epic artist in the history of literature.

Notes

1 'Shavian' denotes a devotee of G. B. Shaw, his writings, or his social and political opinions. In Shaw's *Misalliance* (1910) Hypatia Tarleton, a typical Shaw heroine, exemplifies his lifelong theory that in courtship, women are the relentless pursuers and men the apprehensively pursued.

---

§17. "Careful delineation of incidental pictures, as in 10.362ff., 11.195[-196]. Virgil's art occasionally nods (1.174ff., 8.429–432), but very seldom."

2 Knox is appropriating, humorously, the lyrics 'I can't get away to marry you today/ My wife won't let me!' of a popular comic song by Richard Thompson entitled 'Waiting at the Church'.
3 Despite my best efforts, I am unable to jolt Ronald Knox's memory.
4 Possibly the Irish nationalist politician Charles Henry Meldon (1841–May 1892).

5

Virgil's Appreciation of Scenery

§1. In speaking of Virgil's appreciation of scenery, it must be understood at once that more is intended than merely natural scenery. Virgil, like most of the classical poets, is not alive to that antithesis between the natural and artificial which is characteristic of modern poetry since Wordsworth. He does indeed in two places speak of "vivum saxum", unhewn and unworked stone (1.167, 3.688), just as in the *Georgics* [Georg. 2.469] he refers to "vivi lacus", natural pools as opposed to reservoirs. But in these cases he draws attention to the absence of artificiality only because artificiality is what we should have expected to find: in the one case he is speaking of natural seats formed in the rock, in the other of a natural harbour made by the cliffs at the mouth of a river. But ordinarily the works of man do not mar for him the beauty of a landscape, they rather lend it interest. In 10.806, where the traveller overtaken by the rain-storm hides himself

   Aut amnis ripis, aut alti fornice saxi,

it is usual to translate "Under a river bank, or an arch of deep rock", but I have a strong suspicion that "saxum" here is not a rock, but simply stone, and that the reference is to one of the tall aqueducts which used to traverse, and still may be seen traversing, the Campagna, their high arches being the protection a Roman of Virgil's day might easily make for in a storm, just as we make for a railway bridge.

§2. In any case, there is one particular kind of artificial modification introduced by human requirements into the landscape, which is to Virgil a favourite detail of scenery; and it is an interesting one, because it is quite possibly one of the influences that make us feel in reading the *Aeneid* that we are reading a distinctively Italian poem, sometimes we almost feel inclined to say, a distinctively Medieval poem. I mean Virgil's fondness for towers, and such

---

[§1.] "Love of scenery rather than of nature, since to the ancient poets the works of man are a part of landscape as much as those of nature. In two passages (1.167, 3.668) Virgil does make the modern distinction between the natural and the artificial, but this is not usual with him."

[§2.] "Virgil's especial fondness for towers, illustrated from 6.548."

towers especially as you see perched up on the top of steep hills. This architectural strain in his scenery is perhaps most strongly brought out in the account of the lower world. In the Greek poets you occasionally get a glimpse of the asphodel fields, blazoned with golden flowers, in which the spirits in Elysium are said to walk, but even in Plato you never get any idea of the view presented to the eye by the place in which the wicked are punished, and the souls of ordinary men wander restless. Virgil has anticipated Dante in making Tartarus a place, a place which can to some extent be described. It is not merely that it has gates, the gates of iron and threshold of brass, which we hear of in Homer; that is a sufficiently obvious conception. Aeneas actually

> ... sub rupe sinistra
> Moenia lata videt, triplici circumdata muro,
> Quae rapidus flammis ambit torrentibus amnis,
> ...
> Porta adversa, ingens, solidoque adamante columnae,
> Vis ut nulla virum, non ipsi exscindere ferro
> Caelicolae valeant; stat ferrea turris ad auras, (6. 548[–550]; [552–554])

> [Under a cliff on the left sees a broad city, encircled by a triple wall and surrounded by a rushing torrent of scorching flames ... before him stands a huge gate, with columns of solid adamant so strong that no might of man nor the gods themselves could uproot it with weapons; there stands an iron tower, rising high into the air]

and so on. This is not merely a collection of representative ideas, giving a general impression of the finality and impregnability of the place of punishment, it is an audacious attempt to put it pictorially before the reader's eyes.

§3. But towers dominate Virgil's scenery even in the upper air. The *locus classicus* is of course not in the *Aeneid* at all, but in the Second Georgic. There, in the famous description of the glories of his native land, the poet insists upon the appearance of its towns:

> Tot congesta manu praeruptis oppida saxis,
> Fluminaque antiquos subter labentia muros. (156–157)

> [All the towns built by man's hand on craggy rocks and the rivers which flow beneath their ancient walls.]

[§3.] "Virgil's fondness for towers, illustrated from *Georgics* 2.156–157, *Aeneid* 1.419 [–420] (as opposed to 7.160[–161]), 3.535 [–536], 8.98, 7.631, 7.740. Analogy of the backgrounds used by early Italian painters."

"Congesta manu" – he glories in the artificiality of them; "praeruptis saxis", those sudden hill-heights with the cities nestling on the top of them which we see and envy in the pictures of the Italian Pre-Raphaelites.[1] For this note of scenery is emphatically Italian, you can see that even in the *Aeneid*. When Aeneas in 1.419[–420] comes to Carthage, he climbs the hill:

> ... qui plurimus urbi
> Imminet, adversasque adspectat desuper arces;
>
> [That towers huge over the city and looks down upon the citadel opposite]

you come upon the city *suddenly*, that is; when you have mounted a particular hill, you see its towers rising out of the plain, so that their tops are almost on a level with you, just as an English traveller coming by the road from Amesbury may see Salisbury lying at his feet, and the Cathedral spire confronting his eyes. But in 7.160[–161] as the ambassadors of Aeneas approach the city of Latinus, they see the city itself looming up high in front of them all the time:

> Jamque iter emensi turres ac tecta Latinorum
> Ardua cernebant juvenes, muroque subibant.
>
> [And now the warriors, their long journey ended, were catching sight of the towers and the high roofs of the Latins' city and were drawing close to the wall.]

They see the towers "ardua", high above them, and "subeunt" to the walls, come up to them from underneath. So it is indeed in the very first glimpse the voyagers get of the country that is to be theirs. They reach a harbour (3.530[–531]),

> portusque patescit
> Jam propior, templumque apparet in arce Minervae.
>
> [A harbour opens up before us nearer and nearer, [until] and the temple of Minerva appears on the citadel.]

A temple of Minerva crowns the citadel. And the very rocks which form the harbour are turriti:

> ... gemino demittunt bracchia muro
> Turriti scopuli, refugitque ab litore templum. [3.535–536]
>
> [Crags with towers on top stretched down their arms to form a double wall and the temple stood well back from the shore.]

Conington quite gratuitously takes "turriti" to mean "looking like towers", regardless of the fact that no other instance is quoted of this use of the word. But if we speak of *crinitus* Apollo, we mean that he has hair on the top of him, not that he looks like hair: if we say that a person is *vestitus* we mean that he is covered with clothes, not that he looks like clothes: and surely the natural way of understanding the present passage is to say that the rocks at the side of the harbour were not simply shaped like towers, but were covered with towers, had towers on top of them.

This is, we might almost say, the normal aspect of an Italian city in Virgil; the impression you get of it is that of a lot of towers sticking out of the top of a hill. Even Evander's one-horse town of Pallanteum is seen (8.98) as "muros arcemque procul" [Walls and a citadel at a distance] from the river. "Turrigerae urbes," [Cities crowned with towers] mentioned as being dear to the heart of Cybele in 10.253, are doubtless a mere ritual detail, since Cybele was represented as wearing a crown of towers, but the same epithet applied to the town of Antemnae in 7.631 is surely intended to give an eye-picture. And perhaps the most picturesque of all the local descriptions in the catalogue of Rutulian troops is that of part of Oebalus' contingent (7.740):

Et quos maliferae despectant moenia Abellae:

[And the people whom the walls of apple-bearing Abella look down upon]

a single line suffices to give us the pictures of the walls of Abella rising high above the plain, and the apple-orchards smiling underneath.

§4. Another leading note of Virgilian scenery is the prominence of rivers. This is of course by no means peculiar to Virgil; it is hardly possible to live by the side of a great or famous river without regarding it as in some strange way personal. Rivers in Homer are seldom without their river-gods, and the passage in the *Iliad* where Achilles is pursued by the Scamander betrays an obvious admiration for the river as one of the irresistible forces of nature. But it is Virgil who persistently endows his rivers with human attributes almost whenever he mentions them. The passage in book 8, where Tiber checks his stream so as to let Aeneas row up it without difficulty, by no means stands alone, though this perhaps gives us the most vivid picture (8.62[–64]):[54]

... Ego sum, pleno quem flumine cernis
Stringentem ripas et pinguia culta secantem
Caeruleus Thybris.

[I am that river whom you see scouring its banks and cutting through the rich farmland with a rich stream – the blue grey Thybris.]

---

[54] "Virgil's fondness for rivers, shewn in his violent personification of them, as in 8.62[–64], 7.685, 7.759, 7.801, 8.711[–713]."

The Amasenus is father Amasenus in 7.685, though it is a stream almost unknown in the classical writers. In 7.759 the death of Umbro is bewailed by Fucinus of the glassy wave. And the cold Ufens in 7.801 is said to "find his way along the bottom of the valleys, and hide himself in the deep." In the account of the battle of Actium, we see (8.711[–713])

> ... Magno maerentem corpore Nilum,
> Pandentemque sinus, et tota veste vocantem
> Caeruleum in gremium latebrosaque flumina victos.

[The Nile, huge in body, mourning, opening wide his folds and welcoming with all his drapery the defeated Egyptians into his blue-grey breast of secret waters.]

It is surely by a very bold stroke of personification that even so famous a river as the Nile can be said to throw open his garments, and spreading out his robe to welcome the vanquished troops to the blue bosom of his secret streams. In the triumph which immediately follows, Vulcan has represented Euphrates as flowing less proudly than before, and by a supreme imaginative effort speaks of another river as "scorning to submit to a bridge", "pontem indignatus Araxes" [8.728].

§5. In 9.30[–31], again, the Ganges rises in silence, fed full by seven slow tributaries. In line 125 of the same book, the Tiber actually is so alarmed by the change of the Trojan ships into nymphs that he withdraws his foot ("revocat pedem") landwards from the sea. And in the description of the allies of Aeneas, in 10.205[–206], we find the contingent from Mantua, Virgil's own native city,

> Quos patre Benaco, velatus harundine glauca
> Mincius infesta ducebat in aequora pinu.

[That Mincius, cloaked in blue-green reeds, led down, from his father Lake Benacus, to the sea in hostile ships of pine.]

The magic of the river, the haunting magic that we catch in the line of the *Georgics* already quoted, is naturally not without its share in the carefully calculated effects of the sixth book. Acheron [6.295ff.], the first river you come to, the river over which Charon plies, gives us no impression either of terror or of delight; it is just a very dull estuary, full of mud, and apparently tidal. Phlegethon [6.550–551] flows round the city of Tartarus, his waters run beneath its walls all on fire, like a town river passing a large factory, but they are also rapid, lashing

---

§5. "Further instances of the personification of rivers, from 9.30[–31], 9.125, 10.205[–206]. Importance of rivers in the sixth book, as expressing the various traits in the scenery of the underworld."

their way between the rocks. And then, in order to complete the picture, we must pass on to Elysium, where we find the secret glade and the whispering woods,

> Lethaeumque, domos placidas qui praenatat, amnem. [6.705]

[And the river Lethe flowing by peaceful abodes.]

Acheron is the dreary mouth of the Severn, Phlegethon the stream that flows through some manufacturing town in Derbyshire, Lethe is the Thames at Lechlade.

§6. But undoubtedly the most original feature of Virgil's landscape-painting is his exploitation of the forest. You get the key to this characteristic right at the beginning of the poem, in line 160 and following of the first book. It is a description of the harbour, where Aeneas and his shipwrecked companions first land.

> Hinc atque hinc vastae rupes, geminique minantur
> In caelum scopuli, quorum sub vertice late
> Aequora tuta silent; tum silvis scaena coruscis
> Desuper horrentique atrum nemus imminet umbra. [1. 162–165]

[On either side huge crags and twin peaks loom towards heaven; beneath their crests the waters are quiet and safe all around; and above hang a backdrop of shimmering trees and a grove dark with gloomy shade.]

The description as a whole does not concern us very much, beautiful as it is: parts of it may even be traced to Homer. What I do want to draw to your attention to is that word "scaena". It is simply a word borrowed from the stage; the "scaena" is, literally and exactly, the background, a term which we also use of natural scenery. The great force of it is this, that it shews us Virgil had in his mind's eye a definite picture, arranged as if by the painter: he sees the whole thing before him, and gives every element in the general impression its proper value as a part of the scheme. This is precisely what Homer as a rule, what all the Greek poets as a rule, do not do: it is one of the broad distinctions between ancient and modern poetry that they do not. The classical poet simply enumerates the details that lie before him, sometimes with a pre-Raphaelite exactitude: if it be the cave of Calypso, the vine round the cave, the trees near it, with the wide-winged birds roosting in them, the meadows of violet and parsley, the four springs flowing in all different directions, and so on. It is a singularly rich description, but try for a moment to *picture* to yourself the cave of Calypso, and

---

§6. "Virgil's fondness for woods, marked at the very outset by the passage in 1.160ff. Virgil the first of the ancient poets who goes in for landscape as such."

you will find that you have been left to construct the general impression for yourself. The fact is that the Greeks, whose natural artistic expression was sculpture, not painting, had no great sense of background; the human figure was the important thing, and natural objects, if they were represented at all, were represented with considerable labour, quite disproportionate to the effect produced. Even in Theocritus, except for the scene where the Cyclops sees Galatea playing in the sea, I do not know that you will find a single definitely drawn picture of landscape. But Virgil is on the side of the moderns, in this as in several other respects; he has studied artistic effects; again and again he gives us vignettes, in which the whole scene leaps to the eyes, without ever wasting his words or piling on his details.

§7. Another way of stating this same fact would be to say that inanimate nature, which is apprehended only subjectively by the earliest classical poets, tends to become more and more objective up to Virgil's time. I don't know if that helps you at all. What I mean is, that to Homer, a tree is primarily something to give *you* firewood, or at best something *you* can use as a landmark or worship as the habitation of a god. By the time of Theocritus the conception has advanced; it is now something jolly to lie under, but it is still something jolly for *you* to lie under: only in so far as it is useful or pleasant to one of the characters of the story does it come into the story. But Virgil's use of scenery, and especially of trees, is something different. He describes the landscape, not because it is important to the plot that he should do so, but because the landscape has a dignity of its own, and deserves to be described.

§8. With this background of "silvae coruscae", of waving woods, we start the *Aeneid*, and trees are a constant accompaniment of the story throughout. The ships, for fear of pirates or hostile inhabitants, are secreted (1.310[-311])

> . . . in convexo nemorum sub rupe cavata,
> Arboribus clausam circum atque horrentibus umbris.
>
> [In a wooded cove under the overhanging rocks shut in on every side by trees and their quivering shade.]

But here again, it is not till we have reached Italy that Virgil puts forth his full powers of scenic description. I do not know that any other author catches quite

---

[57.] "This tendency on the part of Virgil illustrated from the case of trees. Function of trees in Homer and Theocritus."

[58.] "Virgil's sense of the magic and mystery of a forest, illustrated from 1.310[-311], 6.179, 7.11, 7.172, 7.505, 7.515, 8.597[-599], 11.523[-525], 6.237[-238], 7.82[-84], 7.565[-567], 6.268[-272], 6.450 [-454], 9.381[-383]."

as Virgil does the horror and magic of a wood. It is yet another link between Virgil and the fairy stories. A wood is always dark and horrid and uncanny. It is "antiqua silva, stabula alta ferarum," as in 6.179, or virgin forest, "inaccessi luci", like those of Circe in 7.11; a temple is "horrendum silvis et religione parentum", its appearance harmonizing with the grim associations of the place (7.172); a Fury can lurk in it, as in 7.505

> ... pestis enim tacitis latet aspera silvis;
>
> [(For) the savage fiend lurks in the silent woods]

and when she blows her horn in line 515,

> Contremuit nemus, et silvae insonuere profundae;
>
> [The trees shivered and the whole forest sounded to its very depths]

The *rendezvous* between Aeneas and Tarchon, the leader of the Etruscans, is

> ... ingens gelidum lucus prope Caeritis amnem,
> Religione patrum late sacer; undique colles
> Inclusere cavi, et nigra nemus abiete cingunt: (8:597[–599])
>
> [A wide sacred grove near Caere's cold river, revered as a holy place by people near and far; on every side a ring of hills enclose it and encircle a grove of dark firs]

and the ambush laid by Turnus is a valley (11.523[–525])

> ... quam densis frondibus atrum
> Urget utrimque latus, tenuis quo semita ducit
> Angustaeque ferunt fauces aditusque maligni.
>
> [Hemmed in on both sides, darkened by the dense foliage of trees; a small path leads to it, making a treacherous approach through a narrow pass.]

It is a place where you never know what may happen, where you are at the mercy of enemies, some human, some more than human. In particular, it is the sort of place where you may expect any sort of dreams or oracles or commerce with the underworld. Such is the cave where Aeneas sacrifices to the infernal gods before descending to Hades (6.237[–238]):

> Spelunca alta fuit, vastoque immanis hiatu,
> Scrupea, tuta lacu nigro nemorumque tenebris,
>
> [There was a deep cave, immense in its vast cleft, jagged and protected by a black lake and dark woods]

and the oracle of Faunus, consulted by Latinus in 7.82[-84],

> ... lucosque sub alta
> Consulit Albunea, nemorum quae maxima sacro
> Fonte sonat, saevamque exhalat opaca mephitim,
>
> [And consults the groves beneath high Mount Albunea, which, mightiest of forests, resounds with its sacred fountain, and breathes forth from her darkness a noxious exhalation]

and the dismal valley of Ampsanctus, by which Tisiphone, her disastrous work accomplished, is hurriedly sent back to her natural home in the lower regions (7.565[-567])

> ... densis hunc frondibus atrum
> Urget utrimque latus nemoris, medioque fragosus
> Dat sonitum saxis et torto vertice torrens.
>
> [A dark forest with its dense foliage presses in upon it on both sides and in the middle a crashing torrent resounds over the rocks with swirling waters.]

Coruscus, horrens, antiquus, inaccessus, horrendus, tacitus, profundus, ingens, sacer, densus, ater, malignus – those are the sort of adjectives by which Virgil's woods are always characterized, while the encircling hills, the deep cave, the rushing torrent, the brimstone lake, keep up the atmosphere of mystery. But when he really wants to produce his most striking effects, it is a wood with paths in it by moonlight.

> Ibant obscuri sola sub nocte per umbram,
> Perque domos Ditis vacuas et inania regna;
> Quale per incertam lunam sub luce maligna
> Est iter in silvis, ubi caelum condidit umbra
> Juppiter, et rebus nox abstulit atra colorem.
>
> [They went on in the darkness in that lonely night surrounded by shadows through the empty halls of Dis and his unsubstantial kingdom; it was just like following a path in the wood under the sinister light coming from a fitful moon when Jupiter has buried the sky in shade and black night has robbed things of their colours.]

That is in 6.268[-272], when Aeneas and the Sibyl go down together to the underworld; could there be a more appropriate setting? Has there ever been a more eerie description? The same scene recurs when he meets the shade of Dido in 6.450[-454],

> ... recens a volnere Dido
> Errabat silva in magna; quam Troius heros
> Ut primum juxta stetit adgnovitque per umbras
> Obscuram, qualem primo qui surgere mense
> Aut videt, aut vidisse putat per nubila lunam:

> [With her wound still fresh, Dido was wandering among them in that great forest. As soon as the Trojan hero stopped beside her, recognizing her dim in the darkness, like someone who sees or thinks he has seen the new moon rise from the clouds at the beginning of the month]

the poor ghost is flitting about among the trees, now appearing, now disappearing, like a young moon between the clouds on a stormy night. And our farewell of Nisus and Euryalus is taken among the same fantastic surroundings; Euryalus loses his way in the wood, and no wonder, for it was (9.381[-383]) a wood

> ... late dumis atque ilice nigra
> Horrida, quam densi complerunt undique sentes;
> Rara per occultas lucebat semita calles.

> [Bristly far and wide with dense undergrowth and dark ilex trees, all of it choked with thick brambles: here and there glimmered a path visible through bushy passageways.]

Could there be a grimmer picture than the dark wood with its thick brambles, and the white path shining here and there in the moonlight?

§9. I do not mean for a moment that Virgil is incapable of recognizing any brighter side about the existence of trees. It were idle to maintain that, for the blessed in Elysium sing together

> Inter odoratum lauri nemus, unde superne
> Plurimus Eridani per silvam volvitur amnis, (6.658[-659])

> [Surrounded by a grove of fragrant laurel whence the mighty river Eridanus rolls upward through the forest]

and Lethe flows, as we have seen, round a

> Seclusum nemus, et virgulta sonantia silvis. (6.704)

> [Secluded grove, and rustling forest bushes.]

[99.] "Virgil is nevertheless conscious of the cheerier aspect of trees, as in 6.658[-659], and 8.91[-96]. He is not at pains to distinguish between different kinds of trees, except in a few cases, such as that of the elm in 6.283: as a rule it is enough to say that Mezentius is lying under a tree (10.835[-836]). Contrast of this with Homer."

And certainly the finest piece of natural description in the *Aeneid* is the sunny journey up the river to Evander's court, with the quiet river underneath, and the thick trees overhead (8.91[–96])

> Labitur uncta vadis abies, mirantur et undae,
> Miratur nemus insuetum fulgentia longe
> Scuta virum fluvio pictasque innare carinas.
> Olli remigio noctemque diemque fatigant,
> Et longos superant flexus, variisque teguntur
> Arboribus, viridesque secant placido aequore silvas.

> [The well pitched ship glides over the waters: the waves are amazed and the woods full of wonder at the uncommon sight of the far-gleaming shields of warriors and painted prows floating on the river. So, they wear out the night and the day with rowing, master all the long windings of the river, and are covered by all types of trees and they cleave green woods on smooth waters.]

"Variae arbores", not even mentioning their names. Sometimes Virgil condescends to specify the kind of tree he is talking about, as in the case of the "ulmus opaca", "ingens", of 6.282[–284], which stands on the nearer bank of Acheron:

> In medio ramos annosaque bracchia pandit
> Ulmus opaca, ingens, quam sedem Somnia vulgo
> Vana tenere ferunt, foliisque sub omnibus haerent.

> [In the middle a huge shadowy elm spreads out its branches as old arms, which people say to be the home of empty dreams, clinging under every leaf.]

But as a rule it is quite enough for Virgil that the thing is a tree, the wounded Mezentius in 10.835 [–836] is sitting merely

> Arboris adclinis trunco: procul aerea ramis
> Dependet galea, et prato gravia arma quiescunt.

> [Resting against the trunk of a tree. Nearby his bronze helmet hangs from the branches and his weighty weapons rest on the grass.]

The mere mention of a tree is enough for the picture, it is for Homer to puzzle our imaginations with a long catalogue of different kinds of trees, such as those in the gardens of Alcinous or round the cave of Calypso. In the Greek poets, you literally cannot see the wood for the trees. But the poet of the *Georgics* has such a fine disregard for mere detail, that in his scenery you cannot see the trees for the wood.

§10. I have taken three of the leading notes of Virgilian landscape, towers, rivers, and woods, without for a moment suggesting that the poet is insensible to the other beauties of Nature, the "florea rura" [1.430] where the bees ply busily in the sun, or the shadows falling longer on the mountain side as evening draws in [*Ecl.* 1.83]. But these things belong rather to the *Eclogues* and the *Georgics* than to the *Aeneid*. The greatness of the nature-description in the Epic poem lies rather in the power of forming a picture in the mind and then transferring it to the mind of the reader, than in any particular minuteness of observation. Here is the contrast with Lucretius, for accuracy of observation is precisely what Lucretius does possess. I remember seeing some time ago a very poisonous little tract for the young, disguised as a story-book, which was called *Eyes and No Eyes*, all about two little boys going down a lane; where needless to say Eyes was always spotting nightingales and scabii and Red Admirals, and No Eyes never had any luck at all in spotting things. But I am sure when they both got home, Eyes carried away nothing from the walk except a lot of insignificant ornithological and entomological details, whereas No Eyes, who had not been foraging about in the ditch the whole time, had probably seen and appreciated the landscape, and became a better man for it. And those two little boys are Lucretius and Virgil. Lucretius is always *observing* and reporting on what he has observed: he hardly ever *sees* or describes what he has seen. Once indeed he does produce a phrase that, coming as it does from a classical poet, fairly takes our breath away; I mean when he talks of lambs playing on hillside and describes them as

. . . velut in viridi candor consistere colli, [DRN 2.322]

[Just like a spot of white standing still on a green slope]

a patch of white picked out on a field of green. But it must be observed that Lucretius uses this, not as a picture, but as an instance of optical illusion. It is with less careful observation, but with much more sense of giving his reader something to look at, that Virgil makes Aeneas see the four white horses on the cliff of Italy, now seen for the first time (3.537[–358]):

Quattuor hic, primum omen, equos in gramine vidi
Tondentis campum late, candore nivali.

[The first omen I saw here was that of four horses white as snow grazing at large over the field.]

---

§10. "Contrast between the faculty of observation and the sense of the picturesque, illustrated by Eyes and No Eyes, or Lucretius and Virgil."

You may say that it is only recorded as an omen, but if you will read on, you will see that if so it was a particularly ineffective omen. Anchises, who is nothing if not a safe prophet, points out that this portends war, since horses are armed for battle, but goes on to qualify the prediction by adding that horses are also used in peace, so possibly it is an omen that there will be no war at all. No, Virgil put in the four white horses because he thought they would be a jolly thing to see on a cliff.

Virgil is the first of the landscape painters, because he likes landscape for its own sake, and the first of the Impressionists, because he is ready to sacrifice the details in order to give you the effect.

Note

1 Fifteenth-century Italian painters preceding Raphael.

6

Virgil's Use of His Sources

§1. The work of most great poets is in some sense indebted to certain sources, which have provided them either with their actual plots, or with a variety of minor incidents in the story. Just as a musician will take a quite uninteresting poem and put it to music in such a way as entirely to overshadow the qualities of the original subject by the brilliance of the new treatment, so the poet does not feel it incumbent on him to invent the outlines of his story for himself, he simply takes an old theme from an old historian, let us say, or collector of folk-lore, and makes it his own by giving to it his own colouring, his own character-drawing, his own handling of the incident. There is hardly any play of Shakespeare which is "original" in the sense of containing an entirely novel situation; his stories all come from North's Plutarch, or Florio's Montaigne, or the *Gesta Romanorum*, or Holinshed's *Chronicle*, or some such "source". It does not very much matter to us who were the first writers who connected the foundation of Rome with names of any of the survivors from the Trojan war, or what influences led Fabius Pictor to identify the founder of the Roman name with one of the beaten side, when it had previously been the fashion to claim Ulysses himself or some party of anonymous Greeks for the same position. Apparently the legend of a Trojan connexion was so far established by the end of the First Punic War, that the Acarnanians, in claiming help from Rome, urged that their ancestors had been the only Greek race not represented by a contingent at the siege of Troy. Among a mass of conflicting legends, some invented for the credit of Rome, some connected with the name of Aeneas through the influence of a widely spread cult of "Aphrodite Aeneias", Virgil had simply to take his choice, and if he conflated two or more of them, or added to them to suit his own purposes, there was no one to accuse him of inaccuracy. Almost all the main outlines of the story are to be found in Dionysius of Halicarnassus, or in a still more accessible form in Conington's

---

[§1.] "Sources of any great poem, in the sense of second-rate authors from whom materials are taken for the story, supremely unimportant. Passing account of one or two of these."

introduction. Nor was it entirely Greek legend which Virgil followed: the story of Dido is Italian, though in this case Virgil has allowed himself very considerable latitude in adapting the story to his purposes. In the original version, Dido committed suicide not for love of Aeneas, who indeed according to then current ideas belonged to a period about 300 years earlier, but in order to avoid the advances of King Iarbas, which threatened her vow of perpetual widowhood, taken over the tomb of the dead Sychaeus. In this as in other incidents, Virgil seems to have been deriving his information from Varro, and using it as best suited his own convenience. These are, strictly speaking, the sources of the *Aeneid*, except for the actual account of the sack of Troy, which was no doubt almost exactly modelled on the Cyclic poem of Arctinus which went by that name. But all these things are no more important to the understanding of the *Aeneid*, than the original treatment of the story by Saxo Grammaticus is essential to the proper appreciation of *Hamlet*.

§2. An enquiry which is far more important is the enquiry into the nature of Virgil's *models*. Whence did he derive, in so far as it was not entirely his own, the atmosphere of his poem, the general scheme of the incident, the colouring of his characters? And to say that in these things Virgil was not entirely original, is by no means the same thing as to say that he plagiarized. It is only the very earliest poets, the most primitive poets, the poets who are writing about a period of civilization which was to all intents and purposes their own, that can be quite uninfluenced by the work of their predecessors. Even in the case of Homer it is doubtful whether we should think his inspiration quite so spontaneous, if we had preserved to us the works of earlier Hexameter bards of the Mycenean Age. And the English or Scottish ballad, though a primitive form of literature if any ever was, is nevertheless a highly conventionalized form of art. The unscrupulous wooer, the indiscreet young lady, the vengeful family of the wronged party, the popinjay which is always letting the cat out of the bag, and having to be called to order – all these figures as well as a host of stock incidents are repeated from ballad to ballad without any sense that they detract from the originality of the individual poem. Much more then in an Epic composed in a literary period, when rich stores of earlier literature lie at the author's disposal, is it inevitable that he should make his own whatever he can of the work of his predecessors, and borrow from them without feeling the need of apology. There is no such

---

§2. "Far more interest attaches to the poet's models. All except the most primitive poets depend for their atmosphere and the arrangement of the incident in the story upon previous writers, even ballad poetry is apt to repeat the same characters."

thing as copyright in classical poetry. Did Milton never imitate Virgil? Did Spenser borrow nothing from Malory, Keats nothing from Spenser?

§3. In this sense Virgil's debt to Homer is so profound and extensive that we sometimes tend to forget it altogether, sometimes to wonder whether there is anything original in the *Aeneid* at all. I have tried in previous lectures to point out how the later poet does differ from the earlier, in some respects even improve on him, and that often in places where he is treading most carefully ground which has already been covered by his predecessor. I have insisted on the higher conception of destiny which animates Virgil's theology, and ennobles his theme, the romantic element of admiration for weakness which attracts our sympathies more definitely to Virgil's heroes than to those of the *Iliad*, the halo of pathos with which Virgil encircles the death of the young, the art with which he contrives to make his story consistent and plausible, the more disinterested feeling he betrays for the beauty and still more the mystery of natural scenery. Those are some of the most prominent differences between the two. But the resemblances lie more on the surface. Broadly speaking, the earlier books, with their account of the wanderings of Aeneas on the high seas are in imitation of the *Odyssey*: the battle scenes at the end of the *Aeneid* are in imitation of the *Iliad*. Odysseus wanders ten years, Aeneas wanders seven; both pass by Scylla and Charybdis, the home of the Cyclops, the isle of Circe; both are pursued by the implacable fury of a god; Odysseus is detained by Calypso, Aeneas by Dido; each loses a companion by misadventure, each goes down to Hades, and so on. The correspondences with the *Iliad* are no less numerous and exact: Achilles holds games over the pyre of Patroclus, Aeneas over the tomb of Anchises: Turnus is carried away from the battle by his patron goddess in the *Aeneid*, just as Aeneas himself is in the *Iliad*; Nisus and Euryalus go out and slaughter the sleeping Rutulians, just like Diomede and Odysseus, and are themselves overtaken and killed, just like Dolon; the action is delayed and the suspense heightened by the absence of Aeneas, as it is by the Wrath of Achilles; Amata tries to keep Turnus back from the battle as Hecuba does Hector; Turnus kills Pallas, as Hector kills Patroclus, and Aeneas, clad like Achilles in armour made specially for him by a god, takes vengeance like Achilles for the death of his friend.

§4. Nor is Virgil's borrowing always borrowing without loss. He sometimes imitates the form of the original without imitating the attendant circumstances which gave that form its significance. Sincerely as we may weep for Pallas, we can

---

[§3.] "Extensiveness of Virgil's debt to Homer, variously illustrated."

[§4.] "Instances where Virgil in borrowing has lost some of the point of the original, from 10.532 [–533], and 9.672, and from the incident of Nisus and Euryalus."

hardly regard his death as the tremendous motive to Aeneas which the death of Patroclus was to Achilles. A short-lived acquaintance picked up on a voyage down the Tiber is hardly a thing to be compared with the heroic attachment between Achilles and his squire. We can pardon the blind fury of Homer's hero when he does return to the fight, but when Aeneas refuses to spare a man's life for a monetary consideration on the ground (10.532[-533]) that

> ... Belli commercia Turnus
> Sustulit ista prior jam tum Pallante perempto,

[Turnus has already put an end to such bargaining in war the very moment he murdered Pallas.]

We can hardly feel that the plea is adequate. What else, we ask, was Turnus to have done? He couldn't very well have stood where he was and let Pallas kill him. There was some excuse for the two Lapithae in Homer, Polypoetes and Leonteus, who in *Iliad* 12.157 held open the gate of the Greek camp to let their comrades get into shelter again, but their counterparts in the *Aeneid* (9.672), Pandarus and Bitias, can only be accused of criminal bravado when they deliberately open the gates of Ascanius' camp in order to smash the besieging army as they rush in. And whereas Diomede and Odysseus were not seriously exceeding their commission as spies when they cut up Rhesus and his followers and drove away their horses, the similar exploit of Nisus and Euryalus looks rather like waste of precious time, when their aim was to penetrate the Rutulian lines and carry through to Aeneas a demand for support with the least possible delay.

§5. It is in these battle scenes that Virgil follows Homer most faithfully, and especially in the mere catalogues of slaughter which are introduced from time to time in order to glorify the rival heroes. Most people complain of boredom in reading these catalogues, and I admit the criticism, but I cannot say that in the long run I find Homer's any less boring. Whole passages which Dr. Leaf[1] sacrifices on the altar of Criticism I would cheerfully devote to the gods of literary appropriateness. Virgil, it is quite true, never really has his heart in the fighting, he never really rejoices to see the blood flow. In fact, by occasional tender touches, he apprises us of the fact that he doesn't quite approve of it. Especially I would notice in this connexion the account of the killing of Lausus by Aeneas in book 10, towards the end. In line 811[-812] Aeneas actually warns the young man that his sense of duty towards his father is carrying him too far:

---

§5. "Especially the battle scenes of the *Aeneid* lack the fighting spirit of the *Iliad*: Virgil never sees red. Instances of an underlying humanitarian attitude, from 10.823ff."

> Quo moriture ruis, majoraque viribus audes?
> Fallit te incautum pietas tua.
>
> [Why are you in such a haste to die? Why do you take on challenges greater than your strength? Your *pietas* deceives you and makes you reckless.]

Lausus naturally refuses to profit by the warning, and meets his death, whereupon Aeneas (823[–824])

> Ingemuit miserans graviter, dextramque tetendit,
> Et mentem patriae subiit pietatis imago.
>
> [Groaned heavily in pity and held out his right hand as the thought of his own *pietas* to his father came into his mind.]

It is a very subtle stroke to make Aeneas' regret depend on the thought of his own ancestral virtues, but the fact remains that he does regret it, and moreover is slightly ashamed of it. You can see that in the very clever touch by which Virgil makes Aeneas get angry with the bystanders – a sure sign that a man is feeling a bit of a fool (830[–831])

> ... Increpat ultro
> Cunctantis socios, et terra sublevat ipsum.
>
> [Further, he rebukes his hesitant men and lifts Lausus off the ground.]

The influences which partly at any rate account for this humanitarianism are not difficult to appreciate. He lived in a time of highly developed civilization, when the whole Roman world was profoundly disgusted with fighting, after the experience of an unusually long period of civil war. You could hardly expect a representative writer of the Augustan age, that age in which *pax* and *otium* seem to be the highest ideal of politics, to take much pleasure in following in the footsteps of the rude old Mycenean bard. See how Tennyson softens down the matrimonial irregularities of Malory's heroes in the *Idylls of the King*, and you will understand something of the delicacy of feeling with which a Virgil must have approached the orgies of carnage, which, as a true disciple of Homer, he felt it to be his duty to reproduce.

§6. Virgil does not care for fighting, and it is doubtful whether on the whole he likes seafaring. At any rate, he has managed to compress into a single book the whole of the wanderings of Aeneas, although they occupied on his own

---

[§6.] "And the sea-travels of the *Aeneid* do not compare, for excitement, with those of the *Odyssey*. But Virgil more real both in his fighting and in his seafaring than Homer."

shewing some seven years out of the nine which are demanded for his story. He has a bit of a rough time, it is true, but he has not all the hair-breadth 'scapes of Odysseus. The Harpies, the distant Cyclops, the unnegotiated passage between Scylla and Charybdis, and the storm off the Syrtes hardly come up to the earlier story so far as excitement goes – the seizing of the sailors by Scylla, Ulysses' own long struggle with Charybdis, the horrible danger in Polyphemus' cave, the slaying of the oxen of the Sun, the outwitting of Circe, the Laestrygons, the raft, and the landing in the river. There is not so much fairy-story about the incidents which befall Aeneas. But though neither fighting nor seafaring are favourite themes with Virgil, I will venture on the paradoxical remark that the seafaring of the *Aeneid* is more real than the seafaring of the *Odyssey*, and the fighting of the *Aeneid* more real than the fighting of the *Iliad*. This paradox I shall not attempt to defend at this moment, but I hope to explain what I mean when we enter more fully into the question of the subsidiary sources of Virgil's inspiration.

§7. To keep for the present to the comparison of Virgil with Homer, we must not omit to consider the more detailed resemblance of phrase and sentiment which betray the dependency of the later poet on the earlier. No one can have failed to observe the remarkable extent of this dependency in the matter of similes. All the business of lions facing huntsmen and jumping on bulls, of wolves getting into sheepfolds and being chased away by shepherds, of deer being harassed by dogs, and boars being surrounded and caught, and the inevitable fires that break out in woods, and winds that agitate the sea – all this comes straight from Homer, or, if it did not, we can find a parallel in Apollonius Rhodius. Here again instances are not wanting in which Virgil's similes seem to have lost something of the appositeness of the originals from which they were derived. Thus the simile in *Odyssey* 6.102 where Nausicaa among her maidens is compared to Artemis among her nymphs is transferred to Dido, who is surrounded by a quantity of young lords [1.496ff.]. This extreme dependence on his originals in the matter of similes is much to be regretted in Virgil, since those in which he seems to be under no obligation to his predecessors are as a rule very interesting. It is to say the least of it a very pretty conceit when in 10.132[–134], Ascanius standing on the wall of the Trojan camp is compared to a gem set in a necklace. And in three of these cases at any rate he seems to have preserved to us

---

[57.] "More detailed resemblances between Virgil and Homer, especially in the similes. The original similes in the *Aeneid* the most interesting, and the most Italian (7.379[–383], 12.473[–477], 10.803ff., 10.132[–134])."

a picture of contemporary Italian scenes. The first is that in 7.379[-383], where Amata, driven to frenzy by Allecto, is said to rage about the city like a top:

> Quem pueri magno in gyro vacua atria circum
> Intenti ludo exercent; ille actus habena
> Curvatis fertur spatiis; stupet inscia supra
> Impubesque manus, mirata volubile buxum;
> Dant animos plagae.

> [Which the boys, intent on their play, make go in a great circle in empty halls; set in motion by the whip it travels on its curved course; the ignorant crowd of children look down puzzled, fascinated by the spinning boxwood; the blows give it life.]

It may well be questioned whether the comparison is a worthy one: it becomes less ludicrous if we suppose that Allecto is conceived as standing over her victim and driving her on: but whatever be said of that it can hardly be denied that the picture itself is an engaging one, and none the worse for being drawn from common life: the empty courts bring Italy to the mind, and we imagine [in] them just such boys as are represented playing irrelevantly in the background of Raphael's Betrothal of the Virgin. The second, in 10.803ff., has already been quoted in another connexion: Aeneas retreats covered by his shield from a shower of weapons, like a traveller sheltering from sudden rain under an arch or a hole in the river bank. Again the "alti fornice saxi" has a ring of Italy about it. And the third is such a sight as Virgil may have seen from his window at the very moment of writing; Juturna drives Turnus' chariot from point to point in the field to avoid Aeneas (12.473[-477]):

> Nigra velut magnas domini cum divitis aedes
> Pervolat et pinnis alta atria lustrat hirundo,
> Pabula parva legens nidisque loquacibus escas;
> Et nunc porticibus vacuis, nunc umida circum
> Stagna sonat.

> [As when a black swallow flies through the great house of a rich master and wings its way through its high halls, and, picking up tiny scraps of food and dainties for her twittering nestlings, her chirping is sometimes heard in empty colonnades and sometimes round watery pools.]

Such fancies as these make us sorry that Virgil did not trust more to his observation and eye for resemblance, and less to classical precedent. It is possible, however, that the secret of his apparent indifference to originality in similes was due to a lack of interest in similes altogether. It is not by any means inconceivable that he put them in out of deference to a literary convention, without having himself any interest in what is, after all, a very tiresome and unconvincing form of poetic artifice. Not that he objected at all to introducing short passages taken direct from Homer elsewhere. There was of course a certain amount of credit attaching to the mere tour de force of working them into his story, and translating them gracefully as he did so. Indeed, he sometimes goes out of his way to quote Homer: it must have been to him almost as gratifying as it was to Bunyan to work in a quotation from the Bible.

§8. Homer failing, Virgil does not despise Apollonius Rhodius as a source of inspiration. There is a very beautiful simile about bees in 12.587[ff.] which is taken directly from him. But more than coincidence of language has been claimed between the two. This debt is one which seems to me to have been exaggerated by critics both of ancient and modern times. The crucial case is of course the story of Dido. It is true that the way in which Venus calls in the aid of Cupid to make Dido fall in love with Aeneas is directly balanced by a similar stratagem in Apollonius, which gives rise to the love of Medea for Jason. It is true that Medea, like Dido, comments favourably at first sight on the deportment of the hero. It is true that both the heroines suffer from insomnia – no uncommon symptom, if we are to believe those who profess to be learned in these subjects, when a woman has fallen in love. It is true that each of the poets has seen fit to occupy practically a whole book with the struggles of a woman's heart. Dido and Medea have the same habit of rushing about from one room to another in a distracted sort of way. But that, so far as the situation goes, seems to be the extent of the resemblance. Dido makes a confidante of her sister Anna, Medea deliberately deceives her sister Chalciope as to the state of her own feelings. Medea is so much in love with Jason that she is prepared to help him win the Golden Fleece and then let him go back to Greece without seeing anything more of him, whereas the whole point of Dido is that she is perfectly prepared to let Aeneas' mission go hang, so long as she can keep him with her. Dido's original scruples are about breaking an oath of perpetual widowhood, she feels like a nun who is breaking cloister: Medea's difficulty is whether she has a right to help the man she loves at the cost of deceiving and displeasing her father. Medea wants to commit suicide, if at all, in order not to trouble Jason; Dido wants to commit suicide precisely in order that she may trouble Aeneas. The love of Medea is only

---

[§8.] "Virgil's use of Apollonius of Rhodes. It is not true that the situation of Dido in book 4 is a mere imitation of that of Medea in the *Argonautica*."

a problem until she has confessed it; the love of Dido does not begin to be a problem to her till after it has been confessed, and consummated, and betrayed. In fact it would be impossible to conceive two heroines in more dissimilar positions.

§9. The real fact of the resemblance, which certainly cannot fail in spite of all the differences, to affect in a strange way the mind of any reader of the classics, is that in both cases we have got right out of the classical atmosphere and into the atmosphere of romance. Conington traced this peculiarity in Virgil, namely, his habit of assigning prominence to women, to the influence of the Greek drama. I think this is highly problematic. After all, with the exception of Dido's case, there are not many instances in the *Aeneid* in which women do become prominent. Amata, the wife of Latinus, plays a considerable part, but she is not so far as sentiment goes any great advance on Homer's Hecuba. Camilla is simply and merely the Penthesilea of the Epic Cycle. Juturna is also instanced, but she is after all a goddess, though only in a small way, and as such she hardly plays any more interesting a part than Aphrodite; indeed she *is* Homer's Aphrodite, Venus herself having taken on in the Virgilian story the role of Thetis. When all is said and done Virgil (who was known to his contemporaries as something of a woman-hater) has left us no portrait of a feminine character which is not thoroughly conventional, except that of Dido. Dido is the distressed lady of romance, and I am bound to say I can see very little in the Greek dramatists which would suggest that such a figure was imitated from them. The grandes dames of Athenian tragedy are not romantic heroines, they are people like Clytemnestra, Electra, Antigone, Jocasta. Antigone is precisely the opposite of romantic, for surely in the eyes of romance a living sweetheart is better than a dead brother. Romance begins with Euripides, but only because he is the first of the moderns: his Alcestis, his Medea, his Creusa, are the first fruits of a general movement in literature which expressed itself later in Theocritus, Apollonius, and Musaeus; that movement through Alexandrine influence communicated itself to the Roman poets from quite early times; Catullus' Ariadne[2] and Ovid's *Heroides* are the outcome of the same movement just as much as Dido. It would be unsafe, then, to say that in making the feelings of a wronged woman a prominent subject in his poem Virgil was, so far, imitating the Greek drama, or

---

§9. "What the two situations really have in common is that they both take the point of view of the woman in the case, in fact they are both romantic. Conington's assertion that Virgil presented us with unconventional portraits of women under the influence of the Greek drama is uncalled for, since there is only one case in which Virgil does give us an unconventional portrait, and the Greek dramatists only begin in the time of Euripides to approach the romantic attitude."

Apollonius: he is simply the child of a romantic reaction which was first foreshadowed in Euripides, probably gained enormously in strength owing to the New Comedy of Menander and others, and came to be the very atmosphere breathed by later poets, whether Alexandrian or Roman.

§10. The remaining instances of alleged imitation by Virgil of Apollonius are of varying degrees of doubtfulness. The following are mentioned by Conington. (1) "The departure of Jason from his father and mother resembles the departure of Pallas from Evander" [8.558–584]. Well, of course there is a parting in both cases, but so far as that went Apollonius could hardly take out a copyright. In Jason's cases it is a mother, in Pallas' a father, who makes the complaint; Alcimede wishes she were dead long ago, before she had seen the day: Evander wishes that he were as hearty as he was some years back, so that he might have had a go at the Rutulians himself, and then goes on to hope that he may live to see Pallas come back victorious, or die soon if he is not to survive. Not a close "resemblance." (2) "The song of Orpheus is contracted into the song of Iopas" [1.742–746]. True, but it is so much contracted that it only occupies four lines, and even in those there are considerable differences. (3) "The reception of the Argonauts by Hypsipyle is like the reception of the Trojans by Dido [1.631ff.], and the parting . . . . . [sic] reappears though in very different colours, in the parting of Aeneas from the Queen of Carthage" [4.365ff.]. The situation is certainly modelled something on the same lines: the heroes are in danger of forgetting the object of their voyage while enjoying the unconventional hospitality of the Amazons. But the parting is as unlike as it could well be: Hypsipyle just sends Jason on his way, expressing a hope that he will get the fleece all right, and that if he is passing Lemnos on his way back, he will drop in and see her. Jason explains that he thinks it will then be time to be getting back to his people; he adds directions as to what she is to do if a son is born to her, and they part the best of friends. So like Dido! (4) "The mythical representations on Jason's scarf answer to the historical representations which distinguished the shield of Aeneas from that of Achilles." This would hardly preclude the supposition that both Apollonius and Virgil were making their own variations on the Homeric theme. (5) "The combat of Pollux with Amycus is reproduced in the combat of Entellus with Dares" [5.424–460]. This is quite untrue; though the same softening influence of romance is, as we have seen, at work in both cases, there can be no doubt at all that both Apollonius and Virgil are imitating Homer independently.

---

§10. "Consideration of Conington's other instances of borrowing in large quantities from Apollonius, with the conclusion that out of 11 instances claimed only 5 need be admitted, and of these 5, 3 are short and unimportant, while the remaining 2 have been radically altered in the process."

(6) That "the Harpies [3.212ff.] of Virgil are the Harpies of Apollonius" is no doubt true, but the further suggestion that the deliverance of Phineus from them gave a hint for the deliverance of Achaemenides, [3.590ff.] – the companion of Ulysses, you will remember, who was marooned on the island of the Cyclops – that suggestion seems highly fanciful. (7) "Phineus' predictions are like the predictions of Helenus" [3.374–462] – only to this extent, that they are both quite obviously founded on the predictions of Circe to Odysseus in the 12th *Odyssey*. (8) "The cave of Acheron in Asia Minor suggests the cave of Avernus in Italy" [6.237–242]. This is very possible, but the passage is in either case a short one, and we have no means of knowing what local Italian legends may have played their part in forming the Virgilian conception of the place. (9) "Evander and Pallas [8.98ff.] appear once more in Lycus and Dascylus." There is a man called Lycus who does send his son with the Argonauts, but there is no speech-making, and no suggestion of a detailed resemblance. (10) "Hera addresses Thetis as Juno addresses Juturna" [12.142–153]. Hera says that she likes Thetis, because Thetis alone repelled the amatory advances of Zeus, Juno simply says, without specifying a reason, that she likes Juturna better than any of the others who have borne children to Juppiter; so the resemblance is not very close. (11). "Triton gives the same vigorous aid in launching the Argo that he gives to the stranded vessels of Aeneas" [1.144ff.]. This is true.

It appears then that out of the eleven instances in which whole incidents or parts of incidents are alleged to have been borrowed by Virgil from Apollonius, a real resemblance can only be traced in five cases: in two of these, the Lemnian women and the Harpies, the incident has been borrowed but has been radically altered in the process; the other three, the cave of Acheron, the assistance of Triton, and the song of Iopas, are short and unimportant accounts. Three of the supposed resemblances are so far off that it is doubtful whether they are more than fortuitous: three can easily be explained by the common debt owed by both poets to Homer.

§11. If we are to institute a comparison between Virgil and Apollonius, I should be inclined to say that Apollonius has something of the surface attraction of Virgil with nothing at all of his depth. In the first of these lectures I took the liberty of comparing Virgil to port. If we still compare Virgil to port, we might say that Apollonius resembled nothing so much as one of the sweet, luscious wines of southern France, Chablis or Sauterne or Haute Barsac. The sweetness, the richness of the port is there, almost to excess; at times it seems positively oily, as if it were a slightly diluted liqueur. But roll it for a moment round your tongue,

---

§11. "Comparison of Virgil and Apollonius, under the similitude of wine."

and you will see at once that the body is not there; it lacks all the qualities which make port port. So it is that Apollonius, with all his smooth, almost glutinous charm, has only to be read with a little thoroughness to make us understand how entirely he lacks all that makes Virgil Virgil.

§12. It is not worthwhile to spend much time in considering the debt of Virgil to his Latin predecessors, partly because it is so slight, as far as extant authors are concerned, partly because so much of early Latin poetry has perished that in any case the proportion of the debt could not be justly estimated. Such as it is, it resolves itself into the borrowing of a few lines, some of which, like "unus qui nobis cunctando restituis rem" (6.846, from Ennius) [The only one who gave us back our country by hesitating] and "Duo fulmina belli, / Scipiadas" (6.842 [–843], from Lucretius) [Two thunder-bolts of war, the Scipios] are not more than quotations.[3] These lines are indeed merely a graceful acknowledgement of the work of his predecessors in the Epic, and would no more justly be accused of plagiarism than quotations in modern poetry, – so Browning recalls "is there a reason in nature for these hard hearts?" from *King Lear* at the end of 'Halbert and Hob', and Wordsworth in his sonnets uses the phrase "incense-breathing morn" in inverted commas, with the admitted reference to Gray's *Elegy*. Others again, such as "tuo genitor cum flumine sancto" (8.72) [And you, Father Thybris, with your holy stream], an echo from Ennius, and 11.97[–98], "salve aeternum mihi, maxime Palla,/ Aeternumque vale" [Forever hail, great Pallas, and farewell forever] are perhaps no more than unconscious repetitions, such as are inevitable in the work of any poet who has studied the writings of his predecessors and has not the leisure to look up their work and see whether he has been anticipated in a particular form of expression.[4] Thus, when Macbeth is meeting Macduff in his last fight, he boasts that he bears a charmed life, which must not yield to one of woman born, and when Macduff points out that this category does not include him, says angrily:

> Accursed be the tongue that tells me so,
> For it hath cowed my better part of man. [V. 8, 17–18]

Milton, by some vague strain of unconscious association of ideas, has imitated this passage twice in two consecutive lines:

[§12.] "Comparison of Virgil with earlier Latin authors necessarily incomplete, but the reminiscences it discloses in the *Aeneid* are either deliberate quotations from them, as 6.842[–843] and 846, or unconscious repetitions, as 8.72, and 11.97[–98]. Illustration of both these phenomena from Wordsworth, Browning, and Milton."

> Adam could not, but wept,
> Though not of woman born: compassion quelled
> His best of man, and gave him up to tears. [XI, 495–497]

Leaving at this point the beaten track of Virgilian criticism, and agreeing with Conington that Virgil imitates Homer far more than he imitates the Alexandrian poets of Greece or his own predecessors in the Roman Epic, while perhaps disagreeing with what seems to me the exaggerated importance he attaches to the influence of the Greek dramatists, we are at liberty to revert to the qualification I made in speaking of the Homeric originals of Virgil's story – to the effect that the seafaring in the *Aeneid* is more real than the seafaring of the *Odyssey*, and the fighting of the *Aeneid* more real than the fighting of the *Iliad*. I do not mean precisely that it is in either case more graphic in Virgil's hands, or that it thrills us more. I mean simply that what is in the case of Homer simply heroic, and therefore unblushingly unlike real life, does in the case of Virgil's treatment more or less correspond to actual fighting and actual seafaring as you might find it in history.

§13. Let us take the case of the seafaring first. The story of the *Odyssey* is a Saga, and one of its principal aims, like that of any other saga, is to carry the reader over a vast quantity of countries, half mythical, half conceived as really existing, each of them with their own special dangers or features of attraction. It is the earliest form of the proverbial sailor's yarn, like the stories which Othello told Desdemona when he was making love to her, about

> The Antropophagi, and men whose heads
> Do grow between their shoulders,[5]

and so on. The *Argonautica* of Apollonius Rhodius is a fairy story – according to Mr. Andrew Lang,[6] the most widely spread of all fairy stories. The ship no longer contains a single figure, that of the famous globe-trotter Odysseus, but a whole crew of oddly-assorted persons each endowed with his own special and sometimes highly extraordinary gifts. We all read those fairy stories when we were young, about the man who wanted to win the King's daughter and to that end had to go through a variety of exploits. He could never have performed all these by himself, but after setting out in his magic ship he was always meeting odd people on the way, and taking them aboard, as they seemed to have nothing better to do. There was the strong man whom he found rooting up a forest, and the swift man who was running a race with a fly, and the crack archer, who was

---

§13. "The seafaring of the *Odyssey* and the *Argonautica* has nothing to do with real life, it is just the seafaring of a fairy tale."

taking aim at a bird mile away, and the man with the wonderful eyesight, and the man who had got all the winds in a bag on his back, and several more. And that is the constitution of the crew of the Argo; Polydeuces the boxer, Hercules the strong man, Lynceus the far-sighted, and there was an archer, but I have forgotten his name.[7] It is a ministry of all the talents, it is the collectivism of the high seas.

§14. Now when you come to the *Aeneid*, you find that it is neither a fairy story nor a Saga. Aeneas' crew have singularly few talents: they go through one or two of the traditional hair-breadth 'scapes of the Mediterranean, but nothing compared with either Odysseus or Jason. The root of all the difference is that they are a much larger number than the Greek heroes. This is no mere remnant of a small island contingent of troops, no cheery adventurers setting out in a single boat to win a single fleece. It is the remnant of a great people; they have their women-folk and their children with them. There are 14 ships at least, as specified in the first book. And the second difference is one of temperament. They are not simply trying to get home; they are not going out on a casual quest from which they can turn back at any moment and find their people sitting up for them. They are men who have both a past and a future, they are homesick exiles, exiled from a land they have never seen, homesick for a home which is not yet in existence. That is the great fact about Aeneas' followers: they are colonists. The crew of Odysseus suffer from sea-sickness, the crews of Aeneas suffer from land-hunger.

§15. Look at his course throughout book 3, and you will see at once that it is a perfectly orderly and natural course to take. Leaving Troy, which is not safe for them, they cross by the nearest sea-way to Thrace. Here they immediately start to build a city. They are warned off by the portent of the bleeding myrtle. But they do not go away just because the place is uncanny; they go away because of the precise nature of the warning given to them:

Heu, fuge crudeles terras, fuge litus avarum. [3.44]

[Ah! Get away from this cruel land, get away from this avaricious shore!]

Go away because the land is "crudelis", has unscrupulous inhabitants, because the shore is "avarum", it's your money they want. Now that is a perfectly sober piece of historical criticism. It is exactly what did happen to everyone in historical

---

§14. "But the companions of Aeneas are no travellers in a fairy tale: it is the migration of a people".
§15. "The story of Aeneas' wanderings not a saga, but a quasi-historical account in which historical motives are assigned for the movements of the exiles."

Greece who ever did try to found a colony on that sea-board; he was cut up by the Thracians. Aristagoras went there, after the failure of the Ionian revolt in 493 B.C., and he died fighting against the Thracians. In 475 Athens tried to plant a colony there, and the design was frustrated by the Thracians. In 465 she again tried it on, at a place called Εννέα Οδοί the colonists were cut off and massacred by the Edonians. And that is just what would have happened to Aeneas if he hadn't moved on.

At this point, I daresay you wouldn't have known what to do. But the ancients did: of course you went and consulted the oracle. So they go to Delos, right in the Cyclades, and the oracle, being after all only an oracle, gives them one of its fatuous old mis-interpretable answers [3.94(–96)]. "Go to the country of your kinsmen" – why of course, says Anchises, any fool knows where that is; Crete, by Jove [3.103ff.]. So off they go to Crete, and find the place empty, owing to recent internal complications, and stake out their claims and build a city in good earnest. They sow their crops, and sit down to see what is going to happen [3.132ff.]. And nothing does happen to the crops, which is unfortunate, and all the cattle get killed off by a plague, and Anchises begins to think this must be the wrong place after all; either he or the oracle must have been at fault [3.137ff.]. In the normal course of things, the next move is to go right back to Delos and get another oracle. Virgil cannot be bothered with all that, so he gives Aeneas a special private revelation to the effect that he is to go to Italy [3.147ff.]. A long way, but they start obediently, and no sooner have they got away from Crete, and come out, mark you, into the open sea, than they are overtaken by a storm, just as S. Paul was, and for three days are driven up and down in Adria[8] [3.192ff.]. Finally they come ashore on the Strophades, and by the time they have been driven off them by the Harpies – trouble with the local fauna this time – they are beginning to want a rest, so they make for the mainland, just opposite the Italian coast, in a convenient position for dashing across with a good breeze [3.209ff.]. Here, at Actium, they have the good fortune to hear that there are kinsmen of theirs close at hand; Helenus, the prophet-son of Priam, has staked out his claim there [3.294ff.]. So they do what all Greek emigrants were in the habit of doing, they paid their relations a friendly call, to see how the land lay. Helenus gives them advice about their next move [3.374ff.]; it's no manner of use attempting anything on the southern shore of Italy, for

> ... cuncta malis habitantur moenia Graiis [3.398]
>
> [In all the towns dwell evil Greeks]

they must go round the toe of Italy, and what's more – here for the first time a directly mythical motive is introduced into this sober historical narrative – they will have to go round Sicily too, in order to avoid Scylla and Charybdis [3.420ff.]. They take the advice, and again they have no sooner put their noses into the open sea, round the end of Sicily, than another storm comes hurrying up, and drives them still worse off their course, all the way to the African coast [3.506ff.]. And here, at Carthage, comes the choice. Shall they be content to give up seafaring, and settle down to amalgamate with the Phenician power, or shall they press on and found a free city on Italian soil. The latter course they finally adopt.

§16. Except for the mention of Scylla and Charybdis – a rationalist would explain even these as a picturesque way of describing a stormy strait – there is no single incident which might not have belonged to the true story of some early Greek settlers. The consultation of the oracle, the successive attempts to found a city, the obstacles which drove them further afield, hostile natives, famine and pestilence, wild beasts, ancestral enemies occupying the country beforehand, contact with the Phenician power – all these can be paralleled from the history of the spread of Greek civilization. The fact that they always get caught by storms at open sea recalls the regular aversion of the Greek seamen from the idea of doing anything but coast-voyages. The very place where they first land in Italy, Cumae, was in fact one of the very earliest places to be colonized by a Greek power. In a word, what Virgil has done is calmly to transport Aeneas and his companions bodily into the middle of the age of Greek commercial expansion, the end of the 8th, together with the whole of the 7th and 6th centuries before Christ. It is one of the most fascinating periods of all history, a time when Samians and Phocaeans and a whole lot of others, all from ridiculously small Greek states, were roving up and down the Mediterranean, some founding colonies of their own, some living by trading with the colonies, at times, for they were not scrupulous, turning buccaneers, and stealing some rich cargo that was being taken to Delphi or Samos. The Phenicians, fierce trade rivals, were ready at any moment to do a bad turn to these intruders on their ancient home. And there was fearful trade rivalry among themselves – a Samian would hardly venture to land where all the cities were inhabited by evilly-disposed Milesians. It may remind us of the Elizabethan days of Drake and Hawkins, when insignificant little places like Plymouth and Fowey would send out their fleets to intercept the treasure-galleons of America on their way to the court of Spain:

---

§16. "In fact, the atmosphere of the third book is a genuine historical atmosphere, that of the 8th, 7th, and early 6th centuries before Christ."

there is the same spirit of enterprise abroad, the same fierce rivalry, the same strong sense of independence. Or we might go further back, and think of the coming of the Northmen and the Danes before the Conquest.

§17. But it is in reality only one situation in this world of sea-adventure that Virgil has seized upon for the purposes of his story. It is the moment, by no means unknown to classical Greece, when the remnants of a great power, not content to brook the sway of an alien conqueror, determine to set out with their wives and families and gods, so far as these things are portable, and found a colony somewhere in a newer world where there is more room to live, where the long arm of the oppressor cannot reach them. What it was that recommended to Virgil's genius this kind of incident to seize upon, it is impossible to say for certain, but perhaps, at the risk of being fanciful, we might hazard the guess that his thoughts were turned to it by an actual case in which it might almost have happened in Virgil's own day. Sextus Pompeius may well have thought at one time, when he practically controlled the Mediterranean with his piratical vessels, of going off on his fortunes and starting the refugees of the Senatorial camp on a new life in a new world. Certainly the thing was in the air, for it occurs at once to Horace when he begins to be despondent at all the misery and crime of the Civil War.

> Nulla sit hac potior sententia, Phocaeorum
>   Velut profugit exsecrata civitas
> Agros atque Lares patrios, habitandaque fana
>   Apris reliquit et rapacibus lupis,
> Ire pedes quocumque ferent, quocumque per undas
>   Notus vocabit aut protervus Africus.
> . . .
> Nos manet Oceanus circumvagus: arva, beata
>   Petamus arva, divites et insulas,
> Reddit ubi Cererem tellus inarata quotannis . . . (*Epodes* XVI, 17–22; 41–43)

> [Let no other plan be adopted but this, that just as
> The community of the Phoceans fled into exile, having cursed
> Their land and ancestral gods, abandoning their temples
> To become the home of boars and rapacious wolves,

---

§17. "Virgil has seized on one particular situation in this period of general unrest, that of a voluntary *anastasis*, or flitting of the survivors of a conquered country to find a new home. The classical instance of this situation was that of the Phocaeans in the time of Cyrus, and was in the air at the period of the Civil wars at Rome, as may be seen from Horace's epodes. Horace is also clearly fascinated by the story of the migration of Teucer."

> Let us go wherever our feet will take us, wherever the Southern,
> Or the boisterous African winds shall call us.
>
> ....
>
> The surrounding Ocean is awaiting us: let us look for
> The fields, the golden fields, the islands of the blest,
> Where the land, though still untilled, produces crops every year.]

You know the rest, the account of the happy isles. You catch exactly the same note in the Teucer Ode in the first book (1.7); Teucer is indeed in exactly the same position as Aeneas. To sail away like the Phocaeans! throwing a lump of lead into the harbour, and then leaving the insulting power of Persia to find nothing in their country but empty houses and untilled fields, to carry off wives and children and Lares to a richer Western land! Where did Horace get it all from? Where did Virgil get it all from?

§18. Well, if they got it from anywhere, of course from Herodotus. The Phocaeans in Herodotus leave their country in the hands of the Persians, they too sail westwards, they come in contact with Carthage, though naturally in a hostile spirit, they too, having settled down among the Agylleans, find the cattle are visited by mysterious diseases, and have to start games to stop the curse. Some of their party get tired of wandering and go home, like the people Aeneas had to leave at Eryx in Sicily (5.751) "animae nil magnae laudis egentis". Aristagoras at a later time, starting from Lemnos, quite close to Troy, goes across to the "litus avarum" of Thrace, and Herodotus records for us his ill-success there. But the whole of this idea of founding a colony in the west is constantly being canvassed in Herodotus. Bias at the Pan-Ionian congress, when the power of Persia is obviously about to crush Greek independence on the Asiatic mainland, advises the Ionians to "set sail, and go to Sardinia, and there found a single city for all the Ionians. Thus they would be freed from slavery and prosper for the future." We must not forget that on the testimony of Anchises Cassandra, like Bias, had from the first urged this Italian scheme (3.183[–185]):

> Sola mihi talis casus Cassandra canebat.
> Nunc repeto haec generi portendere debita nostro,
> Et saepe Hesperiam, saepe Itala regna vocare.
>
> [Only Cassandra prophesized such events. Now I recall how she foretold that this was owed to our people, often talking about Hesperia and about Italian realms.]

---

§18. "In fact we have here Virgil's debt to Herodotus. Instances of the resemblance between the Virgilian and the Herodotean atmosphere."

After the battle of Lade, when the Ionian revolt was suppressed by Persia, Dionysius of Phocaea did actually go off to Sicily and turned pirate; and the Samians also went in large numbers to Sicily and got possession of the town of Zancle, where they settled.

§19. But perhaps the story which bears the closest resemblance at certain points to the *Aeneid* is that of the founding of Cyrene. The impetus to this colonization was not, it is true, given by the attacks of any foreign invader. The colony was ordered simply by the oracle at Delphi, which had not been consulted about any such matter. The order is simply "Colonize Libya", and the unfortunate inhabitants of Thera, to whom it is given, have never heard of Libya. This is precisely what the Trojans feel about Hesperia: Creusa at the end of book 2 mentions to Aeneas that he is to go there [(2.780–)781], but at the time it obviously means to him nothing more than a "western land" not further specified. You get the feeling in 5.83, where Aeneas, lamenting Anchises' death, says, "Alas that it was not granted me in your company

... Ausonium, quicumque est, quaerere Thybrim.

[(to search for) Ausonian Thybris, whatever that name may mean.]

It is like Teucer's "Ambiguam Salamina", a new Salamis, Lord knows where. The Theraean colonists, like the Trojans, try to carry out the oracle, but without proper forethought; as the Trojans waste their time hanging about in Crete, so the Theraeans, instead of reaching the mainland of Libya, colonize a small island off its coast, called Platea. The two stories, I mean, contain the same curious element of uncertainty; they went forth, not knowing whither they went; they have not merely to ask the oracle whither they are to go, but they have to have another special revelation to tell them whether they have got there or not.

§20. In all this, I do not mean that Virgil deliberately imitated Herodotus, or even that he had such and such a passage in his mind when he wrote such and such a passage: I simply mean that the atmosphere of the travels of Aeneas is neither Homeric nor mythical, it is historical and Herodotean. And I should be very much surprised, in consideration of it, if Virgil had never read his Herodotus. In one case indeed facts are actually used for which Herodotus is our primary

---

[§19.] "This specially true of the story in Herodotus of the founding of Cyrene by emigrants from Thera, where we find precisely that element of human uncertainty and divine guidance which characterizes the *Aeneid*."

[§20.] "One instance in which the debt of Virgil to Herodotus seems direct and indisputable, the story of the desertion of Crete (*Aeneid* 3.121ff. and 3.400[–401])."

authority. Of course they may not have been taken directly, they may have been mediated by some secondary authority now lost to us, but it is curious that Conington should not even have noticed, so far as I can see, that we have any account of the incident apart from Virgil and his early commentator Servius. In 3.121ff. the travellers hear that Idomeneus, King of Crete, has left his country, and that it is now uninhabited. They go there, and start a city, as I have already mentioned, and are thwarted in their designs, partly by a failure of the harvests, partly by a disease which attacks both men and crops, and inferentially the cattle also. A little lower down (line 400[–401]) we learn that

> ... Sallentinos obsedit milite campos
> Lyctius Idomeneus.
>
> [And Lyctian Idomeneus has occupied with his army the Sallentine plains.]

He has moved, that is, to the nearest point in the south of Italy; the Sallentine promontory is the heel of Italy, known to the Greeks as Iapygia. Now you turn to Herodotus, book 7, chapter 171, and you find that the Cretans after coming home from the Trojan war, in which they had rendered considerable services to Menelaus, were visited with a pestilence, which affected themselves and their cattle, and had to desert their country, leaving it quite desolate. This was apparently no uncommon thing in Crete; at least, it had certainly happened once before, and it was on this earlier occasion, according to Herodotus, who gives us no information as to the fate of Idomeneus, that the Cretans went and founded a colony in Iapygia. Clearly then Virgil has simply combined these two accounts as he found them set down in Herodotus.

§21. It is interesting to speculate, but it is hardly more than a speculation, whether Virgil shews any traces of the influence elsewhere than in book 3. Thus, it is perfectly in accord with Epic tradition to give a catalogue of the Rutulian troops; Homer himself, or those who made additions to Homer, had introduced such a catalogue into the second book of the *Iliad*. But Homer in no case, I think, mentions the weapons or armour of the various local contingents who came beneath the walls of Troy, nor even of those of the Trojan allies, motley host as they were, in the catalogue of them which immediately follows. Nor do I know where Virgil got the idea of enriching his list of the Italian supporters of Turnus (7.641–817) with detailed description of their accoutrements, unless it were from the passage in Herodotus (7.61–88) where he records with the minutest

---

[§21.] "Speculation as to the possibility of borrowing from Herodotus in other parts of the *Aeneid*. E.g. the catalogue of the Italian host in 7.641–847, and the flashing of the shield in 10.261[–262]."

care the equipment of the grand army of Xerxes. The details do not correspond very closely, but this would hardly have been suitable, since Virgil's warriors are not gathered from the furthest confines of Asia, but primitive peoples of Italy. Even as it is, we almost catch some reminiscences: the Thracian troops in Herodotus (7.75) wear fox-skins on their heads, and fawn-skin boots, just as some of the troops of Caeculus in *Aeneid* 7.688[–690],

> ... spicula gestat
> Bina manu, fulvosque lupi de pelle galeros
> Tegmen habent capiti, vestigia nuda sinistri
> Instituere pedis, crudus tegit altera pero.

[Some carried a pair of hunting spears in the hand and protected their heads with tawny caps made from the skins of wolves, leaving behind the naked print of their left foot while a rawhide boot protected the right.]

The Moschi, too, with their wooden helmets, suggest the followers of Oebalus [7.742]:

> Tegmina queis capitum raptus de subere cortex,

[Whose heads were protected by bark stripped from the cork tree]

and perhaps even the mention of the fact that the Etruscans in 7.665 fight with the "veru Sabello", the Samnite sword, may remind us of τόξα ἐπιχώρια, πέδιλα ἐπιχώρια and κράνεα ἐπιχώρια [Native bows, native shoes and native helmets] of certain Herodotean contingents. And the holding up of the shield by which Aeneas assures the besieged Trojans of his arrival, is surely a form of heliography, such as may remind us of the flashing of the shield on Mt. Parnes, with which the Alcmaeonidae tried to betray their country to the Persian.

§22. I have tried to shew, that whereas the seafaring in Homer and Apollonius is all sailing in fairy-land, the sea-going in the *Aeneid* is sailing the Mediterranean, just such as it was in the times of which Herodotus wrote. And now for the fighting. I cordially admit, that when Virgil imitates Homer in military matters, his work is second-hand, not to say second-rate. But when he leaves Homer, there are certain indications which go to shew that he was far more interested both in tactics and in strategy than the poet who delighted in hand-to-hand conflicts between single-handed heroes, pure carnage and brute force. In its way,

---

[§22.] "Reality, from a certain point of view, of the fighting in the *Aeneid*. The description of the defences of the camp in the early part of book 7 is an anachronism, the siege works belonging rather to the date of Caesar's *Commentaries* than to that of the Trojan War."

the *Aeneid* gives us a very definite picture of a certain strategic situation. Aeneas, going away to ask for help from Evander, leaves the rest of his army encamped, and not merely defended by a low wall, like that of Homer, the sort of thing you can drive a chariot over if you are put to it. It is a real Roman fortification, with its *vallum* and its *agger* and its towers, its *pinnae* or pinnacles, as in 7.159. Like Alesia, when Vercingetorix threw himself into it and was besieged by Julius Caesar, it was partly defended by a river. The attacking force use all the methods with which we are familiar from our early and often painful researches into the *Commentaries* of Caesar. They try to bridge the moat, to pull down the mound, to put up scaling ladders, to advance under their shields in *testudo* formation and avoid the missiles of the defenders [9.505ff.]. All this is of course a gross anachronism; the world had not in Aeneas' time, and did not, till ten centuries later, discover how to besiege a town properly. The Homeric fighting is here inextricably mixed up with the fighting of Virgil's own day. The defence is finally weakened by the fall of a tower, and then, not till then, Virgil falls back on the Homeric story, and makes Pandarus and Bitias throw open the gates and idiotically let Turnus into the fortifications [9.672ff.].

§23. The siege has to be raised when Aeneas comes back, he therefore lands his reinforcements with considerable difficulty, since the Rutulians are waiting for him on shore, and even when a landing has been forced, one part of his troops, the Arcadians, have to struggle up a steep and uncomfortable glen. But the efforts of the relieving party are not without their effect. Turnus (10.308 [-309]) had led out all his array to prevent the landing, rashly deserting the siege: consequently, Aeneas has only to break his way through the Rutulian lines, in order to make it possible for Ascanius and the besieged (line 604[-605]) to break out and join hands with him. This is a detail which probably escapes us in the reading, because we are more interested in the fate of Mezentius, Lausus and the others: but it is none the less the climax of a perfectly reasonable military engagement.

§24. The trophy [11.5ff.] which Aeneas sets up after the battle does not belong either to Homeric warfare or to that of Virgil's own day; it is of the age of a Thucydides or a Xenophon. In the final encounter, when Aeneas advances towards the city, we again have promise of a military description. Turnus, as he explains to us in 11.511[-513], has been informed by scouts of the nature of this advance: the

---

§23. "Further analysis of the strategy of the Rutulian war in the *Aeneid* – the raising of the siege."
§24. "The same continued. Rout of the Italians in the cavalry action in front of the city, and consequent evacuation by Turnus of his ambush on the hills."

cavalry of the enemy have been sent on ahead, to work their way round by the plain, while Aeneas himself with the infantry is coming over the hills. He is therefore preparing to cut him off by an ambush. The cavalry engagement comes off all right [11.597ff.], it consists of a series of charges, the Rutulians being first of all driven back on the walls, and then, taking advantage apparently of the sloping ground up to the city to rally their force, turning back on the Trojan, or rather the Rutulian horsemen. At last, routed largely owing to the death of Camilla [11.831ff.], they are forced to take refuge in the city, and naturally suffer heavy losses in the difficult action of entering the gates while pursued by their opponents. Turnus gets news of the disaster [11.896ff.], and with characteristic impetuosity hurries back to the relief of the city, just in time to let Aeneas and his men pass unharmed through the wood [11.905], where a few moments earlier they would in all probability have been surrounded and cut up by the ambush.

I think in this sense Virgil at least makes some effort to give his fighting a sort of scientific colouring. I do not know whether he had read Caesar; there is certainly not the same reason for supposing so as there is for supposing that he had read Herodotus. But from whatever source he derived his inspiration, it is pretty clear that in both cases he is not content to keep slavishly to Homer, and that in both cases he adapts the Homeric account in such a way as to give his story a more realistic and more historical interest.

Notes

1 Sir Walter Leaf (1852–1927) was an English banker, classical scholar and psychical researcher.
2 C. Valerius Catullus, *Carmina*, Poem 64.
3 Ennius, *Annales* 363Sk. and Lucretius, DRN lib. III, 104.
4 Ennius, *Annales*, fr. 26.
5 *Othello* I. 3. 144–5 (W. J. Craig's *Oxford Shakespeare*).
6 Andrew Lang FBA (1844–1912) was a Scottish poet, novelist, literary critic, and contributor to the field of anthropology.
7 King Eurytus of Oechalia (Thessaly) was a skilful archer and was said to have instructed Heracles in his art of using the bow.
8 Another name for Mare Adriaticum (Adriatic Sea).

Note on the Composition of Book III

§1. It might have been supposed that in the case of so perfect an artist as Virgil, in the work of a poet who is so constantly recollecting himself from line to line, and from book to book, there would have been no question of inconsistencies between one passage and another, of distinguishing this part of the composition from that in point of style and execution. There may have been two dozen Homers; surely there was only one Virgil. And of course there is no real question as to the unity of the whole work, and its single authorship. But in one case, that of book 3, doubts have actually been raised as to whether it is really of a piece with the rest of the poem. Certain discrepancies are alleged on comparison of it with the other books, and adduced not as evidence that it is not of Virgilian authorship, but as evidence that it did not leave Virgil's hand at the same time as the books which precede and follow it. It is apt to be regarded as a *ballon d'essai*, put out some time before the publication of the main body of the *Aeneid* – not otherwise did Tennyson write and publish the single Canto *Morte d'Arthur* long before he had even set about the composition of the other *Idylls of the King*.

§2. What are the difficulties? Well, in 2.781 Creusa's ghost says to Aeneas "et terram Hesperiam venies" [And you will get to the land Hesperia], yet Aeneas does not seem to have caught on, and continues to found abortive colonies elsewhere than in Italy, till in 3.163 the penates appear to him at night and say, "est locus, Hesperiam Grai cognomine dicunt" [There is a place, the Greeks refer to it by the name of Hesperia], which is treated very much as if it were the first time we had come across the idea of Hesperia. That looks, they say, as if the vision of the dead Creusa in book 2 had been composed independently of book 3. Moreover, whereas in 3.257 it is the Harpy Celaeno who tells Aeneas that he will have to eat his tables before he can build a city, and the prophet Helenus who reassures him in 3.394

---

§1. "Was book 3 written at the same time as the rest of the *Aeneid*?"
§2. "Difficulties – (1) in 2.781 as compared with 3.163; (2) in 3.257 as compared with 7.122[–127]; (3) in 3. 390[–391] as compared with 8.42[ff.]; (4) in the general representation of the time occupied by Aeneas' wanderings."

[-395] that the fates will find a way for him to escape this curse, in 7.122[-127], where the table-eating turn does actually come on, Aeneas says

> ... Genitor mihi talia namque,
> Nunc repeto, Anchises fatorum arcana reliquit:
> Cum te, nate, fames ignota ad litora vectum
> Accisis coget dapibus consumere mensas,
> Tum sperare domos defessus, ibique memento
> Prima locare manu molirique aggere tecta.

[My father Anchises as I now recall left me this riddle of fate. 'My son, when you are carried to an unknown shore and there is so little food that hunger forces you to eat your TABLES, then weary as you are, remember to hope for a home and to lay down the foundations of your first buildings and raise a fortification around them.']

Again the discrepancy. The prophecies of Helenus, too, seem unaccountably inadequate in their fulfilment. In 3.390 [-391] he tells Aeneas that the site of his city will be a place where, on landing, he will find a white sow with a litter of 30. This then, we suppose, is to be the site of Aeneas' city Lavinium. In 8.42ff. the river Tiber prophesies the finding of this remarkable litter, and says this will be the place where Ascanius will found Alba Longa, the second city. And the future of the Italian War, which according to Helenus is to be told to Aeneas by the Sibyl, is in book 6 [6. 890–892] actually told him by the shade of Anchises. But the worst is yet to come. According to Conington's estimate, – he is following Conrads[1] – in the third book the wanderings of the Trojans are not supposed to occupy more than two or three years, the only marks of the advance of time being lines 69–70, where the mention of the opening of a new sailing season suggests the beginning of a new year, and in line 284, where a whole winter is said to be passed at Actium. Whereas the general assumption of the rest of the poem is that the space of time during which Aeneas was on the high seas was one of 7 years. Altogether a very pretty set of evidences; the ghost of the Homeric problem rises in our minds; we seem almost to have got back again to Kirchhoff and Leaf.[2]

§3. With regard to the first of these difficulties, I would say that after all Aeneas was not such a hopeless fool as he seems. He would certainly have been a fool, if

---

[§3.] "The first difficulty may be solved by supposing that in hearing Creusa talk of a Hesperian land in book 2, Aeneas did not know Hesperia to be a proper name. The second, though we need not assume with Conington that it was the live Anchises who was supposed to have foretold the eating of tables, certainly does imply a carelessness on the part of the author, but this could only suggest that he wrote book 3 at a different period of his life from book 7, not from books 2 and 4."

he had insisted on setting up shop in Thrace and Crete and so on, after Creusa had told him he was fated to found a city in Hesperia, that is in Italy. But you see, Creusa didn't say he was to go to Italy, she only said he was to go to "a Hesperian land" [2.781]. Of course Aeneas took this prophecy at its face value: to him a Hesperian land meant nothing more or less than a western land. In a word, all he knew after Creusa's prophecy was that it was no good trying the Black Sea. Only later, when Helenus says, "Est locus, Hesperiam Graii cognomine dicunt" [There is a place, the Greeks refer to it by the name of Hesperia] [3.163], only then did Aeneas, knowing that the gender of locus was masculine, realize that Hesperia was the name of an actual place, not a mere geographical adjective.

The second difficulty is a real one. It is not, of course, impossible, that whereas Celaeno merely said there would be no chance of founding a city till after the table-eating incident [3.257], Anchises may have been supposed to prophesy [7.122ff.] that the actual place where the incident occurred would be the actual site of the first city walls. It is absurd, I think, to suppose with Conington that the use of the word "reliquit" – left behind him – in this passage means that the prediction was made by Anchises during life. The prophetic powers of Anchises during life were extremely limited, and hardly extend beyond the interpretation, sometimes a wholly false interpretation, of warning already derived from divine sources. The meaning intended is clearly that Anchises "left" this warning with him when they parted in Elysium. Still, it is undoubtedly strange that Anchises' words should be remembered here by Aeneas, as in a sudden flash of memory, while Celaeno's threats, which must, one would think, have been weighing on his mind ever since they were uttered, are not so much as alluded to. It would be unsafe, however, to deduce from this as a necessary consequence that the third book was written at a time considerably removed from that of the composition of the rest of the *Aeneid*. First, because mere forgetfulness is so frequent a source of inconsistency in all poets, ancient and modern. Secondly because we know on external evidence that the 2nd, 4th, and 6th books were complete at a period in Virgil's life when the second half of the poem had not been begun, so that the third book may well have accompanied or followed closely the composition of those on each side of it, and yet have been some years old when the author started on book 7.

§4. And now for the white sow. In the two passages where this portent is prophetically mentioned, there are two lines the same in each case (3.392[–393], and 8.45[–46]):

Alba, solo recubans, albi circum ubera nati:
Is locus urbis erit, requies ea certa laborum.

[A white sow, lying on the ground, with her young all white around her teats: this will be the place for your city, and there you will find a sure respite from your toils.]

Certain good MSS, however, omit this second line in book 8, and are followed in so doing by Conington. Thus in book 3 the natural interpretation is that the phrases "locus urbis" and "certa requies" refer to Lavinium. In book 8 the line is supposed to have been wrongly interpolated, with reference to Alba Longa. On the other hand, there seems to be far more reason a priori for bracketing the line where it first occurs, in book 3. What Helenus is saying there, is that it will be a long *time* before Aeneas will be able to found his city. He will have to delay in the Sicilian sea, and pass the lake of Avernus and the isle of Circe and so on, "ante quam tuta possis urbem componere terra" [before you can build your city on a safe land] [3.387]. Then he goes on, "signa tibi dicam"; you will find a white sow with a litter of 30. "Signa" of what, we may ask? Assuredly not of the *place*, but of the *time*, when it arrives, at which this long process of waiting will be practically at an end. But the addition of this line, "Is locus urbis erit . . .", quite spoils the sense by introducing the question of the *site* of the future city, a question quite irrelevant to the discussion in hand. Suppose then that the line has been interpolated here, 3.393, in order to answer better to the passage in book 8. If this be the case, Helenus' prediction makes no reference at all to the site of the city, whether Lavinium or Alba Longa, he merely mentions the white sow as an indication that the voyaging of Aeneas is at an end. The god Thybris, speaking in book 8, reveals the further fact, hitherto unsuspected, that this will be the site of Alba Longa. The scribe of the archetype of the MSS quoted by Conington has seen the line already, standing, though wrongly, in the passage in book 3, and leaps to the conclusion that it has no business here. This textual speculation may seem rather far-fetched; if it does not stand, I think we need only accuse Virgil of

---

§4. "The third difficulty, which arises from the non-fulfilment of the prophecies of Helenus, is twofold. The difficulty as to whether it was Lavinium or Alba Longa that was founded where the white sow lay may be overcome by bracketing the line, "Is locus urbis erit, requies ea certa laborum," in Helenus' speech, not, as Conington does, in book 8, where the finding of the sow takes place. Thus Helenus will be understood to have been speaking not of the place but of the time of the first city's founding."

a certain obscurity of statement in book 3, not of any actual inconsistency of ideas on the subject.

§5. There remains the question of the Sibyl. Helenus says (3.458[–459]) that she will describe to Aeneas:

> ... Italiae populos venturaque bella,
> Et quo quemque modo fugiasque ferasque laborem.
>
> [The peoples of Italy and the wars that are to come and how you are to escape and endure all toils.]

It is complained that, as it turns out, Anchises, and not the Sibyl, performs this office for Aeneas. Anchises, when he meets him in Elysium, is said to explain the wars (6.890, [892]):

> ... quae deinde gerenda,
> ...
> Et quo quemque modo fugiatque feratque laborem
>
> [That the hero ultimately had to wage .... And how he could avoid or endure all the trials that lay before him.]

On the other hand the Sibyl does tell him that she sees the Tiber running with blood, that another Achilles awaits him in Latium, that this second Achilles is the son of a goddess, that Juno will continue to persecute him, that the cause of the war will again be a question of marriage, and that his only hope will come from a Greek city [6.86-97]. This may not seem to have given Aeneas his money's worth, but then the Sibyl is expressly said to make these announcements "obscuris vera involvens" [Wrapping truth in darkness] [6.100], and it is pretty clear that when he got to the point Virgil could not find it in his heart to depart so far from traditional conceptions, as to make a priestess deliver an oracle in at all an intelligible way. And then when he was taking Aeneas back again from the lower world it must suddenly have dawned on the poet that after all the visit to these interesting regions had not been of any particular commercial value to his hero, so he hastily adds a note to the effect that Anchises did give him some tips. This is hardly even forgetfulness; it is merely a reconstructing of the plot as it goes on in order to suit the conveniences of the moment.

[§5.] "Another prophecy of Helenus, that the Sibyl will predict to Aeneas the course of the future war, is certainly not literally fulfilled, since it is the shade of Anchises who actually does so. But the discrepancy is not very serious."

Still, it need not surprise us that in such a wilderness of predictions and revelations Virgil should occasionally have forgotten to make the event correspond very closely with the prophecy which foreshadows it. The remaining charge is a far more serious one, that Virgil in the interval between writing the third book and writing the rest of the story changed his mind as to the length of time supposed to be occupied by the wanderings of the Trojans. Is it true that the seven years of Aeneas' voyage are compressed into a couple of years in the actual book in which they are narrated?

§6. There are certain considerations which Conington seems to have overlooked in this connexion. Does not the march of incidents suggest a longer period than the 2 or 3 years so supposed? During this time Agamemnon has gone home and been murdered by Clytemnestra, Clytemnestra has, later, been murdered by Orestes, Neoptolemus has married Hermione, and given her Andromache as a slave, Orestes has murdered Neoptolemus at Delphi, and then Andromache has joined Helenus and they have built a city [3.325–336]. Which is pretty quick work for two years. True, Virgil is not always very careful about his dates, since he makes the Trojans, at the end of several years, find Achaemenides, the companion of Ulysses, on the Cyclops' island, where he says he has been three months [3.645], and this although the visit of Odysseus to the place is in Homer quite soon after the sack of Troy. But inadvertently mistaking the rather confusing chronology of the *Odyssey* is one thing, it is another thing to assume that all this legendary history I have been describing was all over in so inadequate space of time as two years. A further guarantee of lapse of time is the age of Ascanius. In the account of the sack of Troy he is uniformly described as "parvus Iulus" [2. 677, 710, 723], in book 3 he is first mentioned at the court of Helenus, and here, as everywhere in later passages, he has become "puer Iulus" [3.339] [or rather "Ascanius"], or for purposes of scansion "pulcher Iulus". In the seven years of the wandering he has developed out of "parvus Iulus" into the boy who can lead a troop of miniature cavalry, and be entrusted with the nominal command of the Trojan camp. And Andromache herself says he reminds her of her lost son Astyanax, because

. . . nunc aequali tecum pubesceret aevo. (3.491)

[He would have been growing up now, the same age as yourself.]

---

§6. "The fourth difficulty becomes less serious on examination. In writing book 3, Virgil can hardly have meant the wanderings to occupy less than the 7 years he elsewhere allows them, since he makes so much history have intervened [read: intervene] between the start and the landing at Epirus, and regards Ascanius as by that time already pubescens."

"Pubesceret" could hardly by any stretch of imagination be used of a boy much under twelve: properly he should be at least fourteen. Now we know from the *Iliad* that in the tenth year of the Trojan War Astyanax was still young enough to scream when he saw his father's helmet, indeed, Homer obviously regards him as a baby in arms. Allowing for a hazy recollection of the *Iliad* on Virgil's part, or for the possibility that Andromache, womanlike, mortally insulted Ascanius by thinking he was about 8 when he was really about 12, we might suppose the gap to be bridged by 7 years. But that it should be bridged by 2 or even 3 years is surely ludicrous. Andromache gives him an embroidered chlamys [3.484].[3] Why, if he were the age Conington made him out to be in this passage, a pinafore would have been ample.

§7. But indeed, a careful scrutiny of the dates of book 3 will lead us to the inevitable conclusion that, whenever Virgil wrote it, he certainly regarded it as relating the events of 7 years, as when he wrote the rest of the *Aeneid*. Thus: the refugees do not leave the coast of the Troad till the sailing season begins [3.8], so they are in the second year when they go to Thrace. Here they start founding a city, and winter is upon them before they discover the facts about the death of Polydorus which determine them to move on. "Inde ubi prima fides pelago" [3.69] – manifestly in the spring of the third year, since even Conington saw that this was intended as a new sailing-season – they go to Delos, and straight from there to Crete. Again they start building, and also planting (3. 136), and it cannot well have been till the next year, when the harvest began to spring up in the "arva nova" [new land] that the blight broke out [3.139]. Sirius, moreover, was burning the barren fields [3.141] – that is to say, it is now July of the fourth year: they go to Actium, and after much danger by sea at last reach it. Here we must admit a somewhat purposeless delay, since we are told that "interea magnum sol circumvolvitur annum" [Meanwhile the sun rolls on round the great circle of the year] [3.284], which might mean that having set sail in the summer of the fourth year they now spend the fourth winter at Actium, but would be much more natural if we supposed that they did not leave Crete till the spring of the fifth, and spent most of the fifth at Actium, not setting sail till the spring of the sixth. The sixth is spent in coasting along Italy and Sicily, and here we have to leave room for the death of Anchises [3.710] and the first visit to Acestes [1.195], so

§7. "Further, the actual incidents of book 3 involve the lapse of at least five years, and can easily be interpreted as involving the lapse of 7. In fact, though Virgil may have forgotten to make his prophecies tally with their fulfilments in one or two cases, we need not suppose him to have so far altered his conception of the dating of his story as to cram into the course of 2 or 3 years in book 2 what he elsewhere describes as the work of a much longer period."

the 7th has already set in when they arrive at Dido's court. True, this is a liberal estimate throughout, but it seems quite impossible to reduce the time to less than five years at the lowest.

To sum up, then, there may be reason to suppose that the 7th and 8th books were not written at a time closely following the composition of book 3, but we knew already that the two halves of the *Aeneid* were produced at some interval of time. But there is no real reason to think that the third book was written independently of the sixth, and those which go with the sixth, or that it was written with any consciously different ideas of date, such as Conington suggested.

Notes

1. A. Friederich Conrads. His pamphlet, *Quaestiones Virgilianae*, published in 1863, has been called an epoch-making work. Conington in his introduction to the third book follows Conrads in the chronology of the events in Book III. See Virgil, *Opera*, 3rd edn, with a commentary by John Conington, vol. 2 (London: Whittaker, 1876), 192.
2. Johann Wilhelm Adolf Kirchhoff (1826–1908) was a German classical scholar and epigraphist. On Dr Leaf see 149, n.1 above.
3. Chlamys was a broad, woollen upper garment worn in Greece, sometimes purple, and inwrought with gold, worn especially by distinguished military characters.

8

Characteristics of Virgil's Style and Versification

§1. I have already, I think, quoted a particularly idiotic criticism made by Coleridge: "Take away from Virgil his diction and his metre, and what have you left?" Of course, you cannot really take away anybody's diction or metre without taking the whole poem with it, and it is an idle assumption that you can always distinguish in the work of a great poet precisely how much of the effect is produced by what he says, and how much by the way in which he says it. But in so far as, up to now, we have failed to examine the characteristics of the style and diction in which Virgil clothes his thoughts, it remains for us to treat them now, as much as possible, as distinct from the matter they contain.

The most salient characteristic of the Latin language as a whole, whether in prose or verse, is its possibilities in the way of oratory. It is not simply that sonorous periods can readily be composed, owing to the preponderance in Latin of long impressible syllables, though this is certainly a point to be considered. The Greek orator had to labour with the difficulty of composing dignified utterances out of words like παρατετάχαται, the Latin found gems like *formidolosissimorum* lying ready to his hand. There is no vestige of common rhythm, though there is complete metrical correspondence, between an Alcaic stanza running:

τὸ μὲν γὰρ ἔνθεν κῦμα κυλίνδεται
τὸ δ᾽ ἔνθεν· ἄμμες δ᾽ ἀν τὸ μέσσον
   νῆϊ φορήμεθα σὺν μελαίνᾳ,[1]

[One wave swells from this side
The other from that, and we in the middle
Are tossed about in a black ship]

[§1.] Great oratorical possibilities of the Latin language, due (1) to the preponderance of long syllables and consequent sonorousness of the words themselves, (2) to its aptitude for short, pithy, and often epigrammatic statement.

and a Horatian cadence like:

> Quam si clientum longa negotia
> Dijudicata lite relinqueret,
> > Tendens Venafranos in agros
> > > Aut Lacedaemonium Tarentum.²

[As if, with some case decided, he left
the tedious business of his clients,
heading for Venafrum's fields,
or Spartan Tarentum.]

But this was not all; indeed, it had its dangers as well as its defects: if the sonorousness of the Latin tongue is largely responsible for the dignity of Cicero, it is also largely responsible for Cicero's pomposity. But Latin is, further, almost unique among languages in the opportunities it gives of terse expression, of pregnant thoughts, of well-pointed contrasts, of suggestive repetitions, in a word, of phrase-making. That is why Latin always has been and always will be, along with French, the language of inscriptions and epitaphs, of mottoes and epigrams, also, incidentally, of prayer. Take the case of the Collect "Prevent us, O Lord, in all our doings . . ." Here the compilers of the prayer-book were forced to use no less than 44 words in order to translate a prayer which only contained 24 words in the Latin. If Cicero is the master of sounding periods in Latin, Tacitus is the master of telling phrases, but Virgil, though he never wrote a prosaic line, is complete master of both.

§2. Virgil never fails to do justice, even in the less-known parts of the *Aeneid*, to a situation which calls for rhetoric. When Agamemnon and Achilles quarrel about Briseis, they wrangle as two children wrangle in the nursery over the possession of a doll. But when Turnus and Drances contend over Lavinia, they contend as Cicero and Antony, the two greatest orators of their time, contended in the Senate over the destinies of the world. It is impossible to do justice by a mere abstract to these two speeches, or even to that of Latinus, which precedes them. They must be read in full in order to appreciate their claims as masterpieces of Parliamentary oratory. There is however one trick of the rhetorician of which Virgil makes exceptionally good use, which may be worth mentioning. That is

---

§2. Virgil is much more dignified than Homer when it comes to managing a quarrel. One special characteristic of Virgil's forensic passages is his habit of making one of the disputants take up the points of the other in almost exactly the same words. This characteristic illustrated from 11.374 (cf. 389[–91]), 11.366 (cf. 392), 11.362 (cf.399), 11.308[–309](cf. 428[–429]), 11.442, 10.31[–32] (cf. 67), 38 (cf. 73), 25 (cf. 85), 51 (cf. 86), 45[–46] (cf. 88[–90]). Difference between the forensic passages in Virgil and those in Euripides.

the way in which he takes up the points made in the last speech, and turns them inside out in the interests of the opposing argument. Drances has appealed to Turnus, "si patrii quid Martis habes" [If you have any of your fathers' fighting spirit] (11.374); immediately in lines 389[–391] Turnus rounds on him with "An tibi Mavors/ Ventosa in lingua pedibusque fugacibus istis/ semper erit?" [Will your spirit of war always remain in your windy tongue and those nimble feet of yours?] He has urged him (11.366) "pone animos et pulsus abi" [Lay down your pride and since you are defeated, leave the battlefield], the retort is "pulsus ego?" [*I* have been defeated?] and the words which follow in 392. "Nulla salus bello" [War will never save us] is echoed in line 399 from line 362. Then, after a scornful reference to Drances' pleas for liberty of speech, Turnus reverts to the speech of Latinus, who has pointed out the significance of the refusal of aid from Diomede: "Spem si quam adscitis Aetolum habuistis in armis,/ Ponite" [If you had any hope of recruiting the Aetolians as your allies, forget it] (308 [–309]). He admits "Non erit auxilio nobis Aetolus et Arpi:/ at Messapus erit, felixque Tolumnius" [So the Aetolian Diomede and his city of Arpi will not help us; But Messapus and Tolumnius the fortunate will], and so on (428[–429]). Then he returns to Drances' final taunt, that he has refused Aeneas' challenge to single combat. "'Solum Aeneas vocat' – et vocet oro" ['Aeneas is challenging me, and me alone'. Let him challenge, I pray] (11.442). This is not mere sparring at haphazard, it is direct give and take, such as befits accomplished debaters. You will see the same thing in the council of the gods at the beginning of book 10: you will see how Juno takes up every point from the speech of Venus. Compare lines 31–32,

> Si sine pace tua atque invito numine Troes
> Italiam petiere,

[If the Trojans have sought Italy without your approval in defiance of your will]

with line 67,

> Italiam petiit fatis auctoribus: esto,

[He came to Italy with the sanction of fate: so be it]

(*esto* is one of Cicero's pet phrases), or line 38

> ... actam nubibus Irim?

[Iris driven down from the clouds?]

with 73,

> ... Ubi hic Juno, demissave nubibus Iris?

> [Where is Juno in all this, or Iris sent down from the clouds?]

or line 25

> Aeneas ignarus abest

> [Aeneas is far away and knows nothing of this]

with 85,

> Aeneas ignarus abest: ignarus et absit.

> [Aeneas is far away and knows nothing of this. Keep him in ignorance and far away!]

Line 86,

> Est Paphus, Idaliumque tibi, sunt alta Cythera,

> [Paphus is yours, yours are Idalium, and high Cythera]

is a mere repetition of line 51,

> Est Amathus, est celsa mihi Paphus atque Cythera,

> [Amathus is mine, mine high Paphus and Cythera]

but skilfully used to press home Juno's own moral. Finally she meets the appeal of 45[–46:]

> ... per eversae, genitor, fumantia Trojae
> Excidia obtestor,

> [By the smoking ruins of sacked Troy, I beg you, father]

with the scornful *tu quoque* of line 88[–90],

> Nosne tibi fluxas Phrygiae res vertere fundo
> Conamur? Nos, an miseros qui Troas Achivis
> Objecit?

> [Is it I that try to overturn from the foundations the tottering fortunes of Troy. Is it I? Or is it the person who flung the hapless Trojans against the Achaeans?]

exactly the same *tu quoque* with which Elijah silenced Ahab: "I have not troubled Israel, but thou and thy father's house." These strong rhetorical passages would probably be traced by Conington to the influence of Euripides, whose fondness for dialectic passages of thirty lines or so is well known. But Euripides' speeches in this line are nothing if not artificial; their points are clever and sophistic; it has even been maintained that they were all written in such a way as to give the opposition exactly the same number of lines in which to reply as had been used by the side which has already spoken. Euripides was no doubt brought up on the rhetorical exercises of Antiphon and others, who were prepared to prove any thesis from a given set of data, with the maximum of insincerity. But Virgil had heard Cicero.

§3. It is to this rhetorical instinct, or training, in Virgil that we must attribute a very marked tendency of his style, namely, that even where he has quite simple thoughts to express, he prefers to express the same fact in several different ways, one after another, all coupled with *ets* and *ques*, not as if each added anything to the sense of the former, or carried on the action, but as if shewing us that he was capable of stating the facts in any of a variety of ways, and is prepared to let us take our choice between them. An instance where this principle has been carried rather far, is the account of Priam arming himself, during the sack of Troy, to fight Neoptolemus (2.507[–511]):

> Urbis uti captae casum, convulsaque vidit
> Limina tectorum, et medium in penetralibus hostem,
> Arma diu senior desueta trementibus aevo
> Circumdat nequiquam umeris, et inutile ferrum
> Cingitur, ac densos fertur moriturus in hostes.
>
> [When he saw the fall of the captured city, the doors of his palace smashed, and the enemy in the heart of his palace, old as he is, he uselessly casts his long-disused armour about his aged trembling shoulders, fastens his useless sword, and rushes to his death among the packed crowd of his enemies.]

What you want to know, is that when Priam saw that the city was in the hands of the Greeks, he put on his armour to fight, though it wasn't really much use. But for the purposes of the characteristic Virgilian sentence, he has to see the case of the captured city, and the fact that the roofs are falling, and the fact that the enemy have got in, and then he proceeds, although an elderly man, to put on his

---

§3. Another influence of rhetoric on Virgil's style – the habit of stating the same fact twice or thrice over in rapid succession, as if to bring it out in several different lights. Exaggerated instance of this habit in 2.507[–511]. Ordinary instances from 1.5[–7], 1.35, 1.41, etc. An instance of the same tendency becoming tedious, from 1.175.

arms, long disused, quite ineffectually, on to his shoulders which are trembling with age, and gird himself with useless steel, and rush on the enemy, doomed to death. This is not the shortest way of putting it. But you will find this sort of thing, to a greater or less extent, pervading the whole poem. One might almost say that the typical Virgilian sentence was divided into three parts, connected by *et*, *que*, *ac*, or *atque*, each of the three parts containing the same thought expressed under a slightly different aspect. It is not tautology, for it very often makes the sense of an obscure passage easy, or helps us to understand the full significance, from all points of view, of the event described: at the lowest estimation, it is a graceful ornament to the run of the sentences. You can trace it from the very start, in line 5[–7], for example, of book 1:

> dum conderet urbem,
> *Inferretque deos Latio,* genus unde Latinum
> *Albanique patres, atque altae moenia Romae.*

> [Till he should build a city and bring his gods to Latium, whence came the Latin race, the lords of Alba, and the high walls of Rome.]

It does not mean that the carrying of gods into Latium was an event subsequent in time to the founding of the city, though in the latter case it does mean that the Alban fathers were subsequent in time to the Latin race, and the walls of Rome subsequent to the Alban fathers. In line 35,

> Vela dabant laeti, et spumas salis aere ruebant,

> [They were spreading out their sails joyfully, and raising the foaming sea water with bronze prow]

there is no suggestion that the driving of the water before them was not an inevitable consequence of setting sail. In line 41,

> Unius ob noxam, et furias Ajacis Oilei,

> [Because of the guilt and mad passion of one man, Ajax, the son of Oileus]

the *unus* is not a different person from Aiax, nor the *furiae* any more than a different way of looking at the *noxa*. So lines 48–49, 54, 68, 73, 78–80, 97–98, 116–117, 122–123, 140–141, 153, 164–165, 176, 192–193, 195–196, 317, and so on: all of these contain in some measure the phenomenon I am speaking of. It is not a mere Hebrew parallelism, like "He made him lord also of his house, and ruler of all his substance" [Ps. 105:21], it is a perfectly deliberate amplification of the theme wherever it occurs. Sometimes, where commonplace scenes are being described, the effect of it is wearisome or inappropriate, as when Achates in line 175[–176]:

> Succepitque ignem foliis, atque arida circum
> Nutrimenta dedit, rapuitque in fomite flammam.

> [Caught the spark in some leaves, fed it with dry twigs round it and waved the flame amid the kindling wood.]

§4. Indeed, if it is true, as ancient authors tell us, that Virgil was in the habit of deleting an enormous number of lines he had written in the course of revision, we may well believe that the final editing of the *Aeneid*, which never took place owing to his death, would have cut out these amplifications in passages where they are redundant. On the other hand, it is at least possible that some lines were never amplified as fully as Virgil would have liked. This would explain, I mean, the occurrence of half-lines, that old problem of the Virgilian critic, in places where no effect seems to be gained by their occurrence. In 3.340, the broken line

> Quem tibi jam Troja . . .

> [He whom now to you Troy]

is thoroughly in keeping with Andromache's state of mind, and her desire not to dwell on a painful subject. But in other cases, though of course we have no means of knowing that the broken lines were not left in order to vary the metre, some have always found it preferable to suppose that they were meant to be filled in when leisure allowed. If this latter explanation is true, it certainly seems probable that the method of filling up would have been, not to add any new fact, but to give an alternative statement of the last fact mentioned. Thus – not to venture on original suggestions – in 5.594[–595] we have an account of the dolphins sporting in the sea, 'maria umida nando,/ Carpathium Libycumque secant." [Swimming in the waters of the sea, they cleave the Carpathian or Libyan seas], and this would seem to have been all the line as some of the copyists of the best MSS found it. In other MSS it has been filled up, presumably from conjecture, by the addition of the words "luduntque per undas" [And play amid the waves]. It is at least a very good shot: if Virgil ever had finished up the line, these are exactly the sort of words he would probably have used, a mere variation on the same theme, without any advance in the sense.

[54.] Perhaps in his final revision Virgil would have cut out some of these amplifications as redundant. On the other hand, perhaps some of the half lines that stand unfinished would have been finished off by amplification, for instance in 5.594[–595].

§5. But while Virgil, in his ordinary style, is content to be prolix, and would rather say everything four times than have a single fraction of his meaning lost, he is also the precursor of Tacitus, the exploiter of Latin as a vehicle of terse expression, the best of all mines of single-line quotations. There is no poet who is capable of putting so much into a single line as Virgil, when he is at his best. And these effects are produced without any use of the characteristic grandeur of Latin sounds, or any of the hyperbole of Latin oratory. His happiest vein is not simply producing epigrams in the vein of Lucan, lines such as 2.354:

> Una salus victis, nullam sperare salutem,
>
> [The one chance of safety that the defeated have, is to hope for none]

are not lines by which we remember the poet of the *Aeneid*. Nor is it even his deliberate gnomic sayings which chiefly attract our admiration, his

> Heu nihil invitis fas quemquam fidere divis (2.402),
>
> [Alas it is wrong for man to put trust in gods who are against him]

or his

> Quidquid erit, superanda omnis fortuna ferendo est, [5.710]
>
> [Whatever may happen, any fate must be overcome by enduring it]

It is rather the old stock phrases, which somehow seem to lose their charm less in Virgil than in most of the hackneyed poets, the

> Tu ne cede malis, sed contra audentior ito
>
> [Give not way to evil, but face it all the more boldly]

of 6.95, the

> Tendebantque manus ripae ulterioris amore
>
> [And stretched out their hands in longing for the further shore]

of 6.314, the

> Septemque una sibi muro circumdabit arces

[§5.] Virgil's fondness for short and telling phrases. These are not usually epigrammatic or deliberately gnomic, like that in 5.710, but haunting effects produced by extreme simplicity of language, as in 6.95, 6.314, 6.783, 6.820[–821], 6.851[–853], 8.200[–201], 12.435, etc.

[And shall surround seven hills with one wall]

of 6.783, the

> ... natosque pater nova bella moventes
> Ad poenam pulchra pro libertate vocabit,
>
> [When his sons set in motion new wars, it is their own father that will call them to account in the glorious name of liberty]

of 6.820[–821], the

> Tu regere imperio populos, Romane, memento,
> Hae tibi erunt artes, pacisque imponere morem,
> Parcere subjectis, et debellare superbos,
>
> [Your task, Roman, and do not forget it, will be to hold under your sway the peoples of the world. These will be your arts – to impose the custom of peace, to pardon the defeated and vanquish the proud]

of 6.851[–853], the

> Attulit et nobis aliquando optantibus aetas
> Auxilium adventumque dei
>
> [After long prayers, time brought for us too the presence and the help of a god]

of 8.200[–201], the

> Disce, puer, virtutem ex me verumque laborem,
> Fortunam ex aliis
>
> [Courage, my son, learn from me and true hard toil; others will teach you about fortune]

of 12.435[–436], and a hundred others, the whole glory and distinction of which is that there is no word in any of them which could not be translated at sight by any private-school-boy, and that the phrases taken as a whole defy the best efforts of the most competent translators.

§6. Nor is this power of producing effects always so unanalyzable as not to admit of our tracing it further than the whole line, considered as a unit. There are also certain favourite words which from the very fact of their continual

---

[§6.] Virgil's fondness for certain words, to which he gives a dignity of their own by the care with which he uses them. E.g. *magnus*, as in 1.269, 1.300, 5.628, 5.714, 6.11, 6.28, 6.71, 6.83, 6.671. Special meaning of "adventurous" which it sometimes acquires, as in 9.186, 5.751, 4.654, 3.159.

recurrence carry with them indefinable associations, and contribute largely to the magic of Virgil's style. I have already mentioned *fuit*, the pathetic key-word which bears in upon us the utter desolation and homesickness of Aeneas' wanderings. But there are other words, quite as simple and familiar, which attain distinction in Virgil's hands through the carefulness and consistency of his usage. To take the most obvious instance first, let us understand at once that when the word *magnus* occurs in the *Aeneid* it never means large, it always means great. You see what I mean if you look at such uses as that in 1.269[–270]:

> Triginta magnos volvendis mensibus orbes
> Imperio explebit,
>
> [His reign will last for thirty glorious years of revolving months]

those thirty glorious years, or in line 300:

> volat ille per aera magnum,
>
> [through the great expanse of air he flies]

through the wide air, and again "per mare magnum" [Over the great deep] in 5.628, and you have the *magnum inceptum* [The great enterprise] of 5.714, and the *magna mens* [The mighty mind] of the Sibyl (in 6.11) and the *magnus amor* [Overwhelming love] of Pasiphae (in 6.28), the *magna penetralia* [Stately shrine] destined for Apollo (in 6.71) and the *magna pelagi pericula* [Huge perils of the sea] of Aeneas (6.83) and the *magni amnes* [Mighty rivers] of Erebus (6.671), and a hundred other uses, in all of which there is much more in the word than the idea of mere physical extent. Indeed, I believe if you watched the usages carefully, you would find that when Virgil does want to convey the idea of mere physical extent, he almost always employs words such as *ingens* and *immanis*, so as to leave *magnus* free for more solemn occasions. In several well-known passages of course *magnus* is used quite explicitly in the sense of something high and heroic. Thus Nisus says to Euryalus (9.186[–187]):

> Aut pugnam, aut aliquid jamdudum invadere magnum
> Mens agitat mihi,
>
> [My heart has long been driving me to rush into battle or perform some heroic act]

and the people who are left behind at Eryx, because they do not want to face the dangers of the final struggle are called (5.751):

> . . . animae nil magnae laudis egentis,

[Spirits that felt no need for high renown]

and Dido, recalling the exploits of her life, is content to reflect that (4.654)

> Et nunc magna mei sub terras ibit imago,
>
> [My uncompromising spirit will go beneath the earth]

and the Penates can give no better advice to Aeneas than (3.159[–160]):

> ... Tu moenia magnis
> Magna para, longumque fugae ne linque laborem.
>
> [Raise mighty walls for mighty peoples and do not give up on the long toil of fleeing from your homeland.]

§7. And then there is *unus*. Here is a word on which Virgil loves to dwell: (3.435[–436])

> Unum illud tibi, nate dea, proque omnibus unum
> Praedicam,
>
> [One prophecy, son of a goddess, I shall make to you above all others]

and 2.709[–710],

> Quo res cumque cadent, unum et commune periclum,
> Una salus ambobus erit.
>
> [Whatever lies in store, danger or safety, it will be the same for both of us.]

And there is *talis*, "of so high a nature", or "of so low a nature", often thrown in apparently quite gratuitously, as in 1.605[–606],

> ... Quae te tam laeta tulerunt
> Saecula? Qui tanti talem genuere parentes?
>
> [What happy age has brought you to the light of life? What parents of so high nature have produced such a daughter?]

and the similar phrase in 10.597,

> Per te, per qui te talem genuere parentes.
>
> [By your own self and by the parents who brought to life such a man as you.]

---

57. Virgil's fondness for the words *unus*, *talis*, and *si quis*, the last especially in adjurations. Instances from 3.435[–436], 2.709[–710], 1.605[–606], 10.597, 2.521[–522], 2.540[–541], 4.227[–228], 9.203 [–204], 11.416[–418], 12.933[–934], 4.316[–318], 9.493[–494], 10.861, 10.827[–828], 6.367[–368].

Sometimes the emphasis of the line falls on it, in such phrases as the following (2.521[–522]):

> Non tali auxilio, nec defensoribus istis
> Tempus eget,
>
> [This hour does not require such help or such defence]

2.540[–541],

> At non ille, satum quo te mentiris, Achilles
> Talis in hoste fuit Priamo
>
> [Not so did Achilles behave with his enemy Priam, that Achilles whom you falsely claim as your father]

4.227[–228],

> Non illum nobis genetrix pulcherrima talem
> Promisit
>
> [This is not the kind of person his most beautiful mother assured he would be]

9.203[–204],

> . . . nec tecum talia gessi
> Magnanimum Aenean et fata extrema secutus,
>
> [Nor have I behaved in such a way at your side, in following the ultimate fate of noble-hearted Aeneas]

11.416[–418],

> Ille mihi ante alios fortunatusque laborum
> Egregiusque animi, qui ne quid tale videret
> Procubuit moriens,
>
> [Fortunate in his life's labours and the noblest spirit of all, is, for me, the man who has died in order to avoid seeing something like this]

and finally 12.933[–934],

> . . . oro – fuit et tibi talis
> Anchises genitor – Dauni miserere senectae.
>
> [I beg you– you who also had a father of similar age in Anchises – pity Daunus' old age]

In this same passage last quoted, we also meet a peculiarly favourite usage of the *Aeneid*, that of *si quis*, especially in adjuration. The force of it will be best seen from illustrations. In this case it is

> ... Miseri te siqua parentis
> Tangere cura potest, oro ... [12. 932-933]

[If any thought of my unhappy father can move you, I beg you]

But Virgil hardly ever has an adjuration without it, 4.316[-418],

> Per conubia nostra, per inceptos hymenaeos,
> Si bene quid de te merui, fuit aut tibi quicquam
> Dulce meum ...

[By our union, by the marriage we have started, if I have deserved any kindness from you, if you have found anything in me you love]

9.493[-494],

> Figite me, si qua est pietas, in me omnia tela
> Conicite, o Rutuli ...

[Strike me, Rutulians, if you have any *pietas*, cast all your weapons on me]

Nor is it only in adjurations that *si quis* is used with a wealth of delicate tenderness. We have already noticed the pathetic address of Mezentius to his horse (10.861),

> Rhaebe, diu, res siqua diu mortalibus ulla est,

[We have lived long, Rhaebus, if anything at all lasts long for mortals]

and there are similar instances elsewhere, as 10.[827-]828,

> ... Teque parentum
> Manibus et cineri, si qua est ea cura, remitto.

[I return you to the shades and the ashes of your ancestors, if that is a concern of yours.]

and 6.367[-368],

> Aut tu, si qua via est, si quam tibi diva creatrix
> Ostendit.

[Or if there is a way and your divine mother shows you one, you (must ...)]

It was probably to the use of such words, simple in themselves, but instinct with pathos from the force of their surroundings that Tennyson referred, when he was giving unsolicited testimonials to the qualities of Virgil's poetry:

> All the charm of all the Muses often flowering in a lonely word. ['To Virgil']

§8. I have not space, if I had the power, to go into all the subtle characteristics which distinguish the style of Virgil from that of other Roman poets. But there is one little mannerism to which attention may well be called, partly because it is constantly recurring, partly because it lends a distinction to the versification which ought to be capable of imitation in our own verse-copies. This is what one might call the deferred participle, or deferred epithet. Take for an example the account of the Sibyl given by Helenus in 3.458, 460:

> Illa tibi Italiae populos, venturaque bella
> ...
> Expediet, cursusque dabit venerata secundos.
>
> [She will tell you of the peoples of Italy and the wars that are to come . . . if you give her due honour, she will provide a prosperous voyage.]

Venerata, if you are nice to her, but the thought is an afterthought as it were: the natural order would be, "Illa tibi venerata", "She will if you are nice to her", and then the account of what she will do. Or take 4.265[–267]:

> . . . Tu nunc Carthaginis altae
> Fundamenta locas, pulchramque uxorius urbem
> Exstruis?
>
> [Are you now laying the foundations of lofty Carthage and, acquiescent to a wife, erecting a fair city?]

So far as the sense goes, you see, the word *uxorius* goes quite as much with *locas* as with *exstruis*, but it is the poet's pleasure to put it late in the sentence. So 4.[590–]591:

> . . . Pro Juppiter! Ibit
> Hic ait, et nostris inluserit advena regnis

[§8.] Another characteristic of Virgil's style, the deferred participle, adjective, or noun treated as an adjective, which agrees with the subject of the sentence, applies to all of it, but is expressed only in the second, or it may be in the final clause. Instances from 3.458, 460, 4.265[–267], 4.[590–]591, 5.213, 215[–216], 5. 468, 471[–472], etc.

Characteristics of Virgil's Style and Versification

[O god! She cried. 'Will this man leave and be allowed to have made a mockery of our kingdom?]

or 5.213, 215[–216]:

Qualis spelunca subito commota columba . . .
Fertur in arva Volans, plausumque exterrita pinnis
Dat tecto ingentem,

[Just like a dove scared out of her cave . . . flies off in terror from her home to the fields with loud flapping of her wings]

or 5.468, 471[–472]:

Ast illum fidi aequales genua aegra trahentem . . .
Ducunt ad naves, galeamque ensemque vocati
Accipiunt.

[But his loyal comrades lead Dares back to the ships, dragging his weary legs . . . and when called upon are given the helmet and the sword.]

The thing is of frequent occurrence; you will find it for instance in 6.474, 7.84, 7.329, 8.75, 8.562, 11.499, 12.63, and so on.

§9. You might do worse than study the excellence of Virgil's repetitions. I have only time to give some references, if you would care to look them up: 1.239, 1.315, 1.325, 1.341, 1.396, 2.405–406, 3.247–248, 3.435–438 (where you have three repetitions in three lines or so), 3.523, 5.493–494, 7.444, 7.586–587, (this last is a favourite with Homer and Lucretius), 8.352, 8.649, 11.392.

§10. The order of the Virgilian line is a very complicated subject, but there is one point about it which must be firmly understood, and that is the question of which word comes last. The rule of all Latin, whether prose or verse, is that the last word or words should not be a surprise, they must be something which the rest of the sentence led us to expect. That is why in prose the verb comes last – it does come last, you know, in real Latin prose; it is only because you are trying to be too clever that in your composition it comes about six words from the end – it comes last because you could get on without anything else, more or less, but you cannot, unless you are Tacitus at his most journalistic, dispense with the verb. And therefore the verb is the thing you've been waiting for all along, and when it

---

§9. A list of some forms of repetition in the *Aeneid* which are worth imitating.

§10. Order of words in the Virgilian line. In Latin, whether prose or verse, that word comes last which is most easily expected, not that which is most important or most emphatic. In prose this is usually the verb. In verse, the principle which mostly concerns us is that if a noun and adjective agree, and either might go at the end of the line, the noun and not the adjective goes at the end.

crops up at the end you have the feeling, Ah, that's all right. For precisely this reason it is an almost invariable rule in Virgil that when you have a noun and an adjective agreeing with it, the noun and not the adjective comes at the end of the line. Suppose for example a line has to be made out of the words, "et rubros flores sanctis templis praetexere" [And weave red flowers in the holy temples]. You may say, "et sanctis flores rubros (or rubros flores) praetexere templis", or "et rubros templis sanctis (or sanctis templis) praetexere flores". But you must not say, "et templis rubros flores (or flores rubros) praetexere sanctis", or "et flores sanctis templis (or templis sanctis) praetexere rubros", unless you want to give the reader a jump, and thereby impress upon him with intense firmness the sanctity of the temples, or the redness of the flowers. It is perfectly possible to trace Virgil's meaning where such emphasis is intended. Thus in 7.596–597, we have

...Te, Turne, nefas, te triste manebit
Supplicium, votisque deos venerabere seris.

[You, Turnus, are the guilty one, and a harsh punishment awaits you and you will supplicate the gods too late with prayers.]

Why not "serisque deos venerabere votis"? Precisely because the word *seris* is bearing a tremendous emphasis, it is indeed not really an epithet at all, but a predicate. "The prayers you address to the gods will come too late". Ordinarily the noun has to come last, and the adjective first, simply because you want to keep to the end that which is expected: and this is the noun, for you might have a noun without an epithet, but assuredly not an epithet without a noun.

§11. There is another rule, almost as invariable, and when it varies, influenced by the same considerations. If the two words immediately succeeding the caesura are a spondee and a long monosyllable or a short dissyllable, the spondee, if possible, comes first, the monosyllable or its equivalent second. For example, in 11.102, we have the words

Corpora, per campos ferro quae fusa jacebant.

[The bodies which were lying scattered all over the plain slaughtered by the sword.]

"Ferro quae fusa", you see, not "quae ferro fusa". The reason for this, as is excellently pointed out by Calverley[3] in his "Essay on Translating Virgil into Verse", is that Latin poets, scanning by quantity and not by stress, preferred if possible not to

---

[§11.] Another principle of Hexameter verse, that if the foot and a half after the caesura contain a long monosyllable or its metrical equivalent, and a spondee, the spondee goes first and not second, unless the emphasis of the words demands the contrary arrangement.

make the stress of the word as ordinarily pronounced coincide with the syllable on which, in virtue of its quantity and position, the stress of the line fell. "Ferro" had the stress naturally on its first syllable, therefore in the verse it was regularly put in a position where the stress of the line fell not on its first syllable but on its second. Take another instance at random, 4.100,

... Habes, tota quod mente petisti,

[What you looked for with all your heart, you now have]

"tota quod mente", not "quod tota mente", which Ennius would quite undoubtedly would have written. But indeed the rule is so clear that there is no cause to multiply instances. Where there is an exception, it is almost always because one of the two words, either the spondee or the monosyllable, needs to be emphasized; and by the arrangement, "tota quod mente", neither the *tota* nor the *quod* receives any ictus at all. A few lines further up (line 66) we have the words "est mollis flamma medullas" [The flame devours the soft marrow of her bones]. Here it was necessary to emphasize the *est*, because if it had been lightly passed over, one would have assumed that it came, not from *edo* but from *sum*. In 8.510 the poet wished to lay emphasis on the *mixed* [sic] origin of Pallas, so he says, not "mixtus ni matre Sabella", but "ni mixtus matre Sabella" [Were he not of mixed blood, with a Sabine mother]. In 7.261 he was forced to write, "non vobis, rege Latino" [While Latinus is king, you shall not ...], rather than "vobis non, rege Latino", because if he had put it in this second way, it would have looked as if the *non* went with the "rege Latino", not with the main sentence. But I believe there is always some such reason as this to be found when he puts the spondee after the monosyllable and stresses its first syllable.

§12. In conclusion, although the versification of Virgil has really nothing to do with his style, I must add one section on his fondness for elisions. We all know that elisions are commoner in Virgil than in other poets. But we do not always realize the extent of the difference. Ovid, in his Hexameter writings, has about one elision in every five lines: Lucan no more than one in ten. Statius varies, sometimes they are frequent, sometimes you may find about 50 lines without one. But in Virgil, with extraordinary regularity, you find a proportion of one in every 2 lines. You have hardly read more than 20 lines of the *Aeneid* – the *Eclogues* of course are quite different – in order to strike an average.

---

§12. Final principle of Hexameter versification. There should be one elision to every two lines. The exceptions to this are a long passage in the tenth book (130–307) where there are too few, probably owing to hastiness of composition, and one in book 8, lines 567–588, where there are too many, the work in this latter case probably not being Virgil's work at all.

Twice only, so far as I know, is the average disturbed. In a long passage, or rather series of passages, from line 130 to line 307 of book 10, there are only 66 elisions in 178 lines, which gives a proportion of not much more than one in 3. In some parts of this the proportion is very low indeed: in the 27 lines between 185 and 212 there are only 6 all told, and it would be fascinating to suppose that this is an interpolation, as it contains the only reference to Mantua, Virgil's birthplace, found in the whole poem. But it is hardly necessary to imagine more than that at this point the revision Virgil intended was not complete, and that one of the marks of revision would be the deliberate provision of more elided syllables.

The other passage is more interesting. It is that in book 2, where Aeneas is represented as contemplating the murder of Helen. Lines 567–588 are omitted by all the best MSS, and rest almost entirely on the authority of Servius. He says that the lines were written by Virgil, but omitted by Varius and Tucca when the *Aeneid* was published. Nettleship concludes that Virgil meant to write such a passage, but that the text we have is the work of an early interpolator. It is interesting, then, to note that in these 22 lines we meet no less than 24 elisions (where there should be 11) – very much what we might expect from an imitator who was trying to write like Virgil, and had the misfortune to overdo it.

Notes

1   Alcaeus, fr. 326-2-4.
2   Horace, *Odes III*, V. 53–6.
3   Charles Stuart Calverley (1831–84) was an English poet and wit.

Part Two

Critical Essays

9

Ronald Knox's Lectures on Virgil: 'A Wealth of Delicate Tenderness'[1]

Matthew McGowan

In his lectures on Virgil (1912) Ronald Knox mentions only one contemporary classical scholar by name – Arthur Sidgwick (1840–1920) – and he only does so for the sake of a joke:

> The purpose of these lectures is simply to pick out a few of the dominant characteristics of the *Aeneid* which go to make up its greatness and its charm. You will find notes, critical and grammatical expository, in Conington, if you do not mind their being rather elaborate, or in Sidgwick, if you do not mind their being excessively pompous. These lectures will be devoted almost entirely to the appreciation of the *Aeneid*, and that not wholly without a view to the General Paper in Honour Moderations.[2]

It may be that the notes can get a bit windy in Sidgwick's two-volume edition and commentary on the *Eclogues*, *Georgics* and *Aeneid*, a work now almost entirely forgotten and unread.[3] But in 1912 Sidgwick was a popular tutor (especially for Greek), a prominent Liberal, and the President of the Association for Promoting the Higher Education of Women at Oxford, where his name had become a byword in certain circles for 'witty, though always courteous, repartee ("Sidgwickedness")'.[4] Knox's own 'sharp sense of humour and gift for witty discourse' were also to become legendary at Oxford;[5] and it is lines like this to which E. R. Dodds (1893–1979) surely refers when recalling the lectures on Virgil in his own memoir: '[Knox] delighted a small audience of aesthetes and cognoscenti by his witty dissection of conventional opinions on Virgil.'[6]

In truth, the only opinions Knox actually engages in these lectures, and then only rarely, are those of the other scholar mentioned here, John Conington (1825–69).[7] His three-volume edition with commentary on Virgil's complete works was the standard text used by Oxford undergraduates to prepare for

Honour Moderations or 'Mods', the rightly famous exams for second-years studying Classics at Oxford.[8] As Knox notes in the passage quoted above, his lectures on Virgil were designed, at least in part, to help students prepare for Mods at Trinity College in Hilary Term 1911, that is, as both Chaplain, Fellow *and* tutor in Honour Mods.[9] Of course, Knox himself had made no preparation for his Mods while an undergraduate at Balliol College (1906–10), feeling that the reading he had done at Eton in the primary sources had sufficiently prepared him: he considered his grade of 'second' a failure.[10] His cavalier attitude towards Mods does not seem to have coloured his approach to his role as tutor, which he took very seriously and which provides the fundamental context for these lectures. He may have been influenced in his approach to teaching by what he experienced at Balliol, memorably described by Evelyn Waugh: 'in that period the teaching at Balliol was the finest in the country. The dons believed themselves called, not, as in the eighteenth century, to a life of leisure, nor, as in the twentieth, to private research and public performance, but to the domestic task of training their pupils'.[11] In short, Knox's lectures on Virgil cannot be considered apart from the collegial life of Oxford and the training of undergraduates; they were never meant as a contribution to contemporary scholarship on the *Aeneid*, such as it was.[12] In this regard, they are unapologetically parochial, the kind of elevated and artful parochialism peculiar to Oxford.[13] At the same time, they give space to one of the finest classicists of his generation to think deeply and in a sustained fashion about the *Aeneid* – in particular, 'its greatness and its charm' – as the most worthy source of reflection on Greco-Roman literature, politics, religion and philosophy in advance of the epochal transition in history from pagan to Christian culture.[14]

Even if they do not engage with contemporary scholarship on Virgil, they nevertheless reflect the 'traditional view' of early twentieth-century scholars, according to Stephen Harrison, 'that the *Aeneid* asserted the values of order and civilization by depicting their eventual victory'.[15] As Harrison notes, the nineteenth century produced many resources for understanding the *Aeneid*, in particular critical editions and philological commentaries, but had little interest in evaluating the poem as literature.[16] Of course, there were exceptions, notably W. Y. Sellar's *Roman Poets of the Augustan Age: Virgil*, whose sympathetic reading of the poem was congenial to Knox's taste and, on one occasion at least, sets the table for the author's reflections on the meaning of *pietas* that begin the second lecture, 'Virgil's Religious Outlook', discussed below.[17] But a genuinely literary appreciation of the poem begins in earnest in the twentieth century, starting with the appearance in 1903 of two highly influential works of German scholarship: Richard Heinze's *Virgils epische Technik* and Eduard Norden's commentary on *Aeneid* 6.[18] Knox appears to have had no interest in tackling German for his theological studies, which along with learning 'how to "say Mass"' as a newly ordained priest in the Church of England, were of more immediate import to him during his time at Trinity than scholarly works in classics.[19] This was especially true of the 'Higher Criticism' still in vogue among Oxford's more prominent theologians and classicists, an historical method for understanding ancient texts developed in Germany and widespread in England at the time. Its purported findings about which book of the Old Testament or of the *Iliad* was early and which late were often of dubious value and never seemed to agree from one scholar to the next.[20] Though no one today would lump Heinze and Norden in with the higher critics – they were offering something new, and their work fundamentally altered the course of Virgilian scholarship – it is nevertheless difficult to conceive of Knox ever engaging seriously with their work.[21]

Still, Knox acknowledges in *A Spiritual Aeneid* (1918), the story of his religious conversion from High Anglicanism to Roman Catholicism, that at the heart of his lectures on Virgil was 'a merely literary delight I took in the poem'.[22] This delight is clear from his own description of their subject matter:

> They will deal, I imagine, with Virgil's outlook, national and political, with his religious outlook, and his conception of the future life, with the romance and the pathos of Virgil, with his Art and the treatment of the story, with his use of sources and models, with the characteristics of his style and versification – partly with a view to the writing of Hexameter Verse – and also with his appreciation of scenery.[23]

Apart from his 'Note on the Composition of Book III', mention of which is missing here, this sentence offers a fitting summary of the individual lectures collected in this edition, which seem to move from the more general – 'Virgil's Political Outlook' – to the more particular – 'Characteristics of Virgil's Style and Versification'. And yet consistently throughout we are treated to Knox's very personal, indeed particular, appreciation of the epic, where it is taken for granted that the *Aeneid* is so consistently 'great' that nearly any one line can reveal something essential about the whole. Thus, his analysis of the 'use of RES in the plural' includes the remark: 'A careful observation of the small and apparently commonplace words in the Aeneid will very often be a clue to the underlying sentiment of the whole.'[24] For Knox, *res* in the plural obviously does not mean 'things', but something more like 'fortunes', usually with the suggestion of 'a great future, the prospect of world-power', especially when used in combination with *regnum*.[25] I suppose that most – and perhaps all – contemporary commentators on the *Aeneid* would agree with the interpretation here, although few would follow Knox to where he goes next. In reference to the failed fortune of Troy (*Aen.* 6.62: 'hac Trojana tenus fuerit fortuna secuta') and the subsequent emergence of the 'Fortuna Urbis, the fortune that was never known to fail', Knox argues that the underlying idea of the *Aeneid*, which is also the idea of Rome – unstated but always self-evident – is clearly associated with the march of civilization and with optimism:

> It is this continual orientation, this constant turning towards the dawn, that gives the Aeneid at once its atmosphere of optimism, and its sense of grandeur [...] I do not mean that Virgil preaches [...] But I think he does reflect in unconscious ways, like most writers of the period, a sense of profound thankfulness for the restoration of order ... The lesson of the Battle of Actium is to them [i.e. the poets of the Augustan age] always that Antony and Cleopatra stood for the wild untamed East, and in Octavian Western civilization triumphed.[26]

He goes on: 'Whether we approve or disapprove, the fact that the *Aeneid* is an epic of civilization lends it grandeur,' which sentence would hardly have ruffled an audience at Trinity College in Michaelmas Term 1912 and probably convened, to a large extent, with their sensibility. For this was, as Harrison has shown, the 'traditional view' of the poem at the time.[27]

What is clear, to this reader at least, is that the lectures on Virgil pave the way for *A Spiritual Aeneid*, where Knox admits that in the months leading up to being accepted into the Roman Catholic Church in the fall of 1917 he carried the *Aeneid* around 'with something like a demand for spiritual comfort'.[28] In this, as he himself notes, he was not unlike the medieval Christian looking for prophetic guidance in the *sortes Virgilianae*, the practice of bibliomancy or book-divination whereby readers of Virgil would consider the first verse that presented itself as a kind of prognostication of future events. There is, in fact, a sortilegious quality to the Virgil lectures, which prefigures the style of *A Spiritual Aeneid*, where Knox uses the architecture of the epic to structure the journey of his conversion. At the outset of the latter, he provides a key to its symbolism:

> In explanation of the Aeneid-*motif* which runs through the chapter-headings and parts of the book, I had perhaps better give the key to a somewhat obvious set of symbols. Troy is undisturbed and in a sense unreflective religion; in most lives it is overthrown, either to be rebuilt or to be replaced. The Greeks are the doubts which overthrow it. The 'miniature Troy' of Helenus is the effort to reconstruct that religion exactly as it was. Carthage is any false goal that, for a time, seems to claim finality. And Rome is Rome.[29]

On the next page, Knox expands on the last line and offers, for classicists at least, what is perhaps his most striking observation about the *Aeneid* and its hero's journey to Rome:

> I have dared to take my title from a poem even richer in associations [than the *Odyssey* and the journey back home]. For an Aeneid involves not merely coming home, but coming home to a place you have never been in before – one that combines in itself all that you valued in the old home with added promises of a future that is new.[30]

Readers will struggle to find so profound and pithy a summary of the *Aeneid*'s story elsewhere, and the remark is worth the trouble of the memoir; it also sheds light on the lectures. For it is hard to see how Knox gets to this level of understanding on a such a personal matter, especially for a priest, without having been given the chance, some five years before, to prepare the lectures on Virgil. In fact, later in *A Spiritual Aeneid*, he acknowledges as much when reflecting on his time as Chaplain Fellow at Trinity: 'Virgil – or at any rate the Aeneid – I had never learned to value before: it was only when I was forced to look below the surface that I lost my heart to him.'[31] That he was thinking about Catholicism and, perhaps subconsciously, about a path to conversion while preparing his lectures on Virgil is not at all implausible: 'Of the sixth book I managed to make a lecture almost completely devoted to Purgatory.'[32] He is exaggerating, of course, and we know because we have read the lecture, of which barely half may be said to concern purgatory or 'Virgil's conception of a future life'.[33] Those familiar with Knox and his work will recognize here a moment of self-deprecating humour in an otherwise deeply serious story of spiritual conversion.[34]

At the same time, the lectures themselves seem to confirm that Knox's 'merely literary' appreciation of Virgil is also refracted through a thoroughly Anglo-Christian attitude towards scholarship, teaching, and the mundane and metaphysical realities of life in general. Thus, in reference to the Platonic notion of metempsychosis, or the transmigration of souls, on view in the *Aeneid*, Knox can say: 'Virgil, whose soul is naturally Catholic, is up to the distinction between mortal and venial sins: those who die in mortal sin go straight to hell, while everybody else – we must suppose, however good – has to go through some form of punishment.'[35] This passage comes towards the end of his lecture on 'Virgil's Religious Outlook', which begins with a reflection on *pietas* as the defining 'leitmotiv' of the *Aeneid*, among the least controversial assessments of the poem in any place at any time. Knox patiently advances his argument to the point where the epithet *pius* comes to connote a 'moral scrupulousness' which some characters like Mezentius and Dido lack and which Aeneas, naturally, has in spades, and as a result is richly rewarded by the Olympians. In the midst of this discussion, Knox, Chaplain Fellow and newly ordained priest, is comfortable enough with his audience to say, 'There is no getting round Aeneas; you can't take him off his guard. [. . .] That kind of man can never entertain Angels unawares, because he never meets anybody without fully canvassing in his mind the question whether they are Angels or not.'[36] It would be otiose to add that no classicist today would put it quite this way, but Knox's understanding of *pietas* and its relative *pius* in the *Aeneid* is generally accurate and often illuminating. Indeed, he concludes that *pietas* has two basic meanings: first, it carries with it a literal sense of religious obligation, which he explains in the following way:

> the man who knows what sins or impurities need expiation and what piacula are appropriate in each different case is, radically, the man who is pius. In this sense, when we speak of pius Aeneas, we mean practically, 'Aeneas, the trained liturgiologist'. He is the man who . . . always knows how to 'get right with God'.[37]

For Knox, the other meaning has two senses, both moral: first, not bothering about religious observances, as in the case of Mezentius, the *contemptor divom* and 'real villain of the Aeneid',[38] is criminal carelessness for mortals; second, the gods, for their part, have an obligation to show their own 'piety' towards acts of *pietas*, which in this case approaches the meaning of 'pity'.[39] At the same time, the general conception behind divine *pietas* 'is one of justice, rather than of mercy': 'there is a sort of pact or covenant between the god and his worshipper which neither side can creditably break. It is thoroughly Jewish: the Trojans, no less than Israel, are a chosen people, with a land of promise: Aeneas, like Abraham or David, have promises they can claim'.[40]

This is among the more entertaining and enlightening passages of a very entertaining and enlightening lecture, which offers in its second half an extended reflection on purgatory, the afterlife, and the meaning of *Aeneid* 6. Among the many difficulties in the *Aeneid*'s most challenging book is the problem, identified by Conington, of 'the inconsistency . . . between the existence of an abode of permanently doomed spirits, who never get beyond where they are are – "sedet aeternumque sedebit / Infelix Theseus" (*Aen.* 6.617–8) – and the doctrine of Purgatory and reincarnation which the poet takes over from Plato'.[41] Knox appears to solve Conington's problem by reminding his audience that, even in Plato (*Republic* X), not every soul returns to mortal life; some, like Ardiaeus, are punished eternally. Moreover, he adds: 'Virgil makes reincarnation the exception instead of the rule, granted only to the pick of the lot'.[42] In ending the lecture,

Knox ushers those audience members whose minds, like his own, had wandered to the 'Four Last Things' – death, judgement, heaven and hell – to the conclusion that readers of Book 6 are left with 'a comparatively modern view of the future life ... [and] quite startlingly Christian'. He then finishes with the following genuinely original observation:

> In a word, Anchises, living the life of a beatified Saint, has actually witnessed the sufferings of his son in the meantime, and sympathized with them. I know of no other cases in the classics, where knowledge of what is going on in the world is attributed to the departed, even to those who have attained Elysium.[43]

Knox is using his command of Judeo-Christian thought and culture to enlarge his 'appreciation' of the *Aeneid* and to give his audience, on the one hand, something to take into the 'General Paper' in Mods and, on the other hand, to take home and out into the world. Whether he is right or wrong – and I do not think he is wrong – his approach to the text and to the very particular audience he was attempting to reach expands the horizons of Virgilian interpretation by offering a compelling reading of a key religious concept (*pietas*) and some novel and illuminating thoughts on the notion of an afterlife in the *Aeneid*.

As I say, it is hard to imagine a contemporary classicist offering up analysis of this kind with references to 'Angels', 'mortal sin' or the poet's 'Catholic soul', but such remarks are thoroughly at home in Knox's lectures on Virgil and, it must be inferred, in the reading of the *Aeneid* among undergraduates in early twentieth-century Oxford. In this context it was no doubt customary to consider matters of interpretation in reference to other monumental works of western civilization and, especially, in the light of Judeo-Christian scripture. As Knox says early on in the lectures, '[Virgil] is like the Bible, in particular the Book of Psalms'; and then, 'the history of Virgil is hardly less varied or important than that of the Psalms'.[44] This Virgil is obviously very different from the Virgil of Heinze and Norden, but it is worth considering the degree to which Knox is advancing an 'adventist reading' of the poem that entertains, in the words of Philip Hardie, 'the idea that the *Aeneid* is a work peculiarly alive to the impending revolution in history brought about by the advent of Christianity'.[45]

Reading Virgil through a Christian lens is a familiar practice from early on in the tradition, which is by turns happy to view the poet as a pagan prophet of the coming Christ or even a proto-believer with an uncannily Judeo-Christian understanding of justice, mercy and divine salvation.[46] This approach enjoyed a revival in the inter-war period in Europe and the United States,[47] and it is not at all surprising that Knox's views on Virgil overlap in certain respects with an adventist reading.⁴⁸ In the lectures on Virgil, the dialogue between the Greco-Roman civilization represented by Virgil and the Anglo-Catholic Christianity lived by Knox is at times explicit, at other times implied, but every engagement with scripture, or with any Christian notion for that matter, is deeply personal and always the outcome of the importance that Knox attributed to the *Aeneid* in the history of European literature. Early on in the lectures, for example, he points out to his Oxford audience that the poem has been the object of contemplation and devotion from St Augustine, Bede and Dante to Petrarch, Edmund Burke and Tennyson.⁴⁹ From here it is no leap to assert that Knox's lectures on Virgil present the *Aeneid*, at times, from a Christian viewpoint, which is to say from the honest lips of Trinity College's Fellow and Chaplain. At the same time, it is perhaps inaccurate to assume that they offer a consciously 'adventist' reading of Virgil, whereby the audience comes away expecting to find in the *Aeneid* a 'foretaste of Christianity'. For that line of interpretation one needs to wait a generation, again until the inter-war period, where a Christianized approach to the text becomes familiar from the likes of E. K. Rand's *Magical Art of Virgil* (1931) and, especially, Theodor Haecker's *Virgil, Father of the West* (orig. German 1931).⁵⁰ Haecker considered Virgil an 'anima naturaliter Christiana', a soul by nature Christian, a phrase borrowed from Tertullian (*Apologeticus* 17.5) to refer to 'the natural propensity of any human soul to talk of one god'.⁵¹ It is common knowledge that T. S. Eliot relied on the *Father of the West*, even if he dulled the edge of Haecker's expression, to develop the argument of his famous Presidential Address to the Virgil Society, 'What Is a Classic?' (1944), where he concludes that 'Virgil acquires the centrality of the unique classic; he is at the centre of European civilization, in a position which no other poet can share or usurp'.⁵² Of course, Eliot acknowledges his debt to Haecker explicitly for a 1951 radio broadcast, 'Virgil and the Christian World', that takes the adventist reading even further: '[Virgil's] sensibility is more nearly Christian than that of any other Roman or Greek poet ... [the Roman Empire] remains an ideal, but one which Virgil passed on to Christianity to develop and to cherish.'⁵³ In both places, Eliot offers a sophisticated articulation of an adventist reading of the *Aeneid*, which receives a memorable formulation at the close of his Presidential Address:

> the maintenance of the standard [of the classic set by Virgil] is the price of our freedom, the defence of freedom against chaos. We may remind ourselves of this obligation, by our annual observance of piety towards the great ghost who guided Dante's pilgrimage: who, as it was his function to lead Dante towards a vision he could never himself enjoy, led Europe towards the Christian culture which he could never know.⁵⁴

The line about 'our freedom', whose price is the maintenance of Virgil's standard and whose loss is chaos, reverberates today when we imagine Eliot delivering this lecture, the Virgil Society's very first Presidential Address, in London on 16 October 1944, when the war had moved definitively to the continent, even if its outcome was far from assured.[55] The basic thesis of Eliot's now classic essay is that Virgil establishes in the *Aeneid* a pliable and universalizing *idiom* for the cultural, intellectual and spiritual development of Europe; for Eliot, the poem serves as a portal of sorts through which the essential ideas of pagan Greece are translated into the language of Rome, that is into Latin, which is the language of the Church that will provide the words – again, the idiom – that will give shape to Christian Europe and the idea of the west.

I imagine that Knox would have agreed with Eliot, even if he would have found it unnecessary to say so in his Trinity lectures, or to be so explicit about Virgil's connection to the Christian culture he and his audience embodied. Thus, where Eliot and the 'adventist school' generally only seem to look forward from the *Aeneid* to what comes next – a Christian Europe pouring forth from Rome – Knox is alive to the trail of suffering that the poem leaves in its wake, in particular to the tragic loss of young life that hangs over the entire epic. He sums this up as the paradox of Virgil as romantic *and* tragic poet:

> Just as he makes us feel that the winning cause is the cause of destiny, and nevertheless can indulge himself in the luxury of a hero who claims our sympathy by his misfortunes; so Virgil is romantic enough to make us feel that in the end there will be no wrong unavenged, no wrong uncompensated, and nevertheless is constantly touching our feelings with the tenderest pathos at what is to him the saddest of all sights – that of a beautiful life brought to an unmerited and untimely close.[56]

This line of interpretation, focusing on the unsettling moments of the poem and pausing to be overwhelmed by grief, has been at the core of Anglo-American criticism of Virgil for the past fifty years, nay nearly sixty years when one considers that its original and most influential expression appeared in 1963 with Adam Parry's 'Two Voices in Virgil's *Aeneid*'.[57]

In closing, I would like to revisit the topic of Knoxian philology and the author's treatment of some common Latin words with rather uncommon meanings in Virgil with which he ends his last lecture, 'Characteristics of Virgil's Style and Versification'. Reminiscent of his handling of *res*, touched on above, is his treatment of *magnus*. As there, we can observe an uncommon sensitivity in reading Virgil, the *Aeneid* in particular, that makes these lectures worthwhile and, for a certain kind of reader, nearly imperative. Thus, *magnus* is reserved for the meaning of 'great', never 'large' and generally not applied to physical extent, perhaps even explicitly reserved for 'something high and heroic' as in 9.18 (Nisus to Euryalus): 'aut pugnam, aut aliquid jamdudum invadere magnum / mens agitat mihi' (I'm thinking now to take on either a fight or even something heroic).[58] The same can be said for what follows, namely the subtly perceptive treatment of *unus* ('one and only'), *talis* ('of so high a nature' or 'of so low a nature'), and *si quis* ('if perchance'), especially the latter in 'adjurations' where, Knox avers, it 'is used with a wealth of delicate tenderness'.[59] To elucidate the point, he summons Tennyson's 'unsolicited testimonials to the qualities of Virgil's poetry' by quoting from 'To Virgil' (1882) the line: 'All the charm of all the Muses often flowering in a lonely Word'.[60] The quotation is adroitly deployed as it reveals a basic principle of Knox's approach to Virgil, namely that the *Aeneid*'s 'greatness and its charm' often reveal themselves in a single, simple word, and it is incumbent upon the reader – now not merely the Oxford undergraduates so privileged to have heard these lectures live, but also us and all subsequent readers of Virgil – to be sensitive to the immediate and nearly infinite depth beneath the surface of the text. To get to this point in Knox's lectures is to have traced an arc of development from the ingenuous wonder at the sheer capaciousness and grandeur of Virgil, even over Homer, evidently most at home next to the Bible, especially the Psalms, and clearly preparatory for Dante, to the careful, incisive, and illuminating analysis of single words and common expressions. Throughout there is, I dare say, Knox's own 'wealth of delicate tenderness', from which now we all may profit.

Notes

1 In the notes, Ronald Knox's *A Spiritual Aeneid* (London: Longmans, Green and Co., 1918), will be abbreviated *SA*. When quoting from *SA*, I have followed Knox and not italicized the title *Aeneid*.
2 See Chapter 1 in this volume, Ronald Knox, 'Virgil's Political Outlook', 48.
3 Virgil, *Opera*, with introduction and English notes by Arthur Sidgwick, 2 vols (Cambridge: Cambridge University Press, [1890] 1897–99). Pomposity, like modesty, is often a relative term, but for scholars of educational history, especially coeducation at the university level, Sidgwick is an important figure who played a crucial role in the introduction of women to Oxford; see Emily Rutherford, 'Arthur Sidgwick's Greek Prose Composition: Gender, Affect, and Sociability in the Late-Victorian University', *Journal of British Studies* 56, no. 1 (2017): 91–116.

4   Janet Howarth, 'Sidgwick, Arthur', in *The Oxford Dictionary of National Biography* (Oxford: Oxford University Press 2004). Available online.
5   Frank Miller Turner, 'Religion', in *History of the University of Oxford, Vol. VIII*, ed. Brian Harrison (Oxford: Clarendon Press, 1994), 299: 'Knox's sharp sense of humour and gift for witty discourse perhaps brought him as much influence in the University as did his faith. His contribution to the 'funny' Eights Week debates at the Oxford Union carried his reputation to parts of the University never touched by his sermons.' See also Evelyn Waugh, *The Life of the Right Reverend Ronald Knox* (London: Chapman and Hall, 1959), 90.
6   E. R. Dodds, *Missing Persons* (Oxford: Oxford University Press, 1977), 28.
7   Virgil, *Opera*, with a commentary by John Conington and with corrected orthography and additional notes by Henry Nettleship, 4th edn (London: Whittaker, [1858–71] 1884). On its apparent waning utility in Mods preparation, see Frederick Gaspar Brabant, 'Classical Honour Moderations', in *Oxford: Its Life and Schools*, ed. A. M. M. [Algernon Methuen Marshall] Stedman (London: George Bell and Sons, 1887), 234.
8   Contemporary descriptions of Mods seem to know no measure, e.g. Robert. Currie, 'The Arts and Social Studies, 1914–1939', in *The History of the University of Oxford, Vol. VIII*, ed. Brian Harrison (Oxford: Clarendon Press, 1994), 111: 'the most searching examination in Latin and Greek in any university'; L. Pyper, 'Classics Mods become less intense', *Cherwell* 21 (February 2013): 'the hardest set of exams in the world'. Available online.
9   Waugh, *The Life*, 95. Knox records his own ambivalence towards the position in *SA*, 85: 'I had once told a friend that I would never accept a position which involved teaching Honour Moderations.'
10 *SA*, 60; Waugh, *The Life*, 94–5.
11 Ibid., 81. His account fully squares with Knox's own, *SA*, 60–3.
12 This is supported by the fact that the only other roughly contemporary works to appear in these lectures are G. K. Chesterton's 'Ballad of the White Horse' (1911) and Kenneth Grahame's *Golden Age* (1895); see Chapter 3 in this volume, Ronald Knox, 'Virgil's Romance and Pathos'.
13 Waugh, *The Life*, 126: 'Oxford – the little world where "the sun rose over Wadham and set over Worcester" – was more than the background . . . It was an integral and determining part of it.' This applies to his lectures on Virgil but is actually said of Ronald's friendship with Guy Lawrence who, like so many of his brilliant students from Oxford, died in the bloom of youth in the First World War.
14 I treat the question of a 'Christianized' or 'adventist' reading of Virgil below, but for Knox as a classicist, consider his collection of classics prizes at Oxford, listed by Waugh, *The Life*, 89: Hertford (1907), Ireland, Craven and Gaisford in Greek Verse (1908), Chancellor's Latin verse (1910). Waugh's chronology may be off here; cf. *SA*,

61–2, where Knox seems to provide a different timeline and also recounts how he read Plato's *Republic* in Greek 'in a space of nine hours', a feat every classicist today will acknowledge to merit the memory: 'one of the best days I have spent'.
15 Stephen J. Harrison, 'Some Views of the *Aeneid* in the Twentieth Century', in *Oxford Readings in Vergil's* Aeneid, ed. Stephen J. Harrison (Oxford: Oxford University Press, 1990), 5.
16 Ibid., 2.
17 William Young Sellar, *Roman Poets of the Augustan Age: Virgil* (Oxford: Clarendon Press, [1877] 1897), cited in Chapter 2 of this volume, Knox, 'Virgil's Religious Outlook', 22.
18 Richard Heinze, *Virgils epische Technik* (Berlin: Teubner [1903, 1908] 1915), and Eduard Norden's commentary in Virgil, *Aeneis Buch VI*, with the Latin text, a translation and a commentary by Eduard Norden (Leipzig: Teubner, 1903 [1916, 1927]); see Harrison, 'Some Views of the *Aeneid*', 3 n. 11.
19 Knox, SA, 107, 123. Whatever Knox's knowledge – or lack – of the German language was, it is still hard to credit the tale, recorded in Waugh, *The Life* 94–5, that in a paper on Theocritus from his Honour Moderations Knox revealed that he had never heard of Ulrich von Wilamowitz-Moellendorff (1848–1931), among the most famous classicists of his day, who had been to Oxford in 1908 and delivered two lectures that made national news; see Robert L. Fowler, 'Blood for Ghosts: Wilamowitz in Oxford', *Syllecta Classica* 20 (2009): 171–213.
20 Knox, SA, 122–4: 'I was aroused against [the Higher Criticism] in earnest as the result of preparation for delivering lectures on the Iliad . . . And when I came to read the books on the Old Testament . . . all the *petitiones principii*, the splitting up of books into various strata of authorship on the ground of criteria arbitrarily assumed, and then suspecting interpolations everywhere merely in order to make the facts square with the theories, were in evidence here as in my Homeric authors.'
21 Francesco Montarese, 'Ronald Knox and the Study of Classics', in *Ronald Knox: A Man for All Seasons*, ed. Francesca Bugliani Knox (Toronto: Pontifical Institute of Medieval Studies, 2016), 148, comments on Knox's antipathy to the 'higher criticism' and concludes that his 'diffident attitude towards academia . . . may well explain why his views were neglected'. I disagree; Knox may have had a diffident attitude towards academia, but his views on Virgil were neglected because they were never published, until now. Even if he could hardly be considered an academic classicist like his brother Dillwyn, he still enjoyed an excellent reputation in the field so that he was engaged by the Clarendon Press to put together a school edition of *Aeneid* VII–IX (1924) and, upon his death, received the honor of a memorial lecture from the President of the Virgil Society, Robert Speaight, *A Modern Virgilian. A Memorial Lecture to Monsignor Ronald Knox*, delivered to the Virgil Society, on 15 November 1958 (London: Virgil Society, 1959).
22 Knox, SA, 106.

23 See Chapter 1 in this volume, Knox, 'Virgil's Political Outlook', 48–9.
24 Ibid., 56.
25 Ibid., 57; the passages in question, listed in Knox's order: 4.267, 1.278, 7.315, 8.471, 2.783. Contemporary commentaries tend to support this general idea, although I have not found the point made in quite the same way as Knox makes it here.
26 Ibid., 57.
27 Harrison, 'Some Views', 5.
28 Knox, SA, 2: 'if in the course of this book I quote too freely . . . from the poem which is its title, it is because the Aeneid travelled with me in the last two months before the end of my journey, and I read it, as Christians used to, with something like a demand for spiritual comfort'.
29 Preface, ibid.
30 Ibid., 1.
31 Ibid., 106.
32 Ibid.
33 See Chapter 2 in this volume, Knox, 'Virgil's Religious Outlook', 76–83.
34 Similar humor was also on view in ibid., 66: 'Some critic has made a remark to the effect that Aeneas was far more suited to be the founder of a community of contemplative monks than the founder of an Empire. That may be true: but then, it is much easier to found an Empire successfully than to found a successful community of contemplative monks.'
35 Ibid., 77.
36 Ibid., 64. This idea is repeated more adroitly in Knox's school commentary on *Aeneid* VII–IX: 'you must not believe people who tell you that the word *pius*, applied to [Aeneas], refers simply to filial affection. It does, of course, when you are talking about his father; but it means a great deal besides. When you are talking about the gods, *pius Aeneas* means "the devout Aeneas" – you might almost say, "Aeneas, that trained liturgiologist". When you are talking about the dead, it means "the faithful Aeneas". When you are talking about his Trojan followers, it means "the thoughtful Aeneas". When you are talking of people who have done him a service, it means "the fair-minded Aeneas". Always it means the man who knows what is expected of him, sees what is due everybody. Nobody pretends that this makes a very exciting hero for a story'. See Ronald Knox, 'Introduction', in Virgil, *Aeneid, Books VII to IX*, partly in the original and, partly in English verse translation by Ronald Knox (Oxford: Clarendon Press, 1924), 14–15.
37 Chapter 2 of this volume, Knox, 'Virgil's Religious Outlook', 63.
38 Ibid., 184.
39 Ibid., 67.
40 Ibid.
41 Ibid., 81.
42 Ibid.

43 Ibid., 82.
44 Chapter 1 of this volume, Knox, 'Virgil's Political Outlook', 46.
45 Philip Hardie, *The Last Trojan Hero: A Cultural History of Virgil's* Aeneid (London: I. B. Tauris & Co. 2015), 143.
46 For a recent survey of this vast and complex tradition, see Hardie, *Last Trojan Hero*, 127–47 (= ch. 10 '*Imperium Sine Fine*: The *Aeneid* and Christianity').
47 Harrison, 'Views of the *Aeneid*', 3; Hardie, *Last Trojan Hero*, 143.
48 See Knox, *Aeneid* VII–IX, 106 (ad *Aen*. 8.364–5: 'aude, hospes, contemnere ospes, et te quoque dignum / finge deo, rebusque veni non asper egenis'): 'Two of Virgil's uncannily Christian lines; you could write them over a Christian crib.'
49 Chapter 1 of this volume, Knox, 'Virgil's Political Outlook', 47–8.
50 Harrison, 'Views of the *Aeneid*', 3, where he cites Eduard Kennard Rand, *The Magical Art of Virgil* (Cambridge, Mass.: Harvard University Press, 1931), and Theodor Haecker, *Vergil, Vater des Abendlandes* (Leipzig: J. Hegner, 1931), trans. Arthur Wesley Wheen, *Virgil, Father of the West* (New York: Sheed and Ward, 1934).
51 Hardie, *The Last Trojan Hero*, 144. See also Robert Speaight, *Ronald Knox: The Writer* (London: Sheed and Ward, 1966), 118, who plays, somewhat puckishly but productively, with Tertullian's phrase: '[Knox] was, again like Newman, an *anima naturaliter Virgiliana*.'
52 T. S. Eliot, *What Is a Classic? An Address Delivered before the Virgil Society on the 16th of October 1944* (London: Faber and Faber, 1945), quoted here from T. S. Eliot, *On Poets and Poetry* (New York: Farrar, Strauss, and Cudahy, 1957), 70. See Charles Martindale, 'Ruins of Rome: T. S. Eliot and the Presence of the Past', *Arion* 3, no. 2 (1995), 102–40, on Eliot's use of Haecker's work, esp. 104–7.
53 Also printed in Eliot, *On Poets and Poetry*, 135–48; quotation 140, 146.
54 Eliot, 'What Is a Classic', 73–4.
55 For the date I rely on Dennis W. Blandford, *Pentekontaetia: The Virgil Society 1943–1993*, (London: The Virgil Society, 1993), 30: 'The date of the Presidential Address (16 Oct 44) is worth noting, particularly as some Eliot bibliographies quote it incorrectly.' In reference to the dangers still posed by the war, Blandford adds the following, no doubt drawing on personal experience, 32: 'the [Virgil Society's] achievement of 1944 is all the more remarkable when seen against the background. Abroad there were some outstanding successes, and some severe set-backs. At home, there were many reminders of war. In the spring . . . there was the "Little Blitz". In the summer the "doodlebugs" arrived, and continued to arrive for the next nine months: the V1 or flying bomb . . . and the V2 or ballistic missile. London was again evacuated, and it was estimated that by late August 1.5 million Londoners had moved out – twice as many as in 1939. The fact that cultural life continued – indeed flourished – under these conditions only increases our admiration for those who provided it.'

56 See Chapter 3 in this volume, Knox, 'Virgil's Romance and Pathos', 95.
57 Adam Parry, 'Two Voices in Virgil's *Aeneid*', *Arion* 2, no. 4 (1963): 66–80.
58 See Chapter 8 in this volume, Ronald Knox, 'Characteristics of Virgil's Style and Versification', 168. See also *Aeneid* 5.751, 4.654, 3.159.
59 Chapter 8 in this volume, Knox, 'Characteristics of Virgil's Style and Versification', 171.
60 From 'To Virgil, Written at the Request of the Mantuans for the Nineteenth Centenary of Virgil's Death' (1882), which Knox regards as Tennyson 'giving unsolicited testimonials to the qualities of Virgil's poetry' (ibid., 172).

Bibliography

Blandford, Dennis W. *Pentekontaetia: The Virgil Society 1943–1993*. London: The Virgil Society, 1993.

Brabant, Frederick Gaspard. 'Classical Honour Moderations'. In Stedman (ed.), *Oxford: Its Life and Schools*, 218–43.

Bugliani Knox, Francesca (ed.). *Ronald Knox: A Man for All Seasons*. Toronto: Pontifical Institute of Medieval Studies, 2016.

Currie, Robert. 'The Arts and Social Studies, 1914–1939'. In *The History of the University of Oxford: Vol. VIII*, edited by Brian Harrison. Oxford: Clarendon Press, 1994, 109–38.

Dodds, Erik Robertson. *Missing Persons*. Oxford: Oxford University Press, 1977.

Eliot, T. S. *What Is a Classic? An Address Delivered before the Virgil Society on the 16th of October 1944*. London: Faber and Faber, 1945.

Eliot, T. S. 'Virgil and the Christian World'. In *On Poets and Poetry*, 135–48.

Eliot, T. S. *On Poets and Poetry*, New York: Farrar, Strauss, and Cudahy, 1957.

Fowler, Robert L. 'Blood for Ghosts: Wilamowitz in Oxford'. *Syllecta Classica* 20 (2009): 171–213.

Haecker, Theodor. *Vergil, Vater des Abendlandes*. Leipzig: J. Hegner, 1931. *Virgil, Father of the West*, translated by Arthur Wesley Wheen, New York: Sheed and Ward, 1934.

Hardie, Philip. 'Virgil's Epic Techniques: Heinze Ninety Years On'. *Classical Philology* 90 (1995): 267–76.

Hardie, Philip. *The Last Trojan Hero: A Cultural History of Virgil's Aeneid*. London: I. B. Tauris and Co., 2015.

Harrison, Stephen J. 'Some Views of the *Aeneid* in the Twentieth Century'. In *Oxford Readings in Vergil's Aeneid*, edited by Stephen J. Harrison. Oxford: Oxford University Press, 1990, 1–20.

Heinze, Richard. *Virgils epische Technik*, Berlin: Teubner, 1915 [1903, 1908].

Howarth, Janet. 'Sidgwick, Arthur'. In *Oxford Dictionary of National Biography*, 2004. Available online.

Jenkyns, Richard. 'Classical Studies, 1872–1914'. In *The History of the University of Oxford, Volume VII, Nineteenth Century Oxford*. Part 2, edited by Michael G. Brock and Mark C. Curthoys. Oxford: Clarendon Press, 2000, 327–31.

Knox, Ronald A. *A Spiritual Aeneid*, London: Longmans, Green and Co., 1918.

Knox, Ronald A. 'Introduction'. In Virgil, *Aeneid Books VII to IX*, 5–18.

Knox, Ronald A. *God and the Atom*, London: Sheed and Ward, 1945.

Knox, Ronald A. *The Hidden Stream. A Further Collection of Oxford Conferences*. London: The Catholic Book Club, 1952.

Martindale, Charles. 'Ruins of Rome: T. S. Eliot and the Presence of the Past'. *Arion* 3, no. 2 (1995): 102–40.

Montarese, Francesco. 'Ronald Knox as Classicist'. In Bugliani Knox (ed.), *Ronald Knox*, 147–65.

Parry, Adam. 'Two Voices in Virgil's *Aeneid*'. *Arion* 2, no. 4 (1963): 66–80.

Pyper, L. 'Classics Mods become Less Intense'. *Cherwell* 21 (February 2013). Available online.

Rand, Eduard Kennard. *The Magical Art of Virgil*. Cambridge, Mass.: Harvard University Press, 1931.

Rutherford, Emily. 'Arthur Sidgwick's *Greek Prose Composition*: Gender, Affect, and Sociability in the Late-Victorian University'. *Journal of British Studies* 56, no. 1 (2017); 91–116.

Sellar, William Young. *The Roman Poets of the Augustan Age: Virgil*. 3rd edn. Oxford: Clarendon Press, 1897 [1877].

Speaight, Robert. *A Modern Virgilian: A Memorial Lecture to Monsignor Ronald Knox*. London: Virgil Society, 1959.

Speaight, Robert. *Ronald Knox: The Writer*. London: Sheed and Ward, 1996.

Stedman, A. M. M. [Algernon Methuen Marshall]. *Oxford: Its Life and Schools*. London: George Bell and Sons, 1887.

Turner, Frank Miller. 'Religion'. In *History of the University of Oxford: Vol. VIII*, edited by Brian Harrison. Oxford: Clarendon Press, 1994, 293–316.

Virgil. *Opera*. With a commentary by John Conington. Revised, with corrected orthography and additional notes by Henry Nettleship. 4th edn. London: Whittaker, 1884 [1858–71].

Virgil. *Opera*. With introduction and English notes by Arthur Sidgwick, 2 vols. Cambridge: Cambridge University Press, 1897–99 [1890].

Virgil. *Aeneis Buch VI*. With the Latin text, a translation and a commentary by Eduard Norden. Leipzig: Teubner, 1903.

Virgil. *Aeneid Books VII to IX*. Partly in the original and partly in English verse translation. Introduction and translation by Ronald Knox. Oxford: Clarendon Press, 1924.

Waugh, Evelyn. *The Life of the Right Reverend Ronald Knox*. London: Chapman and Hall, 1959.

Ronald Knox's Lectures on Virgil: Their Significance for Scholarly Interpretation of the *Aeneid*

Francesco Montarese

'If you take from Virgil his diction and metre, what do you leave him?', wrote Coleridge in his *Table Talk* of 8 May, 1824.[1] During the course of his Trinity lectures Ronald Knox took issue with Coleridge's aside, twice.[2] Yes, the *Aeneid* demonstrated that Virgil was a master of language and metre but, *pace* Coleridge, it contained an abundance of themes and details that merited attention – political, religious, military, geographical and literary. 'Virgil's love of civilisation,' he wrote, came out 'of all sorts of odd corners of the *Aeneid*.'[3] In what follows I have focused on some examples that illustrate his distinctive approach to the poem and shown, I hope, how they might even now be developed to advantage.

An eye for detail

Ronald Knox, like his three brothers, Dillwyn, Edmund and Wilfrid, was an avid reader of Sherlock Holmes. Evidently, they pored over every detail, for they compiled a list of mistakes and inconsistencies and sent it to Conan Doyle.[4] This attention to detail attained an almost philosophical significance for Ronald. Some years later, on 13 March 1911, while a Fellow at Oxford, he delivered a spoof lecture at the Gryphon Club of Trinity College entitled 'Studies in the Literature of Sherlock Holmes', in which he analysed, with mock scholarly precision, Conan Doyle's tales. In the opening section of the lecture, Knox quoted Holmes's description of his method: 'It has long been an axiom of mine that the little things are infinitely the most important.'[5] No surprise, then, that the same trait came to characterize Knox's study of ancient Greek and Roman literature, nowhere more so than in the Trinity lectures. His meticulous consideration of details in Virgil's poem led him, indeed, to discover that Virgil, like Conan Doyle, had occasionally been imprecise. He observed, for example, that Virgil had not synchronized the chronology of the Achaemenides episode in book 3 with that of Odysseus' wanderings in the *Odyssey*.[6] Later he noted other imprecisions in his 1924 edition of *Aeneid* books 7 to 9.[7] Yet he also took pains to defend Virgil from what he saw as unjust criticisms of inconsistency. For instance, the accepted view in his day had been that the expression 'terra Hesperia' in 2.780 referred to Italy. Not so, Knox objected. It merely indicated that Creusa had told Aeneas that he would fulfil his destiny in some land to the west of Troy.[8] More important than these occasional slips, real or imagined, was the coherence of the poem and its details. Discussing, for instance, the many realistic features in Virgil's accounts of Aeneas' sea voyages, Knox noted that he had introduced geographical details typical of the Mediterranean, particularly those of the seafaring routes followed by ships in antiquity. Other examples occur below.

The chronology of Aeneas' journey in particular aroused Knox's curiosity. Convinced that purported discrepancies – especially those discerned by John Conington – could be resolved by taking into consideration Ascanius' age at each stage of Aeneas' travels, he concluded that the voyage had taken six or seven, and certainly no less than five, years, rather than three, as Conington, following the Virgilian scholar Friedrich Conrads, had suggested.[9] Knox, it should be said, did not address a problem that this chronology presents. He writes that 'the 7th [year] had already set in' when they [i.e., Aeneas and his men] arrived at Dido's, taking at face value Dido's statement that Aeneas was on the seventh year of his travels (1.755–6).[10] What Dido says, though, conflicts *prima facie* with the account of the Trojan women, who claim that they were in the summer of the seventh year of their travels when they had already left Carthage with Aeneas and his men and returned to Sicily (5.626). A solution to the discrepancy between 1.755–6 and 5.626, a discrepancy that Servius had noticed, is to avoid intricate explanations and assume that Aeneas reached Carthage during the seventh year of his voyage – as soon, that is, as the season allowed him to sail from Sicily – and returned to Sicily by late summer of the same year.[11] That Knox did not suggest that there was an inconsistency indicates that he believed that Aeneas, after departing from Sicily immediately after Anchises' death, remained in Carthage for less than a year. Franklin H. Potter made this point several years later in 1926.[12] The issue is of some importance. The length of Aeneas' stay in Carthage determines how we should interpret Aeneas' relationship with Dido and Dido's claim that a marriage had taken place – a claim that Knox, incidentally, rejects.[13]

Critics who disagree with the hypothesis of a shorter stay of Aeneas at Carthage have based their objections on Fama's report at 4.193 ('nunc hiemem inter se luxu, quam longa, fovere') (Now they enjoyed the whole winter together in indulgence) and Dido's contemptuous reaction to Aeneas' departure at 4.309–11 ('quin etiam hiberno moliris sidere classem,/ et mediis properas Aquilonibus ire per altum,/ crudelis?') (What? Are you really equipping your fleet under the winter stars / And in the middle of the north winds hastening to go through the deep, /Cruel man?).[14] Fama's report, however, is not trustworthy because, as Knox points out, she 'pariter facta atque infecta canebat' (Reported in song truth and untruths in equal measure) (4.190).[15] Also, if we assume that Virgil uses *fovere* in Fama's report to mean 'cherish in expectation', as he does when he describes Juno's hopes for Carthage at 1.18, the objection no longer stands. As for the 'hiberno sidere' (Under the winter stars) in Dido's speech, it is plausible that in despair Dido pictures Aeneas as sailing, 'not at the close of summer, but in the near future, when the seas would begin to be forbidding'.[16]

Military details caught Knox's eye. Throughout the poem, he observed, the military equipment, formations, attire and structures described by Virgil are those of contemporary Rome, and so corroborate what critics have often called the 'patriotic' tone of the poem.[17] Unlike Homer, for example, Virgil deployed his Bronze Age warriors in orderly battlelines. The Greeks (2.441) and Volscians (9.505 and 514) adopt the *testudo* formation.[18] The ships at Actium, depicted on the shield of Aeneas (8.693), have turrets, as archaeology shows they had in Virgil's day (see Figure 4). In 12.921–2, Aeneas' launch of his spear is compared to a *murale tormentum* which was invented after his, Aeneas', day. The ceremonial *lusus Troiae* described at 5.545–603 reflects the equestrian performance of the same name revived in the late Republic.[19] Several scholars since have made similar observations about military details. Christine Perkell and Benjamin Thomason, for example, have singled out the four white horses that greet Aeneas and the Trojans on their arrival in Italy (3.539–43).[20] The horses, which Anchises interprets as an omen prophesying both war and the hope of peace, allude to the four-horsed chariots that we know, from other evidence, headed Roman triumphal processions.[21] Another military anachronism, one that has escaped scholarly attention, is the bullock pelt and cap made from the gaping mouth of a wolf's head worn by Ornytus (11.679–81).[22] The use of such imagery owes much to *Iliad* 10.459 where Dolon, a second-rate warrior like Ornytus, wears a wolf skin. The choice of the bullock pelt and cap was probably also motivated by the attire of the *aquiliferi* who bore the standards of the Roman legions. Archaeological evidence shows that *aquiliferi* wore animal pelts.[23] The use of a wolf head as described by Virgil conforms with the wolf's special place in Roman myth and iconography. Details of this kind support Knox's contention that what military anachronisms there are to be found in the *Aeneid* were inspired by Virgil's knowledge of contemporary practice.

Further proof of Knox's attention to detail is the significance that he attributed to Virgil's appreciation of man-made constructions, such as aqueducts and towers, and their significance within their settings. He observed, for instance, that Virgil, in what Knox called one of his, Virgil's, masterful 'impressionist' vignettes, describes a traveller who, searching for shelter from a storm, is torn between two options: 'et tuta latet arce viator / aut amnis ripis aut alti fornice saxi' (10.805–6) (And a traveller hides in a safe shelter either under a river bank or under an arch of lofty stone). Virgil was referring, Knox suggested, to a Roman aqueduct, which, with its high arches, would offer protection in such circumstances.[24] True, to translate *saxum* as 'stone' rather than – the conventional interpretation – as 'rock' may, at first glance, seem questionable, given that *saxum* in the *Aeneid* often denotes rocks or crags.[25] In support of Knox's translation, however, common sense dictates that a traveller in such circumstances would look for shelter under the stone vault of a tall aqueduct rather than under the cover of a lofty rock. A lofty, overhanging, rock on the bank of a river, apart from being an uncommon geographical feature, would afford little protection. Virgil's reference to such a peculiarly Roman structure as arched aqueducts, would be, moreover, perfectly in keeping with his inclination elsewhere in the *Aeneid* to evoke contemporary Rome.[26] Support for Knox's interpretation of 'fornix alti saxi' as an arched man-made structure also comes from within the poem itself, in the description of the entrance to Elysium at 6.631. On this occasion Conington translates *fornix* as 'the arched gateway fronting us'. Again, at 1.424 and 2.608–9, *saxum* denotes an architectural 'construction'.

The towers dotting Virgil's depictions of Italian scenery proved equally intriguing to Knox and led him to make an original observation, one that has not been followed up by later scholars. The sight of towers, he observed, heralded Aeneas' arrival in Italy. The 'very first glimpse the voyagers get of the country that is to be theirs' is that of 'turriti scopuli' (3.536).[27] According to previous translators and commentators, Virgil used this phrase to describe rocks of a tower-like formation.[28] Knox, instead, argued convincingly that it meant, 'furnished with towers', an alternative that Heyworth and Morwood, independently of Knox, have recently deemed plausible.[29] Knox's interpretation has several merits. The standard translation 'tower-like' is not well attested and *turritus* is used with the meaning 'furnished with towers' at 8.693 alluding to the sterns of Antony's ships

Figure 4 A large Roman galley or quinquereme ready for battle at Actium in 31 BC. This relief comes from the Temple of Fortuna Primigenia at Praeneste (Palestrina), now in the Vatican Museums, Gregorian Profane Museum (Inventory no. 31680).

at Actium. The famous relief from Praeneste, now in the Vatican, shows turreted structures on the ships engaged in the battle (see Figure 4).

The detail is corroborated by Cassius Dio (*Roman History* 50.23.3 and 50.18.6) and Lucius Annaeus Florus (*Epitome of Roman History* 2.21.5), who both mention the towers built on Mark Antony's vessels. Moreover, archaeological work at modern Castro has recently unearthed an important shrine of Minerva, as well as some fortifications built by the Messapians, that Virgil had in mind when in 3.536 he described the 'scopuli' as 'turriti'.[30] The name *Castrum Minervae* evokes a fortified structure and the clustering of military terms, as Putnam notes, reinforces the idea that Virgil's *turriti scopuli* indicated a heavily fortified structure.[31]

Towers were, again, the first man-made feature the Trojans glimpsed on their arrival in Latium (7.160). Knox stressed how the phrase 'turris ac tecta Latinorum ardua' – probably to be read as a hendiadys, meaning 'the towers rising from the tops of the buildings' – conveyed beautifully the image of towers rising aloft on top of the hills of Laurentum.[32] The image is conjured up again later by Virgil, when he refers to Laurentum's towers (11.466 and 12.132) and, as a climax, in the description of the Laurentine tower built by Turnus (12.673-4). It is also complemented by two further examples mentioned by Knox: first, the 'turrigerae Antennae' of 7.631, where, once again, the towers on the craggy Monte Antenne intensify the precipitous landscape depicted by Virgil; and, second, the expression 'et quos maliferae despectant moenia Abellae' (And those whom the city walls of apple-bearing Abella look down upon) (7.740), where Virgil displays his familiarity with the produce for which the town was famed and with the landscape in which it was set.[33]

Apart from the evocative description of the iron tower of Tartarus (6.554: 'stat ferrea turris ad auras' (An iron tower reaches out to the sky) and the 'turrigerae urbes' (Tower-bearing cities) in which Cybele delights (10.253), Knox confined his discussion of towers to those standing on Italian hilltops of the kind that he would have seen during his journey to Rome in 1907. He describes them as 'sudden hill-heights with the cities nestling on the top of them which we see and envy in the pictures of the Italian Pre-Raphaelites'[34] (see Figures 5 and 6).

His observations, however, invite consideration of tower imagery elsewhere in the *Aeneid*. One image above all stands out for its frequency, vividness and meaning, namely, the crumbling towers and turrets, and their ruins, in which

Figure 5 Detail from *St Francis in the Desert* by Giovanni Bellini, 1480. Frick Collection, New York.

Figure 6 Detail from *The Agony in the Garden* by Andrea Mantegna, 1457–59. Musée des Beaux-Arts de Tours.

Virgil so evidently delighted. Two illustrations among many will suffice.[35] The first – and perhaps the best illustration – occurs in the narration of the fall of Troy in book 2, the πύργοι (Towers) that were already legendary in Greek epic tradition. Especially noteworthy is the line 'Dardanidae contra turris ac tota domorum / culmina convellunt' (2.444–5) (Against this Dardanians pull apart the towers and whole roofs of houses). Here, as with the 'turriti scopuli' standing on top of the rugged, precipitous, Italian coastline near Castro, the image is that of towers or turrets standing on top of walls, similar, in fact, to those standing at the top of the hill of Hissarlik. The second is to be found at the very end of the poem (12.672–5), when the turret constructed by Turnus collapses. Conington (at 12.676) suggested that Turnus interprets the crumbling of the turret as an omen of his impending doom. This convincing observation encourages the reading of the collapse of the Trojan tower in book 2 as a symbol for the destruction of Troy. Knox's intuition that towers were a recurrent *leitmotiv* of the poem is surely not far from the mark.

Herodotus

A distinctive feature of the Virgil lectures is how much Knox made of the influence of Herodotus in the *Aeneid* or, more precisely, of what he called its 'historical and Herodotean atmosphere'.[36] No hard and fast evidence, he admits, proves that Virgil had read the *Histories* but there are grounds for thinking that he had done so. He was certainly familiar with other Greek historians, a conspicuous example being the striking phrase 'frangere puppim' (Smash your timbers) in 10.297–8, which recalls Thucydides' comments about Brasidas in the *History of the Peloponnesian War* 4.1. With respect to Herodotus in particular, Knox noted that the catalogues of military contingents in *Aeneid* 7.647–817 and in Herodotus, *Histories* 61–9, were similar and that both concluded with the two female leaders, Artemisia and Camilla. Nicholas Horsfall, Barbara Boyd and others have made the same observation.[37] Another interesting correlation to which Knox drew attention was the flight of the Trojans from Troy and Herodotus' account of the Phocaeans fleeing the Persians in the first book of the *Histories*. Two details in particular support Knox's conjecture. The first is a passage in *Histories* 1.163, in which Herodotus described how the Phocaeans sailed to the Adriatic and Tyrrhenian seas and built walls around a new city, one that they would never inhabit, on Crete. Similarly, on their voyage to the Adriatic and Tyrrhenian seas, Aeneas and the Trojans build Pergamea on Crete (3.132–4), only to leave it shortly afterwards. The second is *Histories* 1.165, in which Phocaeans sail away with their entire population and with whatever images of their gods they could take away with them. Aeneas and the Trojans similarly take their *penates* with them when they flee Troy.

There are other possible connections between the two works besides those mentioned by Knox. For example, the parading of Nisus' and Euryalus' decapitated heads on stakes in *Aeneid* 9.465–6, draws possibly on *Histories* 7.238, where Leonidas' head meets the same fate. Both episodes share the same underlying themes, namely heroism and martyrdom. Moreover, in this passage the barbarity of Herodotus' Persians parallels the brutality of Virgil's Latins and especially the Rutulians, and the Etruscan Mezentius, who has joined their side.[38] Again, Virgil's praise of Nisus and Euryalus in 9.446–9 is similar in tone to the famous encomium of the Spartiates at Thermopylae in *Histories* 7.227. The episode of the sacred serpent of the Athenian acropolis shunning all food in *Histories* 8.41 has an echo in *Aeneid* 2.225–7. Laocoon is slain by the sea serpents that slither to the 'saevae arx Tritonidis' (The citadel of harsh Athena) and hide beneath Athena's shield. This episode recalls the chryselephantine statue of Athena on the Athenian Acropolis, which similarly depicts a serpent concealed beneath her shield. The same passage in the *Histories* may also have a connection with the appearance of the serpent in *Aeneid* 5.84–93, where, in a reversal of the doom-laden circumstances in Herodotus, the serpent savours the food rather than snubbing it in the manner of Herodotus' serpent. Aeneas' intimation that the serpent might be a guardian of the 'locus' (place) (5.95–6) – resembles the passage in *Histories* 8.41 in which Herodotus mentions that a great serpent inhabited the Acropolis in Athens. The allusion, if it is one, highlights the success of Aeneas' mission, while the seven coils of the serpent coincide numerically to the duration of Aeneas' journey as well as the seven hills and kings of the city of Rome.[39]

Perhaps most intriguing of all is the connection between, on the one hand, Herodotus' account of the scorn of priests and of their reading of the entrails as expressed by King Cleomenes of Sparta (*Histories* 6.76 and 6.81) and, on the other, the episode of Dido's sacrifices at 4.60–6.[40] Dido takes charge of the rituals herself (4.60 and 4.64) – an unusual thing for a queen to do in the ancient world – and performs sacrifices either throughout the day or, following an alternative interpretation of the phrase 'instaurat diem' (Dido renews the day), at day break each morning.[41] The 'ipsa' in line 60 seems, furthermore, to pick up Herodotus' portrayal of Cleomenes, who, consumed with *furor* just like Dido, performs a sacrifice 'himself' (καὶ αὐτὸς ἔθυσε) at Argos (*Histories* 6.81), despite the priest prohibiting him from doing so.[42] The implication is that, given that the entrails did not reveal what she had hoped for, Dido, with Anna no longer there to inhibit her, took charge of the sacrifice in the hope of making the outcome suit her wishes. Cleomenes had done just the same at Argos. Roman disapproval of such artifice would have brought out the connection between the two episodes all the more clearly.[43] The circumstances of the two scenes are similar in other respects. Both Cleomenes and Dido take charge of a ritual, both sacrifice at the temple of Hera / Juno, both behave deviously towards persons closely related to them (Demaratus and Anna respectively) and both commit suicide in a bout of violent frenzy. The similarities would not have escaped Virgil's contemporaries. Furthermore, book 1 of the *Aeneid* conveys a Spartan aura of military prowess and hostility to foreigners.[44] Virgil likens Venus to a *virgo Spartana* (1.315–16), he refers to the river Eurotas in Sparta (1.498) and associates Venus with Artemis, alluding to Sparta's famous shrine of Artemis Orthia on the banks of that river.

Keywords

Knox's approach is nowhere better illustrated than in the attention that he pays to individual words. He believed that recurring words in the *Aeneid* were often a clue to the underlying sentiment of the whole: 'there are words, quite as simple and familiar', he explains, 'which attain distinction in Virgil's hands through the carefulness and consistency of his usage'.[45] For instance, the simple word *res* (in the plural), he notes, assumes at times the particular sense of 'a great future, the prospect of world power', when used in reference to the Roman Empire, particularly the Roman Empire of the Augustan *aurea aetas*.

Another, more significant, example was Virgil's use of, in Knox's words, the 'run of the mill' adjective *magnus*. In what seems at first glance a startling claim, he suggested that when Virgil wanted to say something was large in the *Aeneid*, he avoided using *magnus*, preferring in such instances *ingens* or *immanis* instead. His observation stands up to scrutiny. There are, I believe, just one or, possibly, two exceptions. The first is *magnus gyrus* (7.379), where *magnus* denotes the breadth of the wide circuit of a top spinning in an empty court. The second exception, granting that it is one, is the expression *magni crateres*, which occurs twice, first at 1.724, where it describes the wine bowls passed round at the first banquet held at Dido's palace, and, then at 3.525, where it describes the bowls that the Trojans used at the sacrifice that they perform on their arrival in Italy. In both passages, especially in the light of 1.728–30, Virgil may have in mind the craters' materials or fine workmanship, rather than their size.[46] Elsewhere the adjective *magnus* unambiguously does not have spatial connotations. In many instances, *magnus* means 'powerful', even 'overwhelming' and 'uncontrollable', occasionally in a negative sense. Several occurrences emerge during Aeneas' encounter with the Sibyl. *Magna mens* at 6.11, as Knox notes, cannot refer, obviously, to the size of the Sybil's mind.[47] In the expression 'magna penetralia' at 6.71, as Knox also notes, *magnus* probably does not mean or only mean 'large', but, instead we may surmise, describes the grandeur of the shrine that Aeneas promises to erect in the Sybil's honour.[48] Further examples – not ones that Knox troubled to indicate – are the comparative *maior* at 6.49, indicating the Sybil's imposing presence, and *magnus* at 6.78–9, which conveys the extraordinary power of Apollo's inspiration of the Sybil.[49] At *Aeneid* 1.171, 'ac magno telluris amore', referring to the Trojans' state of mind as they disembark after the storm Juno inflicted on them, *magnus* means powerful. Perhaps the most vivid example of *magnus* in this sense, one that Knox mentioned, occurs in Virgil's *ekphrasis* immediately preceding Aeneas' encounter with the Sibyl (6.28). Here the phrase *magnus amor* refers to a doomed, destructive ἔρως, one that is all the more overwhelming if, as Knox believed, it was the *amor* suffered by Pasiphae for the bull of Minos[50] or, possibly, for her son.[51] Commentators before and after Knox have usually preferred to see Ariadne rather than Pasiphae as the victim.[52] The more obvious reading of the Latin, though, is that Pasiphae was the victim, given that Ariadne was never 'queen' of Crete and given the several allusions associating Dido to Pasiphae in *Aeneid* 6 and indeed throughout the poem.[53]

The phrase *magnus amor* exemplifies Knox's insight, mentioned above, that ordinary words take on distinctive connotations in the *Aeneid*.[54] In addition to its occurrence at 6.28, it appears on six other occasions.[55] On each occurrence *amor* (ἔρως) denotes an overwhelming passion, acquiring a disquieting undertone of overpowering or uncontrollable frenzy, particularly in that, apart from one occurrence, namely 1.716, the *magnus amor* results in violent death. At 1.344 Virgil uses *magnus amor* to describe the intensity of Dido's ἔρως for Sychaeus. At 1.675 Venus' 'sed magno Aeneae mecum teneatur amore' (May [Dido] share with me the passionate love for Aeneas) stands as a premonition of Dido's tragic ἔρως for Aeneas. The 'mecum' is not easy to explain but it could well hint at Venus' overwhelming love for her son, which results in her being wounded while trying to protect him in *Iliad* 5.[56] The use of *magnus amor* of 1.675 is picked up at 1.716 and applied to Cupid, who, disguised as Ascanius, arouses the affection that Aeneas feels for his son.[57] In 3.330 Orestes is driven by *magnus amor* to commit a sacrilegious act, the murder of Pyrrhus at the altar.[58] In 4.395

('Multa gemens magnoque animum labefactus amore') (Groaning heavily and shaken in his spirit by the passionate love), the phrase, whether it refers to Aeneas or, as some hold, Dido, appears in the context of Aeneas' conflicting obligations towards passion and duty. Finally, on its seventh appearance in book 9.197 it describes Euryalus' state of mind when Nisus tells him that he intends to break through the Rutulian lines and inform Aeneas of the siege. Like all the other occurrences mentioned above, Euryalus' *magnus amor*, this time the love of glory rather than love towards someone, leads to tragedy when their mission fails, with Euryalus dying at the hands of the Rutulian captain Volscens and Nisus at the hands of those defending Volscens. To these examples we might also add 4.532 where *amor* and *magnus* are juxtaposed in a passage describing Dido's frenzied thoughts on the night before she dies.

Is Virgil's insistent use of the expression *magnus amor* yet another example of the Euripidean intertextuality that critics have often noted in the *Aeneid*? The notion of *magnus amor* recalls the ἔρωτες ὑπὲρ μὲν ἄγαν ἐλθόντες (Loves that come to us in excess) of the chorus in *Medea* (627), a stanza (627–35) that also mentions poisoned arrows reminiscent of *Aeneid* 1.688 and 4.68–73 and, as in Virgil's depiction of Dido forsaken, the anger resulting from such passions. The verbal echoes of the *Medea* in book 4 of the *Aeneid* have often been commented upon and Virgil may well have used the expression *magnus amor* in the Dido story to remind readers of *Medea* 627. There the chorus stresses that overwhelming desire was perilous and later Hellenistic philosophers who influenced Virgil were of the same mind. Contributing to this message is Virgil's transformation of Erato, the Muse of love poetry, into Erato the Muse of love of one's *patria* on the arrival of the Trojans at Latium. The ἔρως directed at human beings, or occasionally at things, must, as Aeneas' desertion of Dido exemplifies, give way to love of one's country.[59] This exaltation of, so to speak, patriotic ἔρως explains why those inhabitants of Elysium who await reincarnation are mainly patriots. Passionate ἔρως between man and woman or man and man, by contrast, is destructive, as the series of heroines accompanying Dido in the *campi lugentes* illustrates. In this respect *magnus amor* has a similar meaning to *durus amor* at 6.442.

Religious rituals and traditions

Knox, as we might expect of a man of the cloth, is at his most incisive when commenting on the religious aspects of the *Aeneid*. Discussing the notion of *pietas*, he offers insights into concepts and practices peculiar to Roman religion.[60]

Particularly fruitful is his suggestion that Aeneas was a 'trained liturgiologist' and his definition of a *vir pius* as 'radically, a man who knows what sins or impurities need expiation, and what *piacula* are appropriate in each different case'.[61] One of the several episodes mentioned by Knox in which Aeneas demonstrates his proficiency in religious ritual is the burial of his old nurse Caieta (7.5). Another is Aeneas' anniversary celebration of his father's funeral (5.94–103). Recent critics have made similar observations. Paolo Pocetti observes that Virgil's precise use of religious language is evident in Aeneas's address at Pallas' funeral (11.97–8) when Aeneas uses a two-fold greeting, 'salve, vale', that corresponds to a formula used in funeral tablets of the late Republican period.[62] Aeneas, 'trained liturgiologist' that he was, appears, we may also add, to be following an established custom, the rending of clothes at 5.685–6, comparable to the practice described in the Old Testament.[63]

Virgil's depiction of Aeneas in this guise reveals, of course, that he, Virgil, was well versed in religious customs and ideas. In 7.41, indeed, Virgil, as part of his invocation to Erato, refers to himself as a *vates* and in 6.662 he associates poets with the priests of Elysium. Similarly, the Sibyl calls the legendary poet Musaeus 'vates' at 6.669. But Virgil was also familiar, though Knox did not trouble to make this point, with rituals in cultures other than those of Rome. He refers to religious practices and traditions in Cumae, Etruria, Italian sites (of Latium and Apulia) and Carthage. He alludes, as has been frequently noted, to both of the possible etymologies of the holy site of Cumae, seat of the Sibyl and traditionally the oldest Greek colony in Italy.[64] A further instance of Virgil's precision in such matters is his use of the term *haruspex*, which he reserves exclusively for Etruscan contexts. His religious sensibilities emerge with particular clarity in his description of Aeneas' arrival in Italy. Excavations from *Castrum Minervae* in Apulia have unearthed a statuette of Athena with a Phrygian helmet, no doubt a representation of Iliadic Athena, and an unusual monumental altar.[65] These finds recall the moment when Aeneas recounts that he prayed to Pallas Athena (3.544–5). The mention of Minerva's shrine in 3.530 is readily explained, given the fame of the shrine there to Anatolian Minerva.

Virgil's association of Dido with the moon is a recurrent theme throughout the poem.[66] In particular, Dido's wanderings as described by Virgil, play on the word *erro* and its connection with the moon.[67] This association of Dido with the moon demonstrates Virgil's familiarity with, not only, Ptolemaic religious practices, but Semitic ones too. An example of the former is Virgil's recourse to the Ptolemaic association of Cleopatra, Isis and Selene;[68] an example of the latter is the allusion to Tanith, the patron goddess of Carthage, in his image of the crescent moon (4.511–13; 6.453–4).[69] Finally, Virgil's description of Ornytus riding a Iapygian horse (11.678) indicates the central role that horses played in Iapygian religion. The name of the Iapygian divinity Menzanas meant in local Illyrian dialect 'lord of horses'.[70]

Eschatology

Pietas is the *leitmotiv* of the *Aeneid*, Knox comments, not merely because Aeneas is *pius* in the sense of 'master liturgiologist' or because Virgil is interested in religious rituals and traditions. Virgil's concept of *pietas* goes beyond, he wrote, 'mere scrupulosity, or gratuitous ritualism'. For Virgil it included the concept of loyalty, the role of free will in discerning and observing divine injunctions, deference to fate, the acceptance of collective destiny as well as the performance of purely moral, rather than distinctively religious, duty. In short, Knox concluded, Virgil moralized *pietas* and made the *Aeneid* a 'religious epic'.[71]

Evidence of this extended meaning of *pietas* can be found in Virgil's attention to the moral duties informing his eschatological outlook. Why critics found the eschatology of *Aeneid* 6 unsatisfactory baffled Knox and he would have been equally baffled by recent criticisms along the same lines.[72] He would have rejected any characterizations of Virgil's eschatology, to give a few recent examples, as an 'oscillating eschatological doctrine' or 'a masterpiece of eschatological bricolage', and would have dismissed claims that 'the rich range of inconsistencies [in Virgil's depiction of the underworld] do not suggest a poet aiming at the presentation of some system'.[73] He would have agreed instead with Friedrich Solmsen that Virgil did not, as some scholars maintained, envisage an underworld demarcated into three separate stages or 'phases' – Homeric, moral and philosophical – but rather created a consistent whole informed by Greek philosophical and religious ideas.[74]

Knox's position is not without merits. Virgil's Cerberus, it is true, is perhaps not completely immobile as Horsfall notes in his summary of inconsistencies; the rivers of Hades are at times turbulent, at other moments calm; and the degree to which the shades encountered by Virgil in the underworld were corporal or incorporeal is unclear. These minor discrepancies, however, are not symptomatic of more serious inconsistencies of the kind that some scholars have discerned in his eschatology. For example, O'Hara and Horsfall claim that Theseus is described as being present at 122–3 and also at 617–18, suggesting that he was in two places at once. However, the first of these two passages only describes Aeneas' reference to Theseus' attempt to abduct Persephone while he was still alive and return to the upper world. It does not imply that Theseus himself never left the underworld.[75] Again, Horsfall claims that during his encounter with the Sybil 'Aeneas refers to Lavinium' (6.84), certainly an anachronism, if true, since Lavinium had not yet been built.[76] It is, however, not Aeneas but the Sibyl who refers to the as yet unbuilt and unknown city. As a seer, she had the advantage of seeing into the future, a point that Conington had rightly made in his commentary some fifty years earlier.[77] Another failing of Virgil, according to some scholars, is his distribution of the Furies in more than one location in the underworld.[78] That Virgil, however, deliberately envisaged them in different locations is evident from 6.570, where Tisiphone 'calls' ('vocat') her sisters at 6.570 and, at 6.280, when he says that the Furies gather together in only one place, namely, their bedchambers in the vestibule of Hades, as far away as possible from the wailings of Tartarus.[79] Horsfall, too, finds fault with Virgil's disorderly arrangement of the Furies, claiming that 6.375 implies that the Furies are present or always linger by the river Styx. But this is not so. The line indicates only that the river is associated with them. In the introduction to his commentary on book 6, Horsfall points to another supposed incongruity, namely Sychaeus' presence in the *lugentes campi*, adding that he was – although Virgil does not explicitly say so – 'at Dido's side'.[80] Why, he asks, was he there, given that he did not die of love?[81] Sychaeus, we can reply, may be there as one of the *bello clari*.

Two more alleged inconsistencies mooted by present-day critics were in fact pre-empted in Knox's lectures. 'There are,' Horsfall notes, 'warriors at both 478 and 660, and judges at both 432 and 566.'[82] There is in fact a very good reason, as Knox points out, why there are two sets of warriors and two sets of judges. First, only warriors who lost their lives while fighting *pro patria* end up in Elysium as martyr patriots. Those, like Deiphobus, who died because they were caught up in the fighting are excluded. Not by chance, we can add, the Decii and the Elder Marcellus, who await metempsychosis in Elysium, died fighting for their country. They were instrumental in the development of the Roman empire and, more generally, humanity as a whole. Second, Minos judges those who died before their time and decides whether they should be assigned to the threshold of Tartarus, Tartarus or Elysium, while Rhadamantys decides only the punishment to be exacted on shades who are to be condemned to Tartarus for eternity.

Knox's understanding of Virgil's eschatology can be summarized as follows. All supernatural agencies, mythological or merely personified, who cause distress to mankind and who do not naturally belong to earth, occupy the *vestibulum*, which Knox calls the 'anteroom of hell'. There was no other place for them since they 'would be out of place in heaven, and yet could not be supposed to have deserved the punishments of hell'.[83] Most dead humans who lived for the time that the fates had allotted them end up in Tartarus, since they had committed in one way or another crimes of impiety. Rhadamantys assigns their punishments. Those who died before their allotted time, the ἄωροι, Dido being an example, are judged by Minos and his jury. Those about whom he cannot make up his mind, he assigns to the threshold of Tartarus for eternity, the *lugentes campi* being but one section of this region, the others being the 'circle' of those who committed suicide and the 'circle' of *bello clari*. Of those who reach Elysium, all are destined to undergo metempsychosis after several years of required purification and some years of convivial enjoyment for the span of a total of 1,000 years. How long the purification took depended on how they spent their lives on earth. This last stage is, perhaps, problematic because Virgil does not mention a third judge who determines how long the purification was to last. Possibly Virgil assumed that readers would supply the name of Aeacus, one of the three conventional judges of the underworld. Whatever the reason, Knox evidently thought that Virgil's eschatology was analogous to that of Dante Alighieri, Virgil's 'kindred spirit', as Knox called him. Tartarus corresponded to Hell and its threshold to Limbo; the process of purification through metempsychosis corresponded to Purgatory; and Elysium to Heaven.

Knox assumes, tentatively, that in Virgil's eschatological vision even Anchises, after a long sojourn of 999 years in Elysium, would be reincarnated.[84] Presumably, he surmised, the same would happen to Musaeus, Orpheus, Assaracus and other residents of the Elysium, referred to in book 6, who seem to be distinct from the shades that were about to drink from the river Lethe. He did not, however, rule out that Anchises should be thought of as residing in Elysium for eternity, an attractive option.[85] A third possibility is, therefore, worth considering, one that would reconcile Anchises' cosmogonic account of *ekpyrosis* (6.730–47, particularly 6.745–7) with what Aeneas learns of the underworld and its inhabitants. Those in Elysium who are not explicitly mentioned as undergoing reincarnation go back to the pure fire of soul after 1,000 years. In any case, what is remarkable in this context is how neatly Virgil (and possibly his unknown source or sources) has incorporated the Roman ideas of the *penates*, who are prominent in the *Aeneid* from its very start (1.6), and of *paterfamilias* into a coherent eschatological vision of the underworld. Assaracus, Ilus and Dardanus, all three inhabitants of Elysium, are there as 'fathers' of Rome. And it seems appropriate that the Trojans, Rome's ancestors (Assarachus, Dardanus and Ilus) should also be amongst the 'permanent residents' because they all improved the human condition ('quique sui memores aliquos fecere merendo', 6.664) by furthering the cause of Rome and spreading the benefits of its empire.

This 'fitness of things' that Knox identified in Virgil's eschatological vision is not, contrary to what has often been said, compromised by the presence of heroines grouped around Dido in the *lugentes campi*.[86] Knox made this point.[87] Their inclusion, he argued, in this section of 'limbo' (as he calls the threshold of Tartarus), where they experience only psychological anguish (*poena damni*) rather than physical punishment (*poena sensu*), can be explained by their having died 'of love' before their allotted time.[88] This, after all, had been the fate of Dido, as Virgil says at the moment of her demise (4.696–7). Such souls have committed a crime by ending their lives prematurely but their offence is 'palliated', as Knox put it, because they were overcome by an overpowering passion. Dido, for example, was guilty of impiety in not having duly considered fate, in having manipulated the oracles and in having obstructed the founding of Rome. The *magnus amor* that she suffered for Aeneas excused her decision to kill herself but only partially. Virgil chose his heroines with great care.[89] They had lived similar lives, ones that merited inclusion in the *lugentes campi*.[90] Phaedra's crime against Theseus and Hippolytus is qualified by her overwhelming passion for the latter, one that led her to commit suicide. She died of love. The similarity to Dido's fate is obvious, indeed Phaedra is clearly, at least in her *Hippolytus Kalyptomenos* persona, one of the main intertextual references for Dido's character. They are both victims of Aphrodite/Venus: both try, in vain, to resist passion through a sense of αἰδώς/*pudor*; both feel betrayed by someone close to them; and both are guilty of vengeful deceit at the point of death. That Phaedra should be the first amongst the heroines that Virgil mentions, is then, unsurprising. Procris, the next to appear, also died for love in that her intense ἔρως for her husband Cephalus led her to spy on him while he was out hunting, with the result that he mistook her for a wild animal and shot her. There is, possibly, a further resemblance to Dido. Cephalus seduced Procris in disguise and so, we might surmise, Procris felt deceived by him, as Dido by Aeneas.[91] Eriphyle, too, exemplifies the destructive power of ἔρως; in her case for a necklace[92] – one that ruined her family and led to her premature death at her son's hand. Evadne, who, like Dido, leapt into the flames of her husband's, Capaneus', pyre, is another victim of ἔρως.[93] Hyginus (*Fabulae* 243) reports Evadne threw herself on the same pyre as did her husband, which suggests that Virgil wanted us to think that Dido intended to die with Aeneas in the same manner. Laodamia, dominated by her passion for her husband Protesilaos, who died in the Trojan war, tried to evade the fates 'in expecting her husband to be restored to her' and, unrequited, committed suicide. Virgil may have been alluding here to Hyginus' version of the myth (*Fabulae* 104), where Hyginus recounts that Laodamia followed into a pyre the statue that she had made of her husband and kept in her chamber *sub simulatione sacrorum*. Laodamia's statue of her husband recalls Dido's *effigies* of Aeneas at 4.508.[94] Further, both Laodamia and Dido, following a short-lived worldly ἔρως, longed to rejoin their husbands in the underworld. Pasiphae appears among the group of heroines in the *lugentes campi*, no doubt on account of the destructive ἔρως with which the gods cursed her.[95] In Euripides' *Cretans* she defends herself by declaring that she acted under the influence of the gods (Cretans frag. 472e.6–20).[96] Like the other heroines chosen by Virgil, Pasiphae was therefore not fully responsible for her actions. It could be argued that she does not fit well in this group since the other heroines *died* 'of love', while the only information we have suggests that Pasiphae died from illness. However, if Minos' attempt to have her punished for her love of the bull – again mentioned in Euripides' *Cretans* – was consummated, she too must have died before her allotted time. Finally, just before Dido's entrance, Caeneus appears, though according to what rationale is unclear. Hyginus 14.242 speaks of a tradition according to which Caeneus preferred to commit suicide rather than be 'killed' by the Centaurs, as in Ovid (*Met.* 12.510–35). Did Virgil include him as a victim of ἔρως inasmuch as he yearned to change sex and so change his true nature?[97] Or does his presence allude to Dido's change of roles, from queen to a *virago* leader and back again?[98]

Less convincing is Knox's interpretation of 6.743–4 as a parenthetic aside in which Anchises describes how souls were purified before reaching Elysium.[99] True, Virgil often includes parenthetical asides in speeches, but Knox's suggestion is perhaps overly ingenious, prompted by a wish to exclude purification from Elysium on principle. A forced reading of this kind, however, is not, as we have seen, required to save the consistency of Virgil's accounts of the underworld and of the fates of the souls inhabiting it. Knox does allow that Anchises might have stayed in Elysium and, if that is the case, the vulgate makes sense, as long as we allow for a period of purification through fire and water somewhere within the Elysian fields.

Glimmers of Christianity

It was not Knox's intention to make a Christian of Virgil. What fascinated him were the glimmers of Christian revelation which, he said, were 'naturally' present in Virgil's treatment of morality, the afterlife and human commerce with the gods in the *Aeneid*. He defined Virgil as 'naturally Catholic', as someone who could perceive the difference between a mortal and a tolerable offence in the same way in which Catholics distinguish 'between mortal and venial sins', and he envisaged a place of purgation, comparable to Purgatory, where souls went 'through some form of punishment'.[100] In two passages Virgil appears, he wrote, 'quite startlingly Christian'.[101] 'One is the Sibyl's account of how a Fury with a whip extorts confessions of all the souls in Tartarus of all the crimes' (6.567–9). 'It is not everywhere,' he comments 'that you can find a heathen poet expounding the disastrous consequences of dying with unconfessed mortal sin on your conscience. It is not merely unconfessed crimes, it is unconfessed *piacula*, sins which demand some sort of ceremonial purification.'[102] Christian presentiments are especially evident in an unnoticed detail in Virgil's account of Elysium. On meeting Aeneas, Anchises praises him for his filial obedience for having descended to the Underworld and reveals that he has been aware of his son's sufferings in the world above. Anchises enjoyed, Knox concluded, a state in afterlife akin to that of a beatified saint. He knew of 'no other case in the classics, where knowledge of what is going on in the world is attributed to the departed, even to those who have attained Elysium'.[103]

True to this viewpoint, Knox drew parallels between the *Aeneid* and Scripture. Nisus and Euryalus, he wrote, were the 'David and Jonathan' of the *Aeneid*. He compared Iulus/ Ascanius to Solomon and David to Aeneas. 'It was not David, but Solomon,' he explains, 'who built the house, it was not Aeneas but Iulus who founded the first permanent city of Alba Longa' (1.271, 5.597 etc.).[104] Aeneas' actions, Knox seems to imply, were at times questionable, like those of David, whereas those of Iulus/Ascanius were unimpeachable like Solomon's. Again, 'the Trojans, no less than Israel', he observed, 'are a chosen people, with a land of promise: Aeneas, like Abraham or David, have promises they can claim: the Lord hath made a faithful oath unto David, and he shall not shrink from it'.[105] The relationship between the gods and the exiled Trojans, so essential to Virgil's concept of *pietas*, is a pact, Knox observes, like the Biblical covenant between God and the Israelites, with the qualification that the former relates to justice, whereas the latter relates to divine mercy. On one occasion, however, the difference almost vanishes. Appealing to Jupiter, Aeneas says, 'si quid pietas antiqua labores /respicit humanos' (If somehow ancient *pietas* looks upon humans) (5.688–9). Here the idea of justice has apparently acquired the broader sense of its etymological derivative, 'pity', in the sense of compassion. 'We can almost hear,' Knox comments, 'the Jew speaking: "Remember, O Lord, thy loving-kindnesses, which have been ever of old."'[106]

Five years later, in *A Spiritual Aeneid*, these glimmers of Christianity, apparent both in Virgil's choice of phrase and in the grand story of Aeneas' journey to fulfilment, would enlighten his account of his passage to Catholicism.[107]

Notes

* I should like to thank Alessandro Schiesaro and the anonymous reviewer of the Bloomsbury Academic Press for their comments on drafts of this paper.
1 James O'Hara suggests that Coleridge's criticism might have been prompted by Wordsworth's translation of *Aeneid* 1 and that he simply meant that much is lost in Virgil if read in translation. See James J. O'Hara, 'Virgil's Style', in *The Cambridge Companion to Virgil*, ed. Charles Martindale (Cambridge: Cambridge University Press, 1997), 241.
2 See Chapter 4 in this volume, Ronald Knox, 'Virgil's Art and Treatment of his Story', 110: 'And then remember that imbecile criticism by Coleridge'; and Chapter 8 in this volume, 'Characteristics of Virgil's Style and Versification', 159: 'a particularly idiotic comment by Coleridge'.
3 See Chapter 1 in this volume, Ronald Knox, 'Virgil's Political Outlook', 57.
4 Penelope Fitzgerald, *The Knox Brothers* (London: Flamingo, 2002), 50. They sent the letter in an envelope with 'five dried orange pips', an allusion to a threat letter in the detective story entitled 'The Five Orange Pips' by Conan Doyle, first published in *The Strand Magazine* in November 1891. The episode is discussed in greater detail by Michael J. Crowe in his introduction to his collection of five writings on Sherlock Holmes by Knox in *Ronald Knox and Sherlock Holmes: The Origin of Sherlockian Studies*, ed. Michael J. Crowe (Indianapolis: Gasogene Books, 2011), 7.
5 Ibid., 34.
6 See Chapter 7 in this volume, Ronald Knox, 'Notes on the Composition of Book III', 156, where Knox makes, independently, the same objection as Servius in his commentary to line 590 of the *Aeneid*; see Servius, *In Vergilii Aeneidos librum tertium*, line 590.
7 Knox noted, as he put it, 'a curious want of firmness' in Virgil's handling of the plot of books 7–9. See Virgil, *Aeneid Books VII to IX*, partly in the original and partly in English verse translation. Introduction and translation by R. A. Knox (Oxford: Clarendon Press, 1924), 9–10.
8 Knox, 'Notes', Chapter 7 in this volume, 153–4, explains that, in principle, both Thrace and Crete qualify as Aeneas' destination ('terra Hesperia') since they both lie west of Troy. Creusa's prophetic and enigmatic reference to a 'Lydian Thybris' (2.780–1) would have been interpreted by Aeneas as an injunction to seek a land nearby. For a recent assertion that line 2.780ff. is problematic, see Marianne Shiebe

Wifstrand, 'The Discrepancy between *Aeneid* Book 2 and Book 3 in the Light of the Narrative Structure of the *Aeneid*', delivered at the Vergil Conference in Tromsø on 9 May 2008, available online (5). The lecture is a revised version of her article of the same title that appeared in *Eranos* 81(1983): 113–16.

9   John Conington, 'Commentary' in Virgil, *Opera*, with a commentary by John Conington, 2nd edn, 3 vols (London: Whittaker, 1872 [1858–71]), vol. 2, 192. Robert B. Lloyd, '*Aeneid* III and the Aeneas Legend', *The American Journal of Philology* 78 (1957): 386–7, n. 27, argues that Virgil extended the duration of Aeneas' travels beyond the original two years of the legend. Virgil, I would suggest, wanted the voyage to last seven years in order to match the prophetic significance of the number seven that recurs throughout the poem: the seven kings and hills of Rome (6.783), the seven ships that Aeneas collects after a storm (1.170), the seven stags that he brings down (1.192–4), the seven coils of the serpent (5.84–6) and the seven layers of Aeneas' shield (8.447–9). On the significance of the number seven in the *Aeneid*, see Lee M. Fratantuono and R. Alden Smith, 'Commentary' in Virgil, *Aeneid 5*, text, translation and commentary by Lee M. Fratantuono and R. Alden Smith (Leiden: Brill, 2015), 190–2. For coincidences of the significant number seven with the line numbers of the *Aeneid*, see O. A. W. Dilke, 'Do Line Totals in the Aeneid Show a Preoccupation with Significant Numbers?', *Classical Quarterly* 17, no. 2 (1967): 323, 325. Dilke argues that the coincidences are not casual.

10 Knox, 'Notes', Chapter 7 in this volume, 156. Knox also endorses the assumption that the 'space of time during which Aeneas was on the high seas was one of 7 years' (ibid., 152).

11 Elena Giusti suggests that Virgil intentionally included this discrepancy in order to signal the 'fictitious nature' of the trip to Carthage and show that he was aware of the chronological gap between the mythical Aeneas and Dido; see Elena Giusti, *Carthage in Virgil's* Aeneid: *Staging the Enemy under Augustus* (Cambridge: Cambridge University Press, 2018), 173.

12 See Chapter 4 in this volume, Knox, 'Virgil's Art', 98–9. Knox seems to believe that there was only one, as he puts it, 'indiscretion' in the cave. Aeneas' 'arma', 'exuviae omnes' and 'lectus iugalis' (4.495–6) suggests there was possibly more than one. Potter argues that Aeneas was in Carthage for no longer than ninety days; see Franklin H. Potter, 'How Long was Aeneas at Carthage?', *The Classical Journal* 21 (1926): 623. Giusti, *Carthage*, 272–3, notes that Potter's explanation has not convinced Virgil scholars. Nineteenth-century scholars of the *Aeneid* did not find it difficult to reconcile the chronological indications in book 1 and book 5. Conington, for example, commented that Aeneas had left probably 'as winter was drawing on'; see Conington, 'Commentary' in Virgil, *Opera*, with a commentary by John Conington, 2nd edn, 3 vols (London: Whittaker,1972 [1858–71]), vol. 2, 188.

13 Knox, 'Virgil's Art', Chapter 4 in this volume, 98.

14 Giusti, *Carthage*, 171–2. Fratantuono and Smith suggest that Virgil's intention was to present the episode 'as if the interlude with Dido never happened'; see Fratantuono and Smith, 'Commentary', 593. This conflicts with the fact that Virgil mentions the presents from Dido that the Trojans carried with them, not once, but three times (5.570–2, 9.266 and 11.72–5).

15 Knox, 'Virgil's Art', Chapter 4 in this volume, 99.

16 Potter, 'How Long', 622.

17 See Chapter 6 in this volume, Ronald Knox, 'Virgil's Use of his Sources', 148. Lloyd refers to such a process, which he traces back to Cato, as backward 'illusional projection'; see Lloyd, '*Aeneid III*', 388; and also, Francis Henry Sandbach, 'Anti-Antiquarianism in the *Aeneid*', Virgil Society Lecture, no. 77 (19 March 1966), 36–7.

18 Ibid., 32–3.

19 Anne Rogerson, *Virgil's Ascanius: Imagining the Future in the Aeneid* (Cambridge: Cambridge University Press, 2017), 79–86, esp. n. 2.

20 Christine Perkell, 'Commentary' in Virgil, *Aeneid 3* (Newburyport: Focus Publishing, 2008), 84, and Benjamin Thomason, 'Aeneid III. Aeneas' Voyage Through Imperium' (MA diss., University of Georgia, Atlanta 2004), 115.

21 Roman triumphal processions incorporated the two elements of the omen that the horses provided, i.e. successful strife and hope of peace.

22 Fratantuono speaks instead of a wolf skull; see Leo Fratantuono, 'The Wolf in Virgil', *Revue des études anciennes* 120, no. 1 (2018): 117. But Fratantuono does not observe that the skull must have been removed.

23 Duncan B. Campbell, 'How to Dress a Standard-bearer. Animal Pelts in the Roman Army', *Ancient Warfare Magazine* 12, no. 3 (October/November 2018): 46–9.

24 Francesco Montarese, 'Ronald Knox as Classicist', in *Ronald Knox: A Man for All Seasons*, ed. Francesca Bugliani Knox (Toronto: Pontifical Institute of Medieval Studies, 2016), 57.

25 *Aeneid* 1.167; 1.201; 2.307; 3.84, etc.

26 For the use of *testudo* and the number seven to evoke contemporary Rome, see, respectively, n. 18 and n. 9 above. Virgil's use of the words *toga* and *vitta* is also relevant. Jupiter and Juno predict that the Roman people in years to come will wear the *toga* (1.282 and 12.825). *Vittae* are worn by poets, prophets, inventors and other benefactors of humanity in Elysium (6.665) as well as by the suppliant Latins (7.237) and even by the Greeks in 2.133, who are reported to be about to perform the sacrifice of Sinon according to Roman ritual. At 4.637–8 Dido tells Sychaeus' nurse Barce to put on the *vitta* and then begins to dedicate her offerings to Jupiter. The implication here is that Augustus' golden age will bring together lands which are culturally connected by virtue of being all descended from Jupiter and worship him.

27 See Chapter 5 in this volume, Ronald Knox, 'Virgil's Appreciation of Scenery', 115.

28 LSJ and the *Oxford Latin Dictionary*, s.v. *turritus*, give the meaning of 'in the form of towers'.
29 Knox, 'Virgil's Appreciation of Scenery', Chapter 5 in this volume, 116. See S. J. Heyworth and J. H. W. Morwood, 'Commentary' in Virgil, *Aeneid 3*, with an introduction and a commentary by Heyworth and Morwood (Oxford: Oxford University Press, 2017), 219.
30 Virgil's description matches the archaeology exactly and it is unlikely to be a coincidence. On Castrum Minervae, see Francesco D'Andria, *Castrum Minervae* (Lecce: Congedo Editore, 2009).
31 Michael C. J. Putnam, *Virgil's Aeneid: Interpretation and Influence* (Chapel Hill: University of North Carolina Press, 1995), 60. It is not easy to see what Horsfall had in mind when he wrote 'there would be no sense or purpose in a fortified harbour at this spot (in the text, or on the coast, so near Hydruntum)'. In fact Hydruntum was not especially close. The two settlements are roughly fifteen miles apart along the coast. See Nicholas Horsfall, 'Commentary' in Virgil, *Aeneid 3*, with a commentary by Nicholas Horsfall (Leiden: Brill, 2006), 378. The parallel with *Odyssey* 13.97ff. quoted by Horsfall (ibid.), which is no doubt at the back of Virgil's mind here, is not instructive as far as the meaning of *turriti* is concerned.
32 A passage in Pliny the Younger, *Letters* 2.17, suggests that Laurentum probably stood on a hill.
33 The ancient town of Abella was about ten kilometres northeast of Nola. Virgil considered its territory to be infertile in corn but rich in fruit trees, especially apples.
34 Knox, 'Virgil's Appreciation of Scenery', Chapter 5 in this volume, 115.
35 For other recurring images of turrets and of collapsing towers see, for example *Aeneid* 2.240–7; 9.530–44; 9.46; 9.470–1; 9.575; 9.678; 10.121 and 12.672–5.
36 See Chapter 6 in this volume, Knox, 'Virgil's Use of His Sources', 145.
37 Nicholas Horsfall, 'Camilla, o i limiti dell'invenzione', *Athenaeum* 66 (1988): 31 and n. 6; Barbara Weiden Boyd, 'Virgil's Camilla and the Traditions of Catalogue and Ecphrasis (*Aeneid* 7.803–17)', *American Journal of Philology* 113 (1992): 214–15, 217–18.
38 The death of Herodotus' Masistias (*Histories* 9.22) and possibly that of Artybius (ibid., 5.122) resemble the death of Mezentius in the *Aeneid* (10. 892–4). In both cases death is brought about by a beloved horse rearing after it is shot. By this allusion, Virgil signals the importance of Mezentius' contribution to the Italian cause, comparable to the role that Masistias made at Plataea and Artybius on Cyprus.
39 See note 9 above; and also, Robert Deryck Williams, 'Commentary' in Virgil, *Aeneidos liber quintus*, edited with a commentary by Robert Deryck Williams (Oxford: Clarendon Press 1960), 60.
40 Montarese, 'Ronald Knox', 154–7.
41 It was unusual for anyone else but the priests or interpreters to carry out the sacrifice or inspect entrails.

42 For the kings of Sparta conducting sacrifices in person was a regular occurrence, indeed a duty – provided the sacrifices were scrutinized by the ephors. In fact, Cleomenes is a repeat offender when it comes to sacrilege, as he makes a mockery of the failure of extispicy when about to cross the river Erasinus (*Histories* 6.76).

43 E.g. Tacitus, *Histories* 1.29 on Galba, who 'sacris intentus fatigabat ... deos' (while intent on sacrificing, vexed the gods).

44 Nicholas Horsfall, 'Dido in the Light of History', *Proceedings of the Virgil Society* 13 (1974): 4–6.

45 See Chapter 8 in this volume, Knox, 'Characteristics of Virgil's Style and Versification', 168.

46 Even in the phrases *magnus orbs* (1.602) and the *magnum [mare] Ionium* (3.211), the adjective *magnus* can be interpreted to denote something other than physical size.

47 Knox, 'Characteristics of Virgil's Style', Chapter 8 in this volume, 168.

48 Ibid.

49 Horsfall appears to take *magnus* here as referring to size; see Nicholas Horsfall, 'Commentary' in Virgil, *Aeneid* 6, with an introduction commentary by Nicholas Horsfall, 2 vols (Berlin: De Gruyter 2013), vol. 2, 105.

50 Knox, 'Characteristics of Virgil's Style, Chapter 8 in this volume, 168.

51 The ingenious comparison with Pasiphae's *amor* for her son was first proposed by Brooks Otis, *Virgil: A Study in Civilized Poetry* (Oxford: Clarendon Press, 1964), 284 (and nn. 1 and 2). Alessandro Lagioia, 'Le ali del mito: Dedalo in glosse fra tardoantico e Medioevo', in *Risonanze. Forme e contenuti della memoria dell'antico*, eds Giovanni Cipriani and Antonella Tedeschi (Foggia: Il Castello, 2014), 208, rejects Otis's view on the basis that there is no evidence in literature or art of Pasiphae's love for her son. He overlooks the Apulian red-figure kylix (fourth-century BC), held in the Bibliothèque nationale de France, which shows Pasiphae lovingly holding the infant Minotaur, and, more importantly, a fragment of Euripides' *Cretans*, where someone informs Minos that Pasiphae breastfeeds the Minotaur as an infant (fr. 472). Horsfall, 'Commentary' in Virgil, *Aeneid* 6, 9, argues that 'magnus amor' cannot be a mother's love for her son. However, Venus uses this phrase to refer to her and Dido's 'amor' for Aeneas (1.675).

52 Conington, 'Commentary' in Virgil, *Opera*, with a commentary by John Conington, 2nd edn, 3 vols (London: Whittaker, 1972 [1858–71]), vol. 2, 424, and Sergio Casali, 'Aeneas and the Doors of the Temple of Apollo', *Classical Journal* 91 (1955): 1–9.

53 Pasiphae looks on when Dido and Aeneas meet in Hades (6.447 and 6.450). Rebecca Armstrong, 'Crete in the *Aeneid*: Recurring Trauma and Alternative Fate', *Classical Quarterly* 52, no.1 (2002): 330–1, suggests a Dido–Crete link and, more specifically, a Dido–Pasiphae association. The idea behind such an association could be a monstrous erotic union; see Horsfall, 'Commentary' in Virgil, *Aeneid* 6, 336. The union of Dido and Aeneas, i.e. the union of Carthage and Rome, would be a

monstruous union politically and militarily, or, to quote Philip R. Hardie, *Virgil's Aeneid: Cosmos and Imperium* (Oxford: Clarendon Press,1986), 272-3, a 'bizarre perversion of the cosmic setting', referring to the cave scene, with 'the most serious disruption of the moralised natural order'.

54 Knox, 'Characteristics of Virgil's Style', Chapter 8 in this volume, 167-8.

55 Casali, 'Aeneas and the Doors', 5.

56 Venus herself refers to the episode at *Aeneid*, 10.29. For the connection between the *amor* that Venus feels for Aeneas and the one that Dido feels for Aeneas, see Alessandro Schiesaro, 'Emotions and Memory in Virgil's *Aeneid*', *Bulletin of the Institute of Classical Studies* (2015): 175. Moreover, sinister allusions have been suggested. Philip Hardie, following Ellen Oliensis, 'Freud's Aeneid', *Vergilius* 47 (2001): 39-63, detects incestuous undertones in the presentation of Dido's *amor* for Aeneas as akin to Venus' love for him; see Philip Hardie, 'Virgil's Ptolemaic Relations', *The Journal of Roman Studies* 96 (2006): 26. Schiesaro, 'Emotions and Memory', 175 emphasizing the blurring of Venus' and Dido's *amor*, notes the verbal links (especially through the use of the word *crudelis*) between the Venus-Aeneas encounter in book 1 and *Eclogues* 8.46-50, an account of infanticide. If such Oedipal substitution of Dido for Venus is to be accepted, the intertext may possibly create an aura of danger surrounding Dido as potentially capable of infanticide. On Dido's language of infanticide and the reported practice of infanticide amongst Carthaginians, see Alessandro Schiesaro, 'Under the Sign of Saturn: Dido's Kulturkampf', in *La Représentation du temps dans la poésie augustéenne - Zur Poetik der Zeit in augusteischer Dichtung*, ed. Jürgen Paul Schwindt (Heidelberg: Universitätsverlag Winter, 2005), 91, especially n. 30.

57 Although the concept is a positive one, indicating as it does paternal love, the expression is used here in a context where such an *amor* is being satisfied deceitfully, through *dolus*.

58 Note here the coincidence with the murder of Sychaeus 'ante aras' (At the altar) (1.349).

59 Roma as an anagram of 'amor' was a well-known wordplay in Rome; see Mathias Hanses, 'Love's Letters: an Amor-Roma Telestich at Ovid, *Ars Amatoria* 3.507-10', in *Wordplay and Powerplay in Latin Poetry*, eds Philip Mitsis and Ioannis Ziogas (Berlin: De Gruyter, 2016), 205.

60 See Chapter 2 in this volume, Ronald Knox, 'Virgil's Religious Outlook', 62-3.

61 Ibid, 63.

62 Paolo Poccetti, 'Greeting and Farewell Expressions as Evidence for Colloquial Language: Between Literary and Epigraphical Texts', in *Colloquial and Literary Latin*, eds Eleanor Dickey and Anna Chahoud (Cambridge: Cambridge University Press, 2010), 106-7.

63 E.g. Josh. 7.6; 2 Sam. 13.19; Job 1.20, 2.12.

64 Susan Skulsky, 'The Sibyl's Rage and the Marpessan Rock', *The American Journal of Philology* 108, no. 1 (Spring, 1987), 58.
65 D'Andria, *Castrum Minervae*.
66 The moon is in the background when Aeneas meets his mother Venus in Dido's land. Here he mistakes Venus in disguise to be possibly Diana (1.328-9), the deity most readily associated with the moon. We find moon imagery for Penthesileia on the temple of Juno in Carthage at 1.490 and at 1.499 (where Diana now becomes a simile for Dido); at 1.742 Iopas sings of the moon at Dido's court; at 4.80-1 we find 'luna obscura'; at 4.511 'tria ora virginis Dianae' and at 4.513-14 'messae ad lunam herbae'; and most famously at 6.454, so that the moon illuminates both Dido's first entrance (1.499) and her final departure under Aeneas' gaze (6.454-6). There may be a veiled allusion to the moon also in the 'volvens sanguineam aciem', taking account of the shape of the pupils of the eye, used for Dido at 4.643, in view of Ovid's 'cornua sanguineae lunae' in *Amores* 2.1.23. For the examples above, see Clifford Webber, 'Intimations of Dido and Cleopatra in Some Contemporary Portrayals of Elizabeth I', *Studies in Philology* 96 (1999): 132-5; Hardie, 'Virgil's Ptolemaic Relations', 29-31; and Lee Fratantuono, 'Recens a vulnere: Dido, Ajax, and the Hierarchy of Heroines', *Quaderni urbinati di cultura classica* 106 (2014), 187-8.
67 James D. Reed, and James J. O'Hara follow Timaeus' claim that the Libyans applied the name Dido to the queen because of her wanderings. They also follow the *Etymologicum magnum* in supposing that her name in Phoenician has a meaning equivalent to the Greek πλανῆτις, resulting in Virgil's etymological wordplay on the verb *erro* applied to Dido (4.68-9 [cf. 72], 211, 363-4, 684, 691) and his description of Dido's final 'wandering' appearance in 6.450-4; see James D. Reed, *Virgil's Gaze: Notion and Poetry in the* Aeneid (Princeton: Princeton University Press, 2007), 94; and James J. O'Hara, *True Names: Vergil and the Alexandrian Tradition of Etymological Wordplay* (Ann Arbour: University of Michigan Press, 2017), 173.
68 On Cleopatra, Isis and Selene, see Hardie, 'Virgil's Ptolemaic Relations', 32.
69 On Tanith/Tinnit, see Mark A. Christian, 'Phoenician Maritime Religion: Sailors, Goddess Worship, and the Grotta Regina', *Die Welt des Orients* 43 (2013): 192-5, for evidence of: 1) Tanith's association with the crescent moon; and 2) Tanith as protectress of sailors, just as Dido is in charge of the sailing from Tyre to found a new colony. On Tanith and Dido, see further Ralph Hexter, 'Sidonian Dido', in *Innovations of Antiquity*, ed. Ralph Hexter and Daniel Selden (New York and London: Routledge, 1992), 348-50.
70 Martin L. West, *Indo-European Poetry and Myth* (Oxford: Oxford University Press, 2007), 137.
71 Knox, 'Virgil's Religious Outlook', Chapter 2 in this volume, 83.
72 Ibid, 71.

73 Horsfall, 'Introduction' in Virgil, *Aeneid 6*, xxi, xxv–xxvi. Horsfall, referring (xxiv, n. 1) to Hermann Henselmann, Brooks Otis, James O'Hara and other like-minded critics, continues: 'Virgil writes with a certain disregard [. . .] for precise harmonisation of detail and elimination of inconsistencies. It is perhaps even more important always to bear in mind that we have no reason to suppose that Virgil is attempting to present some sort of creed or belief; that would make the centre of *Aeneid* 6 entirely unlike everything else he wrote.' Horsfall then proceeds to dismiss Solmsen's view – without argument (xxv, n. 1). It would however be odd for a poet who carefully organizes the encounters in Aeneas' *katabasis* so that he can review and retrace his life, to be satisfied with an inconsistent eschatology.

74 Friedrich Solmsen, 'Greek Ideas of the Hereafter in Virgil's Roman Epic', *Proceedings of the American Philosophical Society* 112, no. 1 (February 15, 1968), 14, has been overlooked or dismissed without argument by those suggesting that Virgil might have intentionally introduced inconsistencies. See also Friedrich Solmsen, 'The World of the Dead in Book 6 of the *Aeneid*', *Classical Philology*, vol. 7, no. 1 (January 1972), 31–41. Solmsen's views have much to commend them.

75 James J. O'Hara, *Inconsistency in Roman Epic: Studies in Catullus, Lucretius, Vergil, Ovid and Lucan. Roman Literature and its Contexts* (Cambridge: Cambridge University Press, 2007), 91: 'Did Theseus return from the Underworld, as is implied by 6.122, or does he sit forever in Tartarus?' Also Horsfall, 'Introduction', in *Aeneid 6*, xxv, stresses the inconsistency: 'Theseus is present at 122f. and 617f.' Since Aeneas mentions Theseus together with Orpheus and Hercules (6.119–24), both of whom came back alive from the underworld, Virgil presumably thought that Theseus returned to the upper world and only later, on his death, was condemned to Tartarus for eternity.

76 Horsfall, however, seems to have changed his view in the commentary that follows his introduction (ibid., 122).

77 Conington, 'Commentary' in Virgil, *Opera*, with a commentary by John Conington, 2nd edn, 3 vols (London: Whittaker, 1972 [1858–71]), vol. 2, 430.

78 O'Hara, *Inconsistency*, p. 91; Horsfall too finds fault with the way that the Furies were 'all spread generously about the Underworld 280, 375, 555, 571', but they are not mentioned in Virgil's account of Elysium and the *lugentes campi*. See Horsfall, 'Introduction' in Virgil, *Aeneid 6*, vol. 1, xxiv.

79 Tisiphone is an exception in that she never sleeps. She is always busy punishing the guilty (6.555–6).

80 Horsfall, 'Commentary' in Virgil, *Aeneid 6*, vol. 2, 336.

81 Horsfall, however, appears to have changed his mind in his accompanying commentary, where he challenges earlier objections to Sychaeus' presence in *lugentes campi* on the grounds that he was murdered and his lifespan therefore had been cut short; see ibid., 353.

82 Horsfall, 'Introduction', ibid., xxv; cf. Knox, 'Virgil's Religious Outlook', Chapter 2 in this volume, 71, 75.
83 Ibid, 72.
84 Ibid, 80–1.
85 The expression 'amoena piorum/concilia Elysiumque colo' (5.734–5) used by the ghost Anchises to describe his current abode should perhaps be read as a hendiadys, 'gatherings of the blessed in Elysium'. Perhaps the shades that abide motionless by the river Lethe have a different location in Elysium because they are not as *pii* as the 'blessed'.
86 Horsfall deems that 'Virgil's victims of love as *comparandae* for Dido are a bizarre, disunited collection', despite acknowledging earlier on the same page that 'all their lives are in some way incomplete'; see Horsfall, 'Introduction' in Virgil, *Aeneid 6*, vol. 1, xx. He further remarks that 'the victims of love are a particularly 'untidy' group' (442 ff.), blameless and scandalous, suicides and not' (ibid., xxv). According to Aldo Setaioli, the permanence of the shades in the *lugentes campi* is irreconcilable with metempsychosis since Virgil's eschatological scheme should match the considerably later testimony of Tertullian, *De anima*, 56, which refers to a theory according to which the souls of those who died before their allotted time are bound to remain in Limbo for the natural span of their lives, after which time they move on to purgation; see Aldo Setaioli, 'Inferi', *Enciclopedia virgiliana*, 5 vols in 6 pts (Rome: Istituto dell'Enciclopedia Italiana, 1984–1991), vol. 2, 956–7. But Virgil never suggests that the shades in the *lugentes campi* will move somewhere else. Horsfall, 'Introduction' in Virgil, *Aeneid 6*, vol. 1, xxvi, points out there is 'no indication whatsoever' of the duration of their stay. The strong Odyssean mould of the heroines, however, suggests perhaps that, like their Homeric counterparts, they reside in the *lugentes campi* for eternity.
87 Knox, 'Virgil's Religious Outlook', Chapter 2 in this volume, 74–5.
88 Ibid. According to Jacques Perret, 'Les compagnes de Didon aux Enfers (*Aen*. VI, 445–9), *Revue des études latines* 42 (1964): 260, the common failing of this group of heroines was love, seen as 'source d'une limitation, un pacte vers la terre, d'une fondamentale impureté. Évadné, dans cette perspective, ne fuit pas moins serve que Pasiphaé'.
89 Virgil's list is much shorter than Homer's comprehensive list of heroines in *Odyssey* XI and has more sinister undertones, as appropriate for the *campi lugentes*. Divine ἔρως, a positive force behind many of Homer's mothers of famous heroes, is not celebrated in Virgil. Indeed, it seems only to be considered an attenuating factor preventing them from being relegated to Tartarus. Pasiphae and Caeneus are not in Homer. Phaedra, Procris and Eriphyle appear in Homer, with the last receiving the most negative characterization of the three.
90 Giovanni Garbugino considers the possibility that, as suggested by earlier critics, the list derives from a lost Hellenistic source that fused Homeric and Euripidean heroines; see Giovanni Garbugino, 'Evadne', *Enciclopedia virgiliana*, 5 vols in 6 pts

(Rome: Istituto dell'Enciclopedia Italiana, 1984–91), vol. 2, 437. It would be a remarkable coincidence, however, if Virgil's heroines in the *lugentes campi* all related neatly to the story of Dido only by accident.

91 Other points of contact that critics have noted relate to the arrow wound that both heroines experience, and in particular its accidental origin. This may recall the simile of 4.69–72 where the shepherd accidently shoots the doe with an arrow; see Horsfall, 'Commentary' in Virgil, *Aeneid 6*, vol. 2, 335.

92 The expression 'amor auri' appears in 1.349, where Pygmalion is presented as 'auri caecus amore'.

93 Horsfall, ibid., 335, argues that 'neither Evadne's place in the group, nor her relevance to Dido, are quite clear'. This is perhaps a bit harsh, though he is right in remarking that the wounds Evadne has in common with Dido are not enough in themselves to justify her presence in the group. In any case, we do not need to justify Evadne's presence in the group by supposing Virgil was following a tradition, one of which there is no trace, that depicted her as in love with Polynices; see ibid., 335–6.

94 Laodamia, under pretence of secret rites, devoted herself to the statue. This may well be in the background of Dido's behaviour in the 'magic section' of book 4, in which she pretends to enact a charm to end love, but actually brings a curse on the traitor, as Alessandro Schiesaro, following A.-M. Tupet, suggests; see Anne-Marie Tupet, 'Dido magicienne', *Revue des études latines* 48 (1970): 229–58, 252–3 and Alessandro Schiesaro, 'Furthest Voices in Virgil's Dido', *Studi italiani di filologia classica*, vol. 6, no. 2 (2008): 210–11. This has been challenged by Gabriel A. F. Silva, 'Magic and Memory. Dido's Ritual for Inducing Forgetfulness in Aeneid 4', *Mnemosyne* 73 (2020): 1–14, unconvincingly in my view.

95 The expression 'Veneris monumenta nefandae' early on in the sixth book (6.26) in relation to Pasiphae has already set the theme, i.e. that of the destructive consequences of un-controllable ἔρως. On the Dido–Pasiphae associations, see above n. 53. Pasiphae in Euripides' *Cretans* may have been the prototype of Euripides' Phaedra; see Adele-Teresa Cozzoli, *Euripide: Cretesi. Introduzione, testimonianze, testo critico, traduzione e commento* (Rome: Istituti Editoriali e Poligrafici Internazionali, 2001), 9.

96 See also David Sansone, 'Euripides. Cretans frag. 472e. 16–26 Kannicht', *Zeitschrift für Papyrologie und Epigraphik* 184 (2013): 58–65.

97 Grace Starry West, 'Caeneus and Dido', *Transactions of the American Philological Association* 110 (1980), 316–17.

98 Horsfall, 'Introduction' and 'Commentary' in Virgil, *Aeneid 6*, vol. 1, xxvi, vol. 2, 337. West, 'Caeneus', 323, observes that the fact that Caeneus' last transformation was not fully successful, as shown by the lack of grammatical agreement in 6.448–9, may hint at Dido's change back into the role of a woman, as manifested by her love for Aeneas, as bizarre and unnatural.

99 On Knox's parenthetical asides, see R. J. Tarrant, 'Parenthetically Speaking (in Virgil and other Poets)', in *Style and Tradition: Studies in Honor of Wendell Clausen*, ed. Peter Knox and Clive Foss (Stuttgart: Teubner, 1998), 141–57.
100 Knox, 'Virgil's Religious Outlook', Chapter 2 in this volume, 77.
101 Ibid., 82.
102 Ibid.
103 Ibid.
104 Ibid., 52.
105 Ibid., 67.
106 Ibid.
107 Francesco Montarese 'Ronald Knox', 158–61. Throughout *A Spiritual Aeneid*, Knox used specific lines of the poem to describe events of his own life; see Francesco Montarese, 'Appendix: Uses of the *Aeneid* in *A Spiritual Aeneid*', in *Ronald Knox*, ed. Bugliani Knox, 361–70.

Bibliography

Armstrong, Rebecca. 'Crete in the *Aeneid*: Recurring Trauma and Alternative Fate'. *Classical Quarterly* 52, no. 1 (2002): 321–40.

Boyd, Barbara Weiden. 'Virgil's Camilla and the Traditions of Catalogue and Ecphrasis (*Aeneid* 7.803–17)'. *American Journal of Philology* 113 (1992): 213–34.

Bugliani Knox, Francesca (ed.). *Ronald Knox: A Man for All Seasons*. Pontifical Institute of Medieval Studies, Toronto 2016.

Campbell, Duncan B. 'How to Dress a Standard-bearer. Animal Pelts in the Roman Army'. *Ancient Warfare. The Many Means of Protection* XII, no. 3, (2013): 46–9.

Casali, Sergio. 'Aeneas and the Doors of the Temple of Apollo'. *Classical Journal* 91, no. 1 (1995): 1–9.

Christian, Mark A. 'Phoenician Maritime Religion: Sailors, Goddess Worship, and the Grotta Regina'. *Die Welt des Orients* 43, no. 2 (2013): 179–205.

Coleridge S. T., *Table talk* (8 May 1824), London 1836.

Cozzoli, Adele-Teresa. *Euripide: Cretesi*. Introduzione, testimonianze, testo critico, traduzione e commento. Rome: Istituti Editoriali e Poligrafici Internazionali, 2001.

Crowe, Michael J. (ed.). *Ronald Knox and Sherlock Holmes: The Origin of Sherlockian Studies*. Indianapolis: Gasogene Books, 2011.

D'Andria, Francesco. *Castrum Minervae*. Lecce: Congedo editore, 2009.

Dilke, O. A. W. 'Do Line Totals in the *Aeneid* show a Preoccupation with Significant Numbers? *Classical Quarterly* 17 no. 2 (1967): 322–6.

Fitzgerald, Penelope. *The Knox Brothers*. London: Flamingo, 2002.

Fratantuono, Lee. 'Recens a vulnere: Dido, Ajax, and the Hierarchy of Heroines'. *Quaderni Urbinati di Cultura Classica* 106 (2014): 185–96.

Fratantuono, Lee. 'The Wolf in Virgil'. *Revue des études anciennes* 120, no. 1 (2018): 101–20.

Fratantuono, Lee and R. Alden Smith. 'Commentary'. In Virgil, *Aeneid 5*.

Garbugino, Giovanni. 'Evadne'. *Enciclopedia virgiliana*, vol. 2. Rome: Istituto dell'Enciclopedia Italiana (1984–91): 437.

Giusti, Elena. *Carthage in Virgil's Aeneid: Staging the Enemy under Augustus*. Cambridge: Cambridge University Press, 2018.

Hardie, Philip, R. *Virgil's Aeneid: Cosmos and Imperium*. Oxford: Clarendon Press, 1986.

Hardie, Philip, R. 'Virgil's Ptolemaic Relations'. *The Journal of Roman Studies* 96 (2006): 25–41.

Hanses, Mathias. 'Love's Letters: An Amor-Roma Telestich at Ovid, *Ars Amatoria* 3.507–10'. In *Wordplay and Powerplay in Latin Poetry*, edited by Philip Mitsis and Ioannis Ziogas. Berlin: De Gruyter, 2016, 199–211.

Heyworth S. J. and J. H. W. Morwood. 'Commentary'. In Virgil, *Aeneid 3*.

Hexter, Ralph. 'Sidonian Dido'. In *Innovations of Antiquity*, edited by Ralph Hexter and Daniel Selden. New York and London: Routledge 1992, 332–84.

Horsfall, Nicholas. 'Camilla, o i limiti dell'invenzione'. *Athenaeum* 66 (1988): 31–51.

Horsfall, Nicholas. 'Commentary'. In Virgil, *Aeneid 3*.

Horsfall, Nicholas. 'Dido in the Light of History'. *Proceedings of the Virgil Society* 13 (1974): 1–11.

Horsfall, Nicholas. 'Introduction' and 'Commentary'. In Virgil, *Aeneid 6*.

Knox, Ronald. 'Introduction'. In Virgil, *Aeneid Books VII to IX*, 5–18.

Lagioia, Alessandro. 'Le ali del mito: Dedalo in glosse fra tardoantico e Medioevo'. In *Risonanze. Forme e contenuti della memoria dell'antico*, edited by Giovanni Cipriani-Antonella Tedeschi. Foggia: Il Castello, 2014, 201–44.

LLoyd, Robert Bruce. '*Aeneid* III and the Aeneas Legend'. *The American Journal of Philology* 78 (1957): 382–400.

Martindale, Charles (ed.). *The Cambridge Companion to Virgil*. Cambridge: Cambridge University Press, 1997.

Montarese, Francesco. 'Ronald Knox as Classicist'. In Bugliani Knox (ed.), *Ronald Knox*, 147–65.

Montarese, Francesco. 'Appendix: Uses of the *Aeneid* in *A Spiritual Aeneid*'. In Bugliani Knox (ed.), *Ronald Knox*, 361–70.

O'Hara, James J. 'Dido as "Interpreting Character" at *Aeneid* 4.56–66'. *Arethusa* 26 (1993): 99–114.

O'Hara, James J. *Inconsistency in Roman Epic: Studies in Catullus, Lucretius, Vergil, Ovid and Lucan*. Roman Literature and its Contexts. Cambridge: Cambridge University Press, 2007.

O'Hara, James J. *True Names: Vergil and the Alexandrian Tradition of Etymological Wordplay*. Ann Arbor: University of Michigan Press, 2017.

O'Hara, James J. 'Virgil's Style'. In Martindale (ed.), *The Cambridge Companion to Virgil*, 241–58.

Oliensis, Ellen. 'Freud's *Aeneid*'. *Vergilius* 47 (2001): 39–63.
Otis, Brooks. *Virgil: A Study in Civilized Poetry*. Oxford: Clarendon Press, 1964.
Perkell, Christine, 'Commentary'. In Virgil, *Aeneid Book 3*.
Perret, Jacques. 'Les compagnes de Didon aux Enfers' (*Aen.* VI, 445–9). *Revue des études latines* 42 (1964): 247–61.
Poccetti, Paolo. 'Greeting and Farewell Expressions as Evidence for Colloquial Language: between Literary and Epigraphical Texts'. In *Colloquial and Literary Latin,* edited by Eleanor Dickey and Anna Chahoud. Cambridge: Cambridge University Press, 2010, 100–26.
Potter Franklin H. 'How Long Was Aeneas at Carthage?'. *Classical Journal* 21 (1926): 615–24.
Putnam, Michael C. J. *Virgil's Aeneid: Interpretation and Influence*. Chapel Hill, London: University of North Carolina Press, 1995.
Reed, James D. *Virgil's Gaze: Notion and Poetry in the* Aeneid. Princeton: Princeton University Press, 2007.
Sandbach, Francis Henry. 'Anti-Antiquarianism in the *Aeneid*'. Virgil Society Lecture no. 77 (19 March 1966), 26–38.
Sansone, David. 'Euripides. Cretans frag. 472e. 16-26 Kannicht'. *Zeitschrift für Papyrologie und Epigraphik* 184 (2013): 58–65.
Schiesaro, Alessandro, 'Emotions and Memory in Virgil's *Aeneid*'. *Bulletin of the Institute of Classical Studies* (2015). Supplement 125: 163–76.
Schiesaro, Alessandro. 'Furthest Voices in Virgil's Dido II'. *Studi Italiani di Filologia Classica*, vol. 6, no. 2 (2008): 194–245.
Schiesaro, Alessandro. 'Review of O'Hara *Death and the Optimistic Prophecy in Vergil's* Aeneid'. *Classical Philology* 88 (1993): 258–65.
Schiesaro, Alessandro. 'Under the Sign of Saturn: Dido's Kulturkampf'. In *La Représentation du temps dans la poésie augustéenne. Zur Poetik der Zeit in augusteischer Dichtung,* edited by Jürgen Paul Schwindt. Heidelberg: Universitätsverlag Winter, 2005, 85–110.
Setaioli, Aldo. 'Inferi'. *Enciclopedia virgiliana*, 5 vols. Rome: Istituto dell'Enciclopedia Italiana, 1984-91, vol. 2, 954–63.
Silva, Gabriel A. F. 'Magic and Memory. Dido's Ritual for Inducing Forgetfulness in Aeneid 4'. *Mnemosyne* 73 (2020): 1–14.
Skulsky, Susan. 'The Sibyl's Rage and the Marpessan Rock'. *The American Journal of Philology* 108, no. 1 (Spring, 1987): 56–80.
Smith, P., et al. 'Aging Cremated Infants: The Problem of Sacrifice at the Tophet of Carthage'. *Antiquity* 85 (2011): 859–74.
Solmsen, Friedrich. 'Greek Ideas of the Hereafter in Virgil's Roman Epic'. *Proceedings of the American Philosophical Society* 112, no.1 (1968): 8–14.
Solmsen, Friedrich. 'The World of the Dead in Book 6 of the *Aeneid*'. *Classical Philology* 67 (1972): 31–41.

Tarrant, R. J. 'Parenthetically Speaking (in Virgil and other Poets)'. In *Style and Tradition: Studies in Honor of Wendell Clausen*, edited by Peter Knox and Clive Foss. Stuttgart: Teubner 1998, 141–57.
Thomason, Benjamin Todd. '*Aeneid* III. Aeneas' Voyage Through Imperium'. MA diss., University of Georgia, 2004.
Tupet, Anne-Marie. 'Didon magicienne'. *Revue des études latines* 48 (1970): 229–58.
Virgil. *Opera*. With a commentary by John Conington, 2nd edn, 3 vols (London: Whittaker, 1872 [1858–71]), vol. 2.
Virgil. *Aeneid Book 3*. With a commentary by Christine Perkell. Newburyport: Focus Publishing, 2008.
Virgil. *Aeneid 3*. With a commentary by Nicholas Horsfall. Leiden: Brill, 2006.
Virgil. *Aeneid 3*. With an introduction and a commentary by S. J. Heyworth and H. W. Morwood. Oxford: Oxford University Press, 2017.
Virgil. *Aeneidos liber quintus*. Edited with a commentary by Robert Deryck Williams. Oxford: Clarendon Press, 1960.
Virgil. *Aeneid 5*. With a translation and commentary by Lee M. Fratantuono and R. Alden Smith. Leiden: Brill, 2015.
Virgil. *Aeneid 6*. With an introduction and a commentary by Nicholas Horfsall, 2 vols. Berlin: De Gruyter 2013.
Virgil. *Aeneid Books VII to IX*. Partly in the original and partly in English verse translation. Introduction and translation by Ronald Knox. Oxford: Clarendon Press, 1924.
Webber, Clifford. 'Intimations of Dido and Cleopatra in Some Contemporary Portrayals of Elizabeth I'. *Studies in Philology* 96 (1999): 127–43.
West, Grace Starry. 'Caeneus and Dido'. *Transactions of the American Philological Association* 110 (1980): 315–24.
West, Martin L. *Indo-European Poetry and Myth*. Oxford: Oxford University Press, 2007.
Wifstrand Schiebe, Marianne. 'The Discrepancy between *Aeneid* Book 2 and Book 3 in the Light of the Narrative Structure of the *Aeneid*', delivered at the Vergil Conference in Tromsø on 9 May 2008: available online. This is a revised version of an article that originally appeared in *Eranos* 81 (1983): 113–16
Williams, Robert Deryck. 'Commentary'. In Virgil, *Aeneidos liber quintus*.

The Setting of the Lecture Given by Monsignor Ronald Knox to the Virgil Society on 30 March 1946

John Mair

Francesca Bugliani Knox has established that on 30 March 1946 Monsignor Ronald Knox delivered a lecture entitled 'Virgil and Romance' to the Virgil Society.[1] The present essay is intended to try to place this occasion within its historical and cultural setting, and to this end an account is given of the origins and nature and development of the Society from its inception in 1943 onwards.

For the substance of what follows I am greatly indebted to the work of the late Dennis W. Blandford (1930–2015), the Archivist of the Virgil Society and a gifted teacher of classics. On 12 January 1993, the exact fiftieth anniversary of the inaugural dinner from which the Society is deemed to have sprung, Dennis gave a lecture entitled 'Pentekontaetia: The Virgil Society 1943–1993', and subsequently he produced an enlarged and written version of his talk, complete with very detailed documentation and records.[2] Dennis carried out his work with meticulous care and thoroughness. In only one respect have I been able to offer some supplementary information. This concerns the contribution made by W. F. Jackson Knight, Secretary of the Society from 1943 to 1949, and President from 1949 to 1950. My own first year as a student at the University of Exeter coincided with Jackson Knight's last year of teaching before his retirement, and I benefited from his lectures on Virgil and from his tuition in Latin prose composition. After J. K., as he was almost invariably known, had retired, I visited him from time to time at his home on the edge of the University Estate, and continued to gain from his profound knowledge and insights, and to increase my regard and affection for him both as a scholar and as a wonderful human being.

The foundation of the Virgil Society is generally ascribed to a gathering organized by the Reverend Bruno Scott James and held at Brown's Hotel in

London on Tuesday, 12 January 1943. This event, which probably took the form of a dinner, and its significance will be described more fully below. The prehistory of the occasion is less clear and distinct, but some effort to trace it is needed in order to understand both how the Virgil Society developed in its early years, and hence the milieu in which Monsignor Ronald Knox gave his lecture on 30 March 1946.

It would seem that credit for the inception of a Virgil Society in Britain is largely due to the Reverend Bruno Scott James (1906–84).[3] At the age of seventeen, the young James was admitted as an Anglican monk, but some seven years later he was received into the (Roman) Catholic Church, in which he was soon ordained to the priesthood. In 1935 he became 'the first parish priest and custodian of the Shrine [at Walsingham] since the Reformation'.[4] The small village of Walsingham in North Norfolk is home to two shrines – Roman Catholic and Anglican – established in honour of the Virgin Mary. The Catholic shrine was not – as is occasionally supposed – moribund at the time of Father James's appointment, but there is no doubt that he did much to raise awareness of Walsingham, and to encourage and to develop pilgrimages both to the shrine and to the nearby 'Slipper Chapel', the popular name for a basilica from which pilgrims would advance to the shrine itself.

By 1942 Father James considered that his work at Walsingham was complete, and indeed he contemplated retirement. In recent years, early retirement has become a feature of modern employment, but to leave the field at the age of only thirty-six might seem to be taking the concept a little far. James was apparently concerned about his state of health, but happily such anxieties were largely groundless since a further forty-two years of life upon earth awaited him. At all events, James seems to have used some free time in 1942 to form the idea of a Virgil Society. In this he may have been influenced by the existence of the Vergilian [sic] Society of America, which had been founded in 1937 to celebrate the cultural ties between Italy and America, particularly by means of lectures and conferences, publications, and co-operation in archaeological excavations. This energetic Society continues to flourish, and has a magnificent study centre situated in the Bay of Naples.

Father James permitted himself to think in terms of a society which might hold talks and meetings, and perhaps add a Virgil club and a Virgil library.[5] He put forward his ideas to the Classical Association, but received only a cautious reply, blessing the proposal but offering no more than sympathetic interest.[6] He therefore decided to take matters into his own hands. As he himself acknowledged in *Asking for Trouble*, Bruno Scott James was not an easy person to work with, and he would not have fitted easily into the nowadays esteemed world of team leaders and team players.[7] Nevertheless, he had considerable organizing power, as is evinced by his successful renewal programme for Walsingham, and he now took the initiative by arranging a dinner for certain people whom he considered to be in a position to advance the cause of a society devoted to the study of Virgil. Further, it seems at least conceivable that it was he who arranged for a short article, mentioning the dinner, but mainly extolling Virgil, to be published in the *Times Educational Supplement (TES)* on 9 January 1943, three days before the gathering concerned.[8] H. C. Dent, the editor of the *TES* was a guest at the dinner (see below).

Fortunately, the guest list for this dinner, held on 12 January 1943, has survived.[9] Dennis Blandford provides shrewd pen pictures of the individuals concerned.[10] Here I repeat the list, with a brief indication of the identity of each personage.

1. Miss E. C. Gedge, Treasurer of the Classical Association, and later (1943–6) Treasurer of the Virgil Society.
2. Mrs H. Nicolson = Vita Sackville-West, a prominent intellectual and gardening enthusiast who did not, however, know Latin.
3. Mrs H. B. Wells, née Angela Horatia Emma James, sister of Bruno Scott James, and perhaps envisaged as a hostess for the dinner.
4. T. S. Eliot, a literary critic, playwright and poet.
5. James Lewis May, a Catholic author, critic and translator.
6. Robert Speaight, a Catholic actor, critic, essayist and biographer.
7. W. F. Jackson Knight, Virgilian scholar and author and lecturer at the University College of the South West, later the University of Exeter.
8. Neville West (correctly spelt Nevile), a Catholic teacher of classics at Downside School.
9. John Douglas Woodruff, editor of the Catholic weekly periodical *The Tablet*.
10. H. C. Dent, editor of the *Times Educational Supplement*.

All of the guests were older – some considerably so – than their host, and, given that they were invited by a Catholic convert and priest, it is unsurprising that most of the men listed were themselves Catholics. Exceptions were the Anglican T. S. Eliot, who was, however, 'quite high up the candle', i.e. an Anglo-Catholic, and Jackson Knight, who was a member of the Church of England, and who, within my recollection, from time to time attended Anglican services held in the Mary Harris Memorial Chapel at the University of Exeter, although his main allegiance was to the Spiritualist Church in Exeter city. He was presumably invited as a Virgilian expert and as one whom Father James considered, correctly, to be a valuable ally.

Not all, however, of this cavalcade of guests were actually present at the meal, the exact nature of which is unclear (see below). In particular, none of the three ladies seems to have attended. Earlier in the same day, 12 January, Miss Gedge and Mrs Wells had joined Father James for luncheon, and I suspect that they may well have judged that enough was as good as an – even modest – feast. Mrs Nicolson (Vita Sackville-West) apparently spent the day at her home at Sissinghurst in Kent.[11] Blandford muses on why the invitation to her was not extended to her husband, the diplomat Mr (later Sir) Harold Nicolson, who was proficient in Latin. The answer might be that he was known to be away or abroad on diplomatic business. Mr Eliot also seems to have stayed away from the occasion.[12]

On the other hand, one person who had not been on the guest list above did come. He was David Jones, another Catholic, a poet and an artist within the circle of Eric Gill. He had been invited by Woodruff, whom James presumably thought important or influential enough to be at liberty to extend the list of invitees. In 1975, David Jones remarked that 'there were only about half a dozen chaps there'.[13] This is vague, but may suggest that there were some other absentees. There is also some uncertainty about the nature of the repast. The time of 7.30 pm mentioned at the head of the guest list inclines us to think of a dinner, although two of the guests referred to the meal as a 'tea party'.[14] Perhaps the meal was a form of high tea, although perhaps neither the content nor the appellation of such a collation would have appealed to certain of the guests.[15]

Even if the inaugural dinner did not go quite according to plan, Father James's enthusiasm was unbounded. The initial ardour of some of the attendees seems not to have been maintained, and in the event it was left to James and to Jackson Knight to carry matters forward. James sought to make the best of this and to take the view that he was more free to develop the Society as he saw fit.[16] Nevertheless, both he and Jackson Knight were defeated on one matter which, although in some sense central, was not of ultimate importance. James wished the new body to be called 'The Virgilian Society', but in the end deferred to the general preference for 'The Virgil Society', which had the advantage of avoiding possible confusion with the already established 'The Vergilian Society of America'.[17] Jackson Knight always held that the correct spelling of the poet's name was 'Publius Vergilius Maro' and, with perhaps untypical directness and forthrightness, wrote 'The spelling with an *e* is certainly right, but the wrong spelling with an *i* occurs already at about Vergil's own time.'[18] Other scholars, such as H. J. Rose and Tenney Frank, have also favoured 'Vergil', but 'Virgil' was the form which prevailed.

On the other hand, some positive steps were taken, specifically with regard to appointments. Jackson Knight was offered the Presidency, which he accepted on condition that Eliot took it first.[19] This release of the bird in the hand was to lead to a long delay before J. K. finally succeeded in 1949, after several other notabilities had occupied the office. He did, however, reluctantly agree to become Secretary of the Society – a post for which his brother, G. Wilson Knight, considered him unsuited[20] – but the position did give him a formal status, and he was able to secure valuable support from, and in due course to form a lasting friendship with, Miss J. E. Southan, a library assistant and later Chief Librarian of the Joint Libraries of the Roman and Hellenic Societies. It would seem probable that she discharged many of the clerical duties of the Secretary. Miss Gedge (see above) became Treasurer, a post which became all the more necessary as applications to join the Society poured in: for example, a notice in *The Tablet* about the formation of the new Society drew an enthusiastic response.[21]

The year 1943, which was one of the darkest in the Second World War, saw a number of delays and setbacks. Various proposed deliberative meetings of officials had to be postponed or cancelled, and in the summer James became 'really quite seriously ill'.[22] Finally, however, it became possible to hold a general meeting. This took place on 6 November 1943, under the chairmanship of Douglas Woodruff, who, as an editor (of *The Tablet*) and as a man of affairs, seems to have brought some much needed realism into the Society. Even so, the proceedings proved to be controversial. There were (only) fifteen people present, and of these only three had been present at the inaugural dinner.[23] The attendees did, however, consider that they constituted a Council of the Society. James was present at the meeting and apparently did not demur at the time, but later took great exception to this act of presumption, declaring that a Council already existed, comprising those who had been present at the dinner and others, who included only five of those attending this upstart general meeting.[24] The oddity of this is increased by the fact that neither the President (Eliot) nor the Secretary (Jackson Knight) attended Woodruff's meeting[25] – although, in fairness, J. K. may at the time have been preoccupied with his father's serious illness. It is not my purpose to explore this further, but it does illustrate the kind of thing which can befall small human groupings in possession of an intense inner life.

The general meeting did, however, also have some positive outcomes. In particular it was agreed that 'all lovers of Virgil' would be welcome to join the

Society. This liberality was at variance with the previous view of James that full membership should be restricted, and that some knowledge of Greek and of Greek literature might be a requirement.[26] An annual subscription of five shillings was agreed.[27] A network of branches of the Society should be formed. A new post of Joint Secretary to work in conjunction with J. K. was established, and the first postholder was appointed: he was the experienced and capable Wilfrid Woollen, a former Anglican priest who had converted to Roman Catholicism and who now taught classics at Downside. The Catholic connexion was thus maintained and even extended.

This markedly Catholic ethos continued for some years and was to have some consequences. In 1951, for example, Émile Victor Rieu was the President of the Virgil Society. He was the editor of the *Penguin Classics* and was presently engaged in producing a new English version of the four Gospels.[28] Rieu's Presidential address, given on 10 March 1951, was entitled 'Ancient Poets and Modern Scientists', and gave rise to some disquiet on the part of the by then Assistant Secretary and Treasurer, Mr J. J. Dwyer, who was concerned about the possible effects of the talk upon the susceptibilities of the numerous Catholic members of the Society. A little strangely, Dwyer himself offered to resign over the matter, and indeed did so on 14 May 1952. Rieu himself, who had been an agnostic but had become a member of the Church of England in 1947, magnanimously offered to, and did, withdraw his paper, and to surrender the Presidency, which he had previously accepted, for the year 1952. The Secretary, W. S. Maguinness, who had originally proposed Rieu for the Presidency, came out in sympathy, and resigned from as the end of 1951, but not before, with Rieu, loyally settling the programme for 1952.[29]

The text of Rieu's presidential address survived, and was, some forty-two years later, printed by the Virgil Society.[30] *Tempora mutantur nos et mutamur in illis*, and, on reading this lecture more than twenty-five years still further on from its eventual publication, I find it difficult to see anything exceptionable in Rieu's text. The conclusion would seem to be that, at least in its early years, the Virgil Society was more in thrall to the Catholic conformity of the day than to catholicity in the wider sense. This helps to explain why Ronald Knox, so characterful and withal so orthodox, was to be such a welcome contributor to the Society's programme in 1946.

After this short digression, we return to the earlier history of the Society. After the delays and postponements of the year 1943, the year 1944 saw a wonderful flowering. Eight events in London (one of them undated, and one duplicated) were listed in the Society's programme, the first being given by James Lewis May, one of the invitees to the inaugural dinner. Mr May was a Catholic author, critic and translator, and had written a book about Cardinal John Henry Newman. It may have been as a courtesy to him as the oldest member of the original group that he was invited to give, on 26 February 1944, the opening address, which was entitled 'Virgil and the Ordinary Citizen'. This was well received, and a summary version, the first of many such epitomes, was quickly produced.

On 15 April 1944, Jackson Knight gave the first of his six addresses to the Society, his subject being '*Patriis Virtutibus* – Virgil's Political Philosophy'. On 16 October came the Presidential address by T. S. Eliot, 'What Is a Classic?', an oration which has itself become a minor classic. This was followed on 2 December by some dramatic readings from Virgil, organized by Robert Speaight. Thus was established what has been ever since the pattern of Virgil Society meetings: lectures, with occasional spoken readings from the poet himself. Father James's ideas for a Virgil club and for a Virgil library did not materialize: the Society has never owned, or rented, its own premises, and the practical difficulties – and cost – of managing a club and of setting up and maintaining a library were prohibitive. As it happens, there were, and are, at least in London, abundant library facilities for the study and enjoyment of Virgil's work.

The year 1945 saw a continuation of the previous year's pattern. There were nine meetings, which included, *inter alia*, another talk by Jackson Knight ('*Callida Iunctura*: What Is the Virgilian Kind of Poetry?'), and lectures by Douglas Woodruff ('Virgil and the Middle Ages'), and by Bruno Scott James ('How to Read Virgil'). Father James, whose rapturous embrace of the Society had perhaps not continued in the longer term, never became President of, or held any other principal office within, the Society, but, notwithstanding some misgivings, remained a supporter, at least until he departed for ministry in Naples.

Lastly, for the purposes of the present essay, came 1946, with no fewer than ten scheduled meetings, to which must be added the specially arranged address by Monsignor Ronald Knox, given on 30 March. The most unusual occasion was a weekday Joint Meeting held on Tuesday 7 May, with the British Beekeepers' Association: this was on the initiative of Bruno Scott James, whose swansong this event proved to be. For many, however, the coping stone of the year's programme was probably the address, given on 30 March 1946, by Monsignor Ronald Knox. The son of an evangelically minded Anglican Bishop of Manchester, Edmund Arbuthnott Knox, Ronald Knox combined intellectual gifts of the highest order with the conviction and assurance of the Catholic convert which he became in 1917, when he laid down his Anglican orders and his chaplaincy of

Trinity College, Oxford. It will be seen that with this pedigree and with his carefully considered conversion to the Roman Catholic Church, Knox must have been *persona gratissima* to what seems to have been the dominant, Catholic, element in the Virgil Society.

That this lecture was not announced on the programme card for 1946 is readily explained by the fact that arrangements for it were not made – between Monsignor Knox and Wilfrid Woollen, the Joint Secretary of the Society – until mid-February, by when the year's programme was already under way and a lecture by Miss J. E. Lowe had already been scheduled for the month of March.[31] It is, however, curious that what one would imagine to have been such an important occasion is not recorded by Blandford in *Pentekontaetia*, or mentioned by Speaight in his memorial address, *A Modern Virgilian: A Memorial Lecture to Monsignor Ronald Knox*, given to the Virgil Society on 15 November 1958.[32] In *A Modern Virgilian*, Speaight pays a thoroughly deserved tribute to Knox's lectures given at Trinity College, Oxford as long ago as 1912, but makes no reference to Knox's March 1946 lecture, which was probably within the memory of at least some of his audience. Furthermore, the title of Knox's lecture, 'Virgil and Romance', was almost certainly a revision of 'Virgil's Romance and Pathos', one of the Trinity Lectures which were the very topic of Speaight's address. It may be that Knox, who could be modest and diffident to a fault, had himself asked that his paper should not be published.

It is now time to summarize and to conclude. The Virgil Society was conceived in the dark days of the Second World War, and, after a slow start, quickly blossomed. Its founder, the Reverend Bruno Scott James, enthused, indeed was almost ecstatic, about the potentialities of the Society, but never held any office within it and by late in 1944 was considering resignation.[33] Fortunately he appears not to have taken this step, but seems to have taken no active part in the Society after 1946. Jackson Knight was more restrained in his expression, but had a hardly lesser view of the possibilities: he saw the Society as having a potentially global influence as a centre of quality and excellence.[34] In this he was fortified by the initially rapid growth of the Society, which by late 1944 had some 450 members. This figure then fluctuated, and rose more slowly to an officially certified figure of 652 in 1967.[35] It then gently declined, to the point where in the 1980s serious thought was given to winding up the Society.[36] Happily, that was averted and at present the number of Society members has stabilized at about 120.

The wording of what might nowadays be characterized as the 'mission statement' of the Society has changed little over the years, and this is currently stated as follows: 'The purpose of the Virgil Society is to unite all those who cherish the central educational tradition of Western Europe. Of that tradition Virgil is the symbol.' This aim has, perhaps, been imperfectly realized. Nevertheless, there have been positive outcomes. Over the years, well over 300 lectures have been delivered, and the great majority have been either summarized and circulated, or, since 1962, published in the Society's *Proceedings*. Within the Society there have been many fruitful exchanges of information and opinions. There have never been any entrance qualifications for admission, and people of many different backgrounds have joined the Society, to the great gain of fellow members and of themselves.

Notes

1. See, in this volume, Francesca Bugliani Knox, 'Introduction: The Context of Ronald Knox's Lectures on Virgil', 22.
2. Dennis W. Blandford, *Pentekontaetia: The Virgil Society 1943–1993* (London: The Virgil Society, 1993).
3. Bruno Scott James, *Asking for Trouble* (London: Darton, Longman and Todd, 1962). James's book is a memoir rather than an autobiography, and is tantalizingly deficient in factual information, especially in respect of dates and names. The form 'Scott-James', occasionally found in Virgil Society literature, is incorrect.
4. Ibid., 119.
5. Blandford, *Pentekontaetia*, 7.
6. Ibid.
7. James, *Asking*, 136.
8. Blandford, *Pentekontaetia*, 7–8, 76.
9. Reproduced in *Pentekontaetia*, 9.
10. Ibid., 10–17.
11. Ibid., 10.
12. Ibid., 11.
13. Ibid., 8.
14. Ibid.
15. For convenience I continue to use the term 'dinner', regardless of the actual menu.
16. Blandford, *Pentekontaetia*, 21.
17. Ibid., 19–20.
18. Ibid.; W. F. J. Knight, *Roman Vergil*, 2nd edn (London: Faber and Faber, 1944), 36.
19. Blandford, *Pentekontaetia*, 20.
20. 'In the event he was prevailed on to act as Secretary, an office for which he was unfitted by both circumstance and temperament: he only took it on under pressure';

'He was burdened by a responsibility which he did not like and for which he was not by nature equipped'. See G. Wilson Knight, *Jackson Knight: A Biography* (Oxford: The Alden Press, 1975), 268, 270. Nevertheless, acceptance was almost a political imperative for J. K.: had he not agreed, he could easily have been sidelined by other parties in the Society; and then his prospects for the Presidency, which he dearly desired, might have vanished altogether.

21 Blandford, *Pentekontaetia*, 21.
22 Ibid.
23 Ibid., 23–5.
24 Ibid., 24–5.
25 Ibid., 24.
26 Ibid., 22.
27 In terms of inflation, this equates to approximately £12.13 at 2021 values, and is thus remarkably close to the present level of £12.00 per annum.
28 Rieu was editor of the *Penguin Classics* until 1964. He produced translations of the *Odyssey* (Penguin 1946), of Virgil's *Eclogues* (*Virgil: The Pastoral Poems*, Penguin 1949), of the *Iliad* (Penguin 1950) and of the *Argonautica* of Apollonius of Rhodes (*The Voyage of Argo*, Penguin 1959); and of *The Four Gospels – A New Translation* (Penguin, 1952).
29 For the whole episode, see Blandford, *Pentekontaetia*, 37–40.
30 Émile Victor Rieu, 'Ancient Poets and Modern Scientists', *Proceedings of the Virgil Society* XXI (1993), 35–52.
31 Blandford, *Pentekontaetia*, 119. On Miss Lowe's lecture entitled 'The Problem of Dido and Aeneas' and its manuscript, see the Appendix to this volume: 'J. E. Lowe, Ronald Knox and the Virgil Society Lecture Entitled "The Problem of Dido and Aeneas"'.
32 Robert Speaight, *A Modern Virgilian: A Memorial Lecture to Monsignor Ronald Knox* (London: Virgil Society, 1959). This was a different address from Speaight's Presidential Address which he had already delivered, on 18 January 1958, and which was entitled 'The Virgilian *Res*'.
33 Blandford, *Pentekontaetia*, 16–17 and 26. James himself claimed to have founded and piloted the Society through the early years (*Asking for Trouble*, 162).
34 Wilson Knight, *Jackson Knight*, 276–8.
35 Blandford, *Pentekontaetia*, 72–3.
36 Ibid., 48–52.

Bibliography

Blandford, Dennis W. *Pentekontaetia: The Virgil Society 1943–1993*. London: The Virgil Society, 1993.

James, Bruno Scott. *Asking for Trouble*. London: Darton, Longman and Todd, 1962.
Knight, G. Wilson. *Jackson Knight: A Biography*. Oxford: The Alden Press, 1975.
Knight, W. F. Jackson. *Roman Vergil*. 2nd edn. London: Faber and Faber, 1944.
Rieu, Émile Victor. 'Ancient Poets and Modern Scientists'. *Proceedings of the Virgil Society* XXI (1993), 35–52.
Speaight, Robert. *A Modern Virgilian: A Memorial Lecture to Monsignor Ronald Knox*. London: Virgil Society, 1959.

Appendix: J. E. Lowe, Ronald Knox and the Virgil Society Lecture Entitled 'The Problem of Dido and Aeneas'

Francesca Bugliani Knox

In 2019 Laurence Kenworthy-Browne presented me with a handwritten, anonymous manuscript entitled 'The Problem of Dido and Aeneas'. He had received it from his sister Christina Kenworthy-Browne CJ, archivist and librarian at the Bar Convent in York, who taught classics for many years at St Mary's Convent school, Ascot. Sr Christina had received the manuscript as a gift from Lady Helen Asquith – daughter of Katharine Asquith and sister to Lord Oxford – who was a classics teacher and also worked in the Ministry school inspectorate. According to Laurence Kenworthy-Browne, Lady Asquith gave Sr Christina the manuscript in the late 1960s or early 1970s, claiming that it was the text of a lecture by Ronald Knox.

There were two good reasons to consider the possibility that the manuscript could be the text of the lecture Knox had delivered to the Virgil Society. First, the Virgil Society listed a lecture entitled 'The Problem of Dido and Aeneas' in the programme for the year 1946 as having been delivered in March around the time when Knox was preparing his own address to the Virgil Society. Second, the lecture recorded in the manuscript discussed the story of Dido and Aeneas in ways that sometimes resembled Knox's treatment of the episode in his Trinity Lectures; and it also emphasized Virgil's use of 'keywords' and discussed the concept of *pietas* along the same lines as Knox in the Trinity Lectures. On the other hand, two reasons – besides a difference in style – called for caution. First, the handwriting did not resemble Knox's and anyway Knox always typed out fair copies of his lectures and indeed of his sermons. Second, the Virgil Society archives attributed the lecture entitled 'The Problem of Dido and Aeneas' to a certain J. E. Lowe.[1]

Why was there no record in the Virgil Society archives of the lecture by Knox? Could there have been a mistake in attributing 'The Problem of Dido and Aeneas' to J. E. Lowe? Eventually I was able to consult the typescript of the 'Problem of

Dido and Aeneas' deposited in the British Library in the early 1950s by L. A. S. Jermyn, secretary of the Virgil Society until 1953. The typescript bore the name of J. E. Lowe, who at the time was still alive. I compared the British Library typescript with the handwritten manuscript and concluded that 'The Problem of Dido and Aeneas' had been written and delivered at the Virgil Society by Miss Joyce Egerton Lowe on 16 March 1946.[2] The handwritten manuscript presented to me was almost certainly its original version, presumably written by Lowe. The typescript held in the British Library was a later transcription, that included all the corrections the author had inserted in the manuscript and some minor amendments. As for Knox's lecture, I found confirmation in *The Tablet* archives that, as he had stated in his letters, Knox had indeed given a lecture at the Virgil Society entitled 'Virgil and Romance', even though no record of it exists in the Virgil Society archives.[3] He did so – unusually for the Virgil Society timetable, which set an interval of at least one month between lectures – on Saturday 30 March 1946, only fourteen days after Miss Lowe's lecture on Saturday 16 March of the same year.

How Helen Asquith came across Lowe's manuscript is unclear. Lowe was a Catholic convert (1918), taught Latin at a Catholic Training College in Cavendish Square and knew Ronald Knox. He wrote a foreword to her book *Church Latin for Beginners*, published by W. and G. Foyle in 1923. She wrote a play – a sort of detective play – in which 'Ronnie' features as one of the characters. She very probably knew Laurence Eyres and Helen Asquith, both, like her, Catholic converts and teachers of classics. Possibly her lecture came to be among Knox's papers at Mells because at some point she gave or sent it to him; Helen Asquith may then have passed it on to Sr Christina. Alternatively, Helen Asquith might have received it directly from Lowe and then given it to Sister Christina to keep.

Notes

1 Dennis W. Blandford, *Pentekontaetia: The Virgil Society 1943–1993* (London: The Virgil Society, 1993).

2 J. E. [Joyce Egerton] Lowe (b. 1892), Lecturer in Latin, Catholic Training College (Cavendish Square) and part-time assistant of Latin at UCL, graduated from Bedford college in classics (1914). Her publications: *Church Latin for Beginners: An Elementary Course of Exercises in Ecclesiastical Latin* (London: Burns Oates and Washbourne, 1923); *Fifty Latin Grammar Texts* (London: W. and G. Foyle, 1929); *Magic in Greek and Latin Literature* (Oxford: Blackwell, 1929); *Folia Latina, an Easy*

Latin Reader (London: Burns Oates, 1930); *Ecclesiastical Greek for Beginners*, with an introduction by C. C. Martindale (London: Burns Oates London, 1931); *The Key of the Door, a Play in Three Acts* (London: Garamond Press, 1935).

3 See also, in this volume, Francesca Bugliani Knox, 'Introduction: The Context of Ronald Knox's Lectures on Virgil', 22.

Index

Abella, walls of 116, 200, 217 n.33
Abraham 51, 53
   Aeneas, similar to 67, 184, 213
Acarnanians (people of Acarnania), appeal of 127
Acestes, King of Segesta 64, 157
Achaemenides, one of Ulysses' crew in the *Aeneid* 58, 137, 156, 196
Achates, companion of Aeneas 105, 165
Acheron, river 72, 95, 117, 118, 123, 137
Achilles 59, 94, 105, 116, 130, 170
   compared to Aeneas 129
   and *poena damni* 74–5
   quarrel with Agamemnon 160
   shield of 50, 136
   and Turnus, 88, 155
Actium 141, 152, 157
   battle of 50, 57, 117, 182, 197, 199
Actor, Aeneas' companion 89
adjurations, *see under* '*Aeneid*'
Aeacus, King of Aegina 210
Aeneas 1, 4, 7, 11, 12, 51, 52
   and Anchises 3, 14 n.22, 49
   callousness of 54
   compared to David and Abraham 67, 184, 213
   contrasted to Jason 136
   counterpart of Hector 88
   his cult of 'Aphrodite Aeneias' 127
   his desertion of Dido 55, 97–103, 206
   favoured of heaven 54, 66
   heliography of 147
   as a liturgiologist 10, 63, 184, 191 n.36, 207–8
   as a man of destiny 9, 53, 56, 68, 196
   numerous sacrifices of, *see under* 'sacrifices'
   pater Aeneas 64
   persecution of, by Juno 67, 71, 155
   pietas of 10, 61, 65–6, 82–3
   raising a siege 148–9
   remorse of, on killing Lausus 130–1
   representative of the vanquished side 88
   resemblance to Julius Caesar 50, 53–5
   revelations received by 66, 141, 156
   his shield, symbolic meaning of 50, 51
   trustee of fate 52–3
   unimportance of, in the *Iliad* 105
   wanderings of 50, 129, 131–2, 140–4, 152, 157–8, 196–7
Aeneid
   adjurations in 52, 169, 171, 188
   allegorical exegesis of 11
   anachronisms in 147–8, 197–8, 216 n.26
   aqueducts in 113, 198
   characters in 105–8
      female characters 135
   defining idea of 57, 182
   as an epic of civilization 57–9, 183
   grandeur of 57, 59
   and Greek drama 136
   Herodotean atmosphere of 144–7
   keywords in 56, 181, 187–8, 167–72, 204–6, 241
   military details in 148–9, 197–8
   not a fairy story 132, 140–3, 147
   optimism of 57, 59, 182
   pietas in, *see* '*pietas*'
   plot of, *see* 'plot of the *Aeneid*'
   political interest of 49–59
   published after death 46
   reality of fighting in 147–9; *see also* 'fighting'
   revision, incomplete, of 165, 176
   significance of the number seven 215 n.9
   single authorship of 151
   third book of, *see* 'composition of the third book of the *Aeneid*'
   towers in 113–16, *see also* 'towers'
   Virgil's wish that it be destroyed 46

Africa 53, 66, 108, 142
Agamemnon, King of Mycenae 156
Agrippa, Marcus Vipsanius 50
Agylleans, inhabitants of Agylla (Cerveteri) 144
Ahab, seventh King of Israel 162
Ajax 105, 164
Alba Longa 52, 152, 154, 164, 213
    Alban Fathers 164
Alcaic stanza 159
    correspondence with Horatian cadence 160
Alcimede, mother of Jason 136
Alcinous, garden of 123
Aldenham Park 20
Alesia, ancient town on Mont Auxois 148
Alfenus Varus, jurist and writer 45
Alfred, King 90
Allecto, a fury 64, 133
Allia
    infaustum nomen 49
    Romans defeat at 49
Amasenus, river 117
Amata, wife of Latinus 129, 133, 135–6
Ambraciot gulf 50
Ampleforth Abbey 19, 22, 24, 39, 40
    Ampleforth Journal 22
amplification, *see under* 'rhetoric'
Ampsanctus, valley of 121
Amycus, Aeneas' companion 86, 87, 136
Anchises 49, 53, 66, 76, 94, 129, 141, 144, 170
    association of, with Iulus 52
    'beatification' of 81, 185
    comparison of, with saints 82
    death of 145, 157, 196
    his injunction to Aeneas 3, 4
    his knowledge of terrestrial events 82, 213
    his prediction regarding the four horses 197
    purgatory of 80, 210
    purification of 212
    reincarnation of 210
    as a reliable prophet 3, 50, 125, 152, 153, 155
    shade of 82, 152
Andromache, wife of Hector 105, 156, 157, 165

Anglo-Catholicism 18, 183, 186, 231
Anna, Dido's sister 103, 134, 204
Antemnae, Roman town 116
Antigone 135
Antiphon, Athenian orator 163
Antony 50, 55, 160, 198, 199
    and Cleopatra 57, 182
ἄξιος use of, in Homer 71
Aphrodite 135, 211
    see also 'Venus'
Apollo 49, 50, 57, 61, 168
    crinitus 115
    priest of 61
    and Sybil 205
Apollonius, of Rhodes 82, 87, 110
    alleged imitation by Virgil 134–5, 136–8
    Argonautica 139–40
    compared to Chablis 137
    similes in 132, 134
    Virgil's debt to 134, 135
appropriation, *see under* 'Virgil'
aqueducts, *see under* '*Aeneid*'
Araxes, river 117
Arctinus, of Miletus 128
Ariadne 205
Argiletum, ancient street in Rome 50
Argonauts 136, 137
Aridaeus
    character in Plato 81, 184
Aristagoras, of Miletus 141, 144
Aristotle 47
art of Virgil 97–111
    'artistic prudence' 76
    dramatic instinct 102–3
    flaws in 110
    moral principle in 83, 98–9
    provoking outrage 103–4
    and romanticism 85
    skill in characterization 105
    violation of good taste 97–8
    see also 'Dido and Aeneas'
Artemis (Diana), goddess 132, 204
Artemisia, queen of Halicarnassus 202
Ascanius (Iulus) 49, 51, 132
    age of 156
    attitude of, towards bonfire 51
    compared to Solomon 52, 213
    founder of Roman dynasty 51, 52

hopes of 52
invented by Virgil 51–2
killing of the doe, by 107
likeness of, to Astyanax 156
parvus Iulus 156
poor joke of, about eating tables 51
his prominence 51–3
puer Iulus 156
pulcher Iulus 156
spes surgentis Iuli 52
Asquith Julian, 2nd Earl of Oxford and Asquith 24, 25, 29 n.23, 39, 40
Asquith, Lady Helen 241, 242
Asquith, Lady Katharine 24, 241
Assaracus 78, 210
Astyanax 109, 156, 157
Asylum 50
Athena (Athene) 108, 203, 206, 207
   anger of 108
   see also 'Minerva'
Auden W. H.
   Memorial for the City 12
Augustan age 131, 204
   moral standards of 98, 99
   poets of 57, 99
Augustine of Hippo, Saint
   influence of Virgil on 47
Augustus, Roman Emperor 45, 46, 49, 50, 51, 54, 55
   and Juno 69
   tribute to 58
Avernus 48
   cave of 137
   lake 154

ballads, conventionality of 105
Balliol College, Oxford 17, 18, 26 n.7, 180
barbarism 57–8
Bar Convent (York) 241
Barker, Nicolas J., historian 24, 25, 32 n.57, 33 n.63
Bath 24
Bede, Venerable 47, 48, 186
Bellini, Giovanni, painter 200
bello clari 75, 209, 210
   and the doctrine of intention 75
Benacus, lake 117
Bentley, Richard 4
Bias of Priene, sage 144

Bible
   Douay version 20
   Epistle to the Hebrews 53, 91
   1 Kings 18:18 162
   New Testament 19, 20
   Old Testament 8, 10, 181, 190 n.20, 207
   Psalms 10, 67, 164, 185, 188, 213
      psalms 45 and 68 46
   1 Samuel 16:9 86
   Vulgate 20
Bitias, companion of Aeneas 130, 148
Blandford, Dennis W. 192 n.55, 229, 231, 232
   Pentekontaetia: The Virgil Society 1943–1993 229, 236
Blériot, Louis 18
Bossuet, Jacques Bénigne 47
Boyd, Barbara 202
Brennus, chieftain of the Senones 49
Briseis, character in the *Iliad* 160
Browning, Robert
   'Halbert and Hob' 138
   Pippa Passes 18
Bunyan, John 134
Burke, Edmund 47, 48, 186
Butler, James Montague 17
Byron, Lord 50

Cacus, a giant
   defeat of, by Hercules 58
Caeculus, son of Vulcan 47
Caesar, Julius 45, 148, 149
   and Aeneas 50, 53–5, 100
   battle of Zela 55
   Commentaries 148
Caieta, Aeneas' nurse
   burial of 64, 207
Calchas, Argive seer 108
Caliban 4, 59
Calverley, Charles Stuart 176 n.3
   'Essay on Translating Virgil into Verse' 174
Calypso 96, 102, 129
   cave of 118, 123
Camilla 57, 95, 107, 135, 149, 202
Capaneus, husband of Evadne 211
Capitol, Hill of Rome 49, 50
Cares, supernatural agencies 72

Carlyle, Thomas 46
  writer of Carlylese 48
Carmental gate 50
Carthage 7, 55, 101, 103, 142, 144, 172, 207
  Aeneas' length of stay in 196–7, 198
  as a false goal 21, 182
  and Italian scenery 115
  temple of Juno in 220 n.66
  walls of 58, 90, 108
Cassandra, priestess 95, 144
  unpersuasiveness of 108
Castro (*Castrum Minervae*) 199, 202
catalogues
  tedious nature of 130, 202
Catholic soul of Virgil 10, 77, 183, 185, 213
Catholicism (Roman) 10, 19, 230–2, 234, 236, 242
  Knox's conversion to 1, 11, 18, 21, 181, 182–3, 214
Catiline, Lucius Sergius 45, 50
Cato, Marcus Porcius 50, 70, 91
Catullus 61, 135
  Ariadne 135
  exponent of *lepos*
Celaeno, a harpy 66, 151, 153
Cephalus, King of Athens 211
Cerberus, hound of Hades 208
ceremonial
  ancient and modern 63, 64, 82
  Christian 63
Chalciope, sister of Medea 134
Charlemagne 3
Charles I, King 7, 90
Charlie, Prince 90
Charming, Prince 86
Charon, ferryman of Hades 52, 117
Chesterton, G. K. 90
chlamys, given to Ascanius by Andromache 157
Christianity 1, 8, 185, 186
Church Times, The 3
Cicero 19, 45, 91, 160, 161, 163
  exponent of *humanitas* 61
Cinderella 86
Circe 120, 129, 132, 137
  isle of 129, 154
civilization, triumph of 57–9
  end and beginning of 12
  European 2, 9

Claudii, Roman patrician family 49
Clausus, the Sabine 49
Cleomenes, King of Sparta 203, 204, 218 n.42
Cleopatra, 57, 207
  and Antony 57, 182
  and Caesar 54, 100
  compared to Dido 54–5, 100
Cloanthus, companion of Aeneas 49, 106
Cloelia, Roman heroine 50
Cluentii, Roman family 49
Clytemnestra 75, 135, 156
Coleridge, S. T. 195
  imbecility of 110, 159
colonization, Greek 142, 145
composition of the third book of the
    Aeneid
  chronology of the third book 156–8
  inconsistencies 151–7
Conington, John 59 n.2, 63, 73, 75, 76, 128, 139, 146, 179–80, 198, 202, 209
  elaborateness of his notes 48
  his edition of the *Aeneid* 21, 40
  on the imitation by Virgil of Apollonius of Rhodes 136–7
  Knox's disagreement with 72–3, 79–82, 118–19, 135–6, 152, 154–5, 156, 157–8, 163, 184–5, 196
conjugium 99
Conrads, Friedrich 152, 158 n.1, 196
Constantine, the Great 8
Cordelia 92
Coroebus, son of King Mygdon of Phrygia 94
covenant
  between gods and men 10, 67–8, 83, 184, 213
Crassus, Marcus Licinius 45
Cretans 146
Crete 65, 141, 145, 153, 157, 202, 206
Creusa 56, 66, 135, 151
  Hesperia 145, 153, 196, 214 n.8
crime
  crime de la passion 74–5
  expiation of 80–1
  impiety of 76
Cromwell, Oliver 46, 90
culpa 99
Cumae 142, 207

Cupid 134, 206
Cybele, mother of the gods 70, 116, 200
Cyclades 141
Cyclops 58, 119, 129, 132, 137
   island of 137, 156
Cyrene, founding of 145

Daedalus 95
Daily Mail, The 8, 48
Dante Alighieri 8, 9, 74, 83, 114, 186, 188, 219
   Inferno 72, 74, 114
   Purgatorio 8, 10
   his understanding of Virgil 8, 71–2
   Virgil's debt to 5, 47
Dardanus, son of Zeus 210
Dares, Trojan boxer 87, 88, 136
Dascylus, King of Mysia 137
David, King 52, 67, 219
   compared with Aeneas 67, 184, 219
   and Goliath 86, 103
death
   premature in *lugentes campi* 211–12
   as a supernatural agency 72
Decii, Roman family 209
Deiphobus, son of Priamus 75, 81, 109, 110, 209
Delos 66, 141, 157
Demosthenes 19
destiny 9, 10, 53, 54, 56, 95, 187, 196, 208
   and free-will 69
      example of Dido 69–70
   future destiny of infants 72–3, 81
   and the gods, 67–8
   and providence 10, 68
   Virgil's strong sense of 85
Diana 64, 67, 220 n.66
   see also 'Artemis'
Dido
   compared with Cleomenes 203–4
   compared with Cleopatra 54, 100
   contrasted with Hypsipyle 136
   contrasted with Medea 134–5
   early legends of 128
   forecasting exploits of Hannibal 50–1
   gentleness of her character 54
   her love for Aeneas 99
   in *Heroides* 99
   'minx-like' qualities of 100–1
   and moon imagery 122, 207–8, 220 n.66, n.67
   not the heroine of the *Aeneid* 65, 102
   outbursts of 102–3
   and Pasiphae 74, 205, 218 n.53
   punishment of, in Hades 74–5, 81
   real crime of 69–70, 74
   romantic character of 135
   sacrifices of, *see under* 'sacrifices'
   shade of 121–2
   and Sychaeus 65, 69, 128, 205, 209
   treatment of, by Aeneas 54, 55, 100
   unreasonableness of 100–1
   unsubstantiality of, before Virgil 105
   variety of views about 97, 99, 100, 101
Dido and Aeneas 97–103
   child of 99
   marriage of 98–9
   similar to Caesar and Cleopatra 54, 100
   their problematic love 55
   why Aeneas deserts Dido 54
dignus, *see* 'mereor'
Dio, Cassius 199
Diomede, Greek hero 87, 105, 129, 130, 161
Dionysius, of Halicarnassus 127
Dionysius, of Phocaea 145
disease, as supernatural agency 72
Dodds, E. R. 179
Dolon, son of Eumedes 87, 129, 197
Doyle, Conan 195, 196, 214 n.4
dragon 72, 86
drama, Greek
   Virgil's alleged debt to 135–6
Drances, Latin opponent of Turnus 107
   debate with Turnus 89, 160–1
Dryden, John 3, 6, 8, 12
   his version of the fourth *Eclogue* 8–9
Dwyer, J. J. 234
Dyrrhachium, battle of 50, 54

Eclogues, *see under* 'Virgil'
ekpyrosis 210
Electra, daughter of Agamemnon 135
Elijah, prophet 162
Eliot, T. S. 5, 186, 187, 231, 232, 233, 235
   Four Quartets 12
   and Virgil 9
   'Virgil and the Christian World' 2, 186
   'What Is a Classic' 2, 186, 192 n.55

elisions in Virgil, *see under* 'style of Virgil'
Elysium 70, 73, 74, 75, 77, 114, 118, 153, 209
    Anchises in 50, 155, 185, 210–11, 213, 22 n.85
    inhabitants of 63, 71, 76–82, 122, 206, 209
    likened to heaven 73, 219; *see also* 'heaven'
    purification in 78–9, 212
empire 3, 45, 66, 108
    ideology of 3–4
    pax romana 4
    Roman 1, 3, 9, 70, 186, 204, 209, 211
    successors of the Roman Empire 4
    translatio imperii 3
    translatio studii 3
Ennius 138, 175
Entellus, Trojan hero 87–8, 136
Epeus, builder of the Trojan horse 87–8
epic 1, 3, 59, 99, 110, 146, 182, 202
    religious 82–3, 206
Epirus 50, 51, 108, 156
Er, son of Armenius 81
Erato, a Muse 206, 207
Eros 205–6
Eryx, city 109, 144, 168
eschatology of Virgil 71–83, 209–12
    alleged inconsistencies in 208–9
    Conington's difficulties with 79–81
    compared with Dante's 210
    perceived inconsistencies in 76–83
    poena damni 76
    poena sensus 74–5, 211
    suicides, punishment of 74, 81
    summary of 209–11
esto, 'pet phrase' of Cicero 161
Eton College 17, 18, 180
Etruria 207
Euphrates, river 117
Euripides 163
    Cretans 211, 212, 218 n.51, 223 n.95
    first of the 'moderns' 135
    his influence on Virgil 135–6
    Medea 136
    and romance 135, 136
Eurotas, river 204
Euryalus
    apparent foul play on Euryalus 103–4
    mother of 62, 65
    see also 'Nisus and Euryalus'
Evander, King of Pallanteum 56, 58,116, 136, 137, 148
    Aeneas' visit to 50, 123
    and the death of Pallas 93–4
    story of killing of Cacus told by 58
Eyes and No Eyes, 124
Eyres, Laurence 19, 20, 24, 25, 39–41, 242
    correspondence with Knox 19
    editor of *In Three Tongues* 20
    and Knox's lectures on the *Iliad* 18
    and Knox's lectures on *Odyssey* 18, 19
    and Knox's lectures on Virgil, 22–4, 39–40

Fabius Pictor, Quintus 127
fairy-stories 85, 86, 92, 105, 120
    Aeneid, not a fairy story 132, 139–40, 147
Fama 197
fate
    in Homer 68
    in Virgil 68–9, 70
Faunus, oracle of 121
fighting 139
    Virgil's dislike of 130–1
First Punic War 127
Fletcher, C. P. L. 28 n.19
Florio, John 127
Florus, Lucius Annaeus, historian 199
forests, *see* 'woods'
fortifications, Roman 148
Fortuna Urbis 57, 69, 182
Fowey 142
Frank, Tenney 233
Fraser, Simon, 15th Lord Lovat 19
French, suitability of, for epigrams 160
Fucinus, river 117
Fufetius Mettius 50
Fulgentius, Latin writer 11
fuit, pathetic use of 90–2, 168
funeral 207
    games 87, 108
Furies 72, 209

Galatea 119
Gallus, Gaius Cornelius 45
Ganges, river 117

Gauls, victory of, at Allia 49
Gedge, E. C., Treasurer of Catholic Association 231–3
George III, King 90
Gesta Romanorum 127
Ghent, altarpiece in St Bavo's Cathedral 1, 2
Gibbon, Edward 102
Golden Age 8, 59
golden fleece 134
Goneril 92
Gorgons 72
Grahame, Kenneth, *The Golden Age* 85–6
Graves, Charles 28 n.19
Gray, Thomas 138
Gryphon Club 23, 195
Gyas, boat captain 106

Hades 83, 120, 129, 208, 209, 218 n.53
    Aeneas'meeting with Deiphobus in 109
Haecker, Theodor 2–3, 186
Hannibal, exploits of, adumbrated by Dido 50–1
Hardie, Philip 185, 219 n.53 n.56, 220 n.66
Harpies 72, 132, 137, 141
Harrison, Stephen 180, 182
Heaney, Seamus 9
heaven 76–7
    inhabitants of 76
    merits leading to 76
Hector 59, 88, 92, 129
    ghost of 66
Hecuba, Queen of Troy 8, 48, 135, 129
Hegel, heterodoxy of 48
Heinze, Richard 180–1, 185
Helen of Troy 66, 77
Helenus, Trojan prince and seer 51, 66, 91, 105, 108, 141
    predictions of 137, 152
Hell 8, 73, 74, 77, 76, 80
    anteroom of 72, 209
    inhabitants of 76, 81
    limbo, *see* limbo
    sins against *pietas* 76; *see also* 'sin'
    torments of 76
    see also 'Tartarus'
Henry, James 79
Hercules 67, 140, 221 n.75
    type of civilization 58

Hermione 156
Herodotus
    his description of equipment 146–7
    Histories 202, 203, 217 n.38
    Knox's interest in 19, 29 n.23, 203–4
    Virgil's debt to 144–8
Hesperia 144, 145, 151, 153, 196, 214 n.8
Heyworth, S. J. 198
Higher Criticism 181, 190 n.20 n.21
Hippolytus, son of Theseus 211
Hissarlik, ancient city 202
Holinshed, Raphael 127
Holmes, Sherlock 108, 195, 214 n.4
Homer
    his attitude towards fate 68
    his lack of romanticism 86–7
    Virgil compared to 87–8, 89
    Virgil's debt to 129–34
    see also '*Odyssey*' and '*Iliad*'
Honour Moderations at Oxford University 26 n.7, 37, 48, 179, 180, 190 n.19
Hopkins, Clare 37
Horace 28 n.19, 37, 38, 45, 98, 122, 143
    Epodes XVI.17–22; XVI.41–3 143–4
    exponent of *urbanitas* 11, 61
    Odes III. v. 53–6 160
    Virgil's friendship with 45
horse, the wooden 8, 48, 108
    Iapigyan 208
horses, white, omen of 124–5, 197
Horsfall, Nicholas 202, 208–9, 217 n.31, 221 n.73, 222 n.86, 223 n.93
Housman, A. E. 4
Hyginus 211, 212
Hypsipyle, Queen of Lemnos, contrasted with Dido 59, 136

Iapygia 146, 208
Iarbas, King of Getulia 102, 128
Icarus 95
Idomeneus, King of Crete 146
Iliad 3, 7, 47, 50, 92, 105, 106, 157, 205
    compared with the *Aeneid* 57, 67, 71, 86–9, 94, 116, 129–30,140, 197
    lectures by Knox on 18, 27 n.14, 190 n.20
    as tragedy 92
    see also 'Homer'
Ilioneus, companion of Aeneas 52, 91, 105

Ilus, King of Ilium 52, 78, 210
imperialism 3–4, 59
impiety 70, 76, 210, 211
Iopas, song of 136, 137, 220 n.66
Isaiah 1, 8–9
Isis, the goddess 207
Italy 1, 91, 108, 133, 141, 142, 147, 153
    Aeneas destined to found a kingdom in 53–9
    towers in 199
Iulus, *see* 'Ascanius'

James, Bruno Scott 229, 230, 231, 235, 236
    Asking for Trouble 230, 237 n.4
    'How to Read Virgil' 235
Janiculum, Hill of Rome 50
Jason 134, 140
    contrasted with Aeneas 140
    contrasted with Pallas 136
    scarf of 136
Jebb, R. C. 20
Jocasta, Queen of Thebes 136
Johnson, Samuel 1
Jones, David 232
Jourdain, Eleanor, *see* 'Moberly, Charlotte'
Julii, Roman patrician family 52
Juno 6, 56, 67, 68, 69, 71, 108
    and death of Turnus 68
Juppiter 53, 54–5, 64, 68–9, 70, 91,100, 137
    Aeneas' appeal to 67
    his anger 71
    and the descendants of Aeneas 56
    priest of 63
    his prophecy 58
    and the rights of Iulus 53
justice 67, 91, 184, 185, 213
Juturna, goddess 68, 89, 133, 135, 137
Juvenal 47

Keats, John 129
Kenworthy-Browne, Christina CJ 241
Kenworthy-Browne, Laurence 22, 241
Kirchhoff, Adolf 152
Knight, W. F. J. 229, 231, 232
    '*Callida Iunctura*: What Is the Virgilian Kind of Poetry?' 235
    '*Patriis Virtutibus* – Virgil's Political Philosophy' 235
Knight, Wilson G. 233

Knox, Dillwyn 20, 190
Knox, Edmund 17, 195
Knox, Edmund Arbuthnott, bishop 235
Knox, Lindsey 17
Knox, Ronald: life
    Anglo-Catholic at Oxford 5, 18, 180, 183, 184, 186, 36
    at Aldenham 20
    Catholic chaplain at Oxford 19
    as a classical scholar 1, 5, 17–18, 180
    as a classics teacher 18–19, 22, 27 n.12
    his conversion to Roman Catholicism 1, 2, 10, 18, 19, 21, 181, 182, 183, 214
    Greek and Latin compositions of 17, 18, 19, 20, 21, 27 n.11, 20 n.21
    lectures on the *Iliad* 18, 27 n.1
    lectures on the *Odyssey* 18, 27 n.14
    lectures on Virgil, *see under* 'Knox, Ronald, lectures on Virgil's *Aeneid*'
    New Testament, professor of the 19
    Romanes lecture 20
    at St Edmund's college 18, 22, 27 n.18
    scholarships won 17–18, 26 n.6 n.7, 189 n.14
    at Summer Fields 17, 20
    as translator 28, 30 n.29
    translator of *Aeneid*, Books VII–IX 6, 18, 22
    translator of *De imitatione Christi* 20
    translator of *Pippa Passes III: Evening: Talk by the Way* 18
    translator of the New Testament 20
    at Trinity College Oxford 5, 18, 23, 40, 180, 181, 182, 195, 236; *see also* 'Trinity College Oxford'
    Virgil's importance for 18, 20–2
Knox, Ronald: lectures on Virgil's *Aeneid*
    composition of the third book 151–8
    delivered at Trinity College 18, 22, 23, 37–8
    editing criteria of 39–41
    Eyres's transcription of 22, 24, 39
    origins and fortunes of 17–36
    pathos and romance in the *Aeneid* 85–96
    political outlook in the *Aeneid* 43–60
    pre-publication history of 22–5

religious outlook in the *Aeneid* 61–84
scenery in the *Aeneid* 113–26
sources of the *Aeneid* 127–50
Virgil's storytelling 97–112
Virgil's versification and style 159–76
Knox, Ronald: other works
   Aeneid, Books VII to IX 22, 190 n.21, 191 n.36, 196, 214 n.7
   A Spiritual Aeneid 11, 21, 26 n.7, 30 n.38, 181, 182, 183, 214, 224
   A Still More Sporting Adventure 21, 30 n.36
   The Belief of Catholics, 29 n.22
   'The Fifth Georgic: a Cento from Virgil' 21
   In Three Tongues 20, 23, 28 n.19, 30 n.32
   Let Dons Delight 7
   The Mystery of the Kingdom 29 n.22
   Publius et Amilla 17
   Remigium alarum 18
   Signa Severa 17
   Studies in the Literature of Sherlock Holmes 195
   'Virgil and the Future Life' 10, 22
   'Virgil and Romance' 22, 31 n.42 n.47
Knox, Wilfred 17

Lade, battle of 145
Laestrygons, giants 132
Landino, Cristoforo 11
Laocoon 8, 48, 108, 203
Lapithae, mythical race 81,130
Latin, valuable features of 159–63
Latinus, King 7, 58, 89, 107, 121, 135, 160, 161, 175
Laurentum 199, 217
Lausus, son of Mezentius 93, 95, 107,103, 131, 148
Lavinia 54, 67, 68, 160
   heroine in the *Aeneid* 4, 65
Lavinium, town 152, 154, 209
Leaf, Sir Walter 130, 149 n.1
Lemnos 136, 144
Leonteus, commander of the Lapiths 130
Lethargy, a supernatural agency 72
Lethe 77, 80, 118, 122, 210, 222 n.85
Levi, son of Jacob 53
Libya 82, 145

limbo 72–5, 81, 210, 211, 222 n.86
   inhabitants of 72–5
   lugentes campi in 75
   see also 'bello clari'
Little John 105
Livia, wife of Caesar Augustus 45
Livingstone, Sir Richard Winn 37
Lowe, J. E. 236, 241–2, 242 n.2
   'The Problem of Dido and Aeneas' 22, 31 n.46
Lucan 47, 166, 175
   Pharsalia 70
Lucca Conference, 55 BC 45
Lucretius 45, 59, 92–3, 138, 173
   contrasted with Virgil 124
   De rerum natura 59
   death of 45
   sanctitas of 61
lugentes campi 74, 206, 210, 211–12, 222 n.86 n.89, 222–3 n.90
   heroine inhabitants of
      Caeneus 212, 223 n.98
      Dido 74, 206, 211, 212
      Eriphyle 211
      Evadne 211, 223 n.93
      Laodamia 211–12
      Pasiphae 212
      Phaedra 211
      Procris 211
      Sychaeus 209
Lunn, Arnold 19
Lupercal, cave on the Palatine Hill 50
Luperci, priests 50
Lycus, son of Dascylus 137
Lynceus, one of the Argonauts 140

Macaulay, Thomas Babington 102
Macbeth 138
Macduff, Lord 138
Maclaren, Gertrude 20
Maclean, Alan D. 24, 25
Macmillan, Harold 24, 25, 33 n.63
Maecenas 45
Mandelstam, Osip 3
magic, white 62, 103
magnus, true meaning of 167–9, 187–8, 204–5
magnus amor in the *Aeneid* 205–6
Maguinness, W. S. 234

Magus, a soldier in Turnus' army 52
Malory, Thomas 129
   Idylls of the King 131
Manes, deities 52, 62, 78
Manlius, guardian of the Tarpeian Citadel 50
Mantegna, Andrea, painter 201
Mantua 45, 117, 176
Marcellus, Marcus Claudius (43–23 BC), nephew of Augustus 45, 94
   death of 94
Marcellus, Marcus Claudius (*c*. 268–208 BC), Roman general 209
Mary, the Blessed Virgin 46
May, James Lewis 231, 236
Medea, contrasted with Dido, *see under* 'Dido'
Melchizedek, the king-priest 53
Meldon, Charles Henry 108, 111 n.4
Mells (Somerset) 24, 242
   archives at 39
Memmii, Roman family 49
Menander, Greek dramatist 136
Menelaus, King of Sparta 77, 146
Menzanas, Messapian deity 208
Mercury, Roman god 55
mercy 67, 184, 185, 213
   see also 'justice'
Meredith, George 102
mereor, keyword in the *Aeneid* 70–1
merits, doctrine of 1, 73, 75–6
   patriots, in relation to 75
   pii vates, in relation to 76
Messapus, King of Etruria 161
Messina, straits of 108
Mezentius, Etruscan King 70, 95, 107, 123, 148, 184, 203
   death of 271 n.38
   and the death of his son Lausus 93
   pathetic address to his horse 171
   villain of the *Aeneid* 65, 107, 184
Michael, the Archangel 72
Milton, John 1, 102, 110
   'Lycidas' 1
   Paradise Lost 102
Mincius, river 129
Minerva
   Castrum Minervae 199, 207
   Pallas Athena 207
   shrine of 115, 199, 207
   see also 'Athena'
Minos, judge in Hades 72–4
Misenus, steersman of Aeneas 64, 105
Mnestheus, hero of the Memmii 49
Moberly, Charlotte Anne, and Eleanor Jourdain
   An Adventure 21
models followed by Virgil 128–47
   Apollonius, of Rhodes 134–8
   Herodotus 144–7
   Homer 128–34
   Latin predecessors 138–9
moon imagery, *see under* 'Dido'
Montarese, Francesco 5, 190 n.21
Monte Antenne, Hill of Rome, 200
morality
   moral duties 70–1, 83, 85, 208
   varying standards of 98
Morwood, J. H. W. 198
Moschi, Iron Age people of Anatolia 147
Mourning fields 75
   see also '*lugentes campi*'
Munro, H. A. J. 20
Murray, Gilbert 19
Musaeus, polymath 135, 207, 120
Mussolini, Benito 1
Mynors, Roger 24, 25, 32 n.59, 33 n.61 n.62

Napoleon Bonaparte 54
Nausicaa, daughter of King Alcinous 132
Neoptolemus, son of Achilles 8, 48, 66, 156, 163
Neptune, god 66
Nestor, King of Pylos 88, 105
Nettleship, Henry 40, 176
Nicolson, Harold 231, 232
Nile 117
Nisus and Euryalus 65, 87, 95, 103–5, 106, 110, 203
   both put in the position of Dolon 86–8, 129
   similar to David and Jonathan 213
   similar to Odysseus and Diomede 129, 130
   see also 'Euryalus'
Norden, Eduard 180–1, 185
North, Thomas 127

Oakley, Thomas 20
obtrectatores Virgiliani 47
Odysseus 87, 89, 92,130, 137, 139, 140, 156, 196
  his adventures 132
  compared with Aeneas 129
  as man of 'sound common sense' 105
Odyssey 19, 77, 129, 132, 139, 156, 196
  as romance 92
  seafaring in 139
  see also 'Homer'
Oebalus, King of Sparta 116, 147
Ogilvie, Robert Maxwell 10
O'Hara, James J. 214 n.2, 208
Olympus 65, 83
oracles 120
  Dido and 69, 211
  sibylline 9
Orestes, son of Agamemnon and Clytemnestra 156, 205
originality, definition of 127
Ornytus, soldier under Aeneas 187, 208
Orpheus, augur and seer 78, 136, 210
Ovid 1, 57, 97,175
  Ars amatoria 98
  Heroides 99, 135
  Metamorphoses 212

Palinurus, helmsman of Aeneas' ship 52, 54, 64, 70, 105
Palladium, small statue of Athena 108
Pallanteum, ancient city near Tiber 50
  Aeneas' visit to 50
  towers of 116
Pallas, son of Evander 52, 67, 92, 130, 138, 175, 207
  death of 52, 93–4, 95, 129–30
  parting of Evander from 136, 137
Pandarus, companion of Aeneas 130, 148
Parry, Adam 187
Pasiphae 74, 212, 218 n.51 n.53, 222 n.89, 223 n.95
  magnus amor of 168, 205
paterfamilias, idea of 210
pathos of Virgil 25, 48, 85, 89, 92–5, 172, 187
  sorrow for Marcellus' death 94–5
Patroclus 87, 92, 94, 129, 130
Paul, Saint 6, 47

shipwreck of 141
visit of, to Virgil's tomb 4, 76
pax et otium 131
penates 50, 65, 66, 151, 169, 203, 210
Penelope 98
Penthesilea, Amazonian queen 135
Perkell, Christine 197
Persia 144, 145
Persians 147, 202, 205
Petrarch 186
  Africa 47
Phenicians 142
Phineus 137
Phlegethon 117, 118
Phocaeans 142, 143, 144, 202, 203
piacula 63, 82, 184, 207, 213
pietas 10, 61–2, 65, 76, 100, 185, 206, 241
  leitmotif of the *Aeneid* 61–2, 183, 208
  'pity', derived from *pietas* 67
  true significance of 65–7, 70–1, 82–3, 184
  see also 'eschatology of Virgil'
pius 61–2, 63, 183–4
  Aeneas as 63–4, 184, 191 n.36, 207
  ethical connotations of 65
  meaning loyal 64
  religious meaning of 63
  translation of 61
Plato 26, 102, 114
  doctrine of transmigration of souls 77–8, 81, 82, 183–4
  Virgil's debt to 77, 81, 83
plot of the *Aeneid*
  plausibility of 108–9
  and scenery 119
  Virgil's treatment of 55, 97–111
Plutarch 53, 63, 127
Plymouth 142
Pocetti, Paolo 207
Polites, a prince of Troy 66, 95
Pollio, Caius Asinius 45
Pollux 136
Polydeuces (Pollux) 86, 87, 140
Polydorus, son of Priam 66, 95, 157
Polymestor, King of Thrace 95
Polypoetes, a Lapith 130
Pompeius, Sextus 143
Pompey 45
Pope, Alexander 4

Potter, Franklin H. 196, 215 n.12
Prayer-book, the 77, 160
Pre-Raphaelites (Italian) 115, 118, 200
Priam 8, 48, 66, 95, 141, 163
Propertius 3, 47
prophecies 49
   of Anchises 50
   of Apollo 49–50
   of the *penates* 50
   of Vulcan 50
Prospero 4, 59
Protesilaos, husband of Laodamia 211
providence 64
purgatory
   Catholic doctrine of 10–11
   inhabitants of 77
   and the interpretation of *Aeneid* VI.739-744 78–9, 82
   and Platonic transmigration of souls 78, 81, 82, 83
   purification in 78–9, 81, 82, 210, 212, 213
   shortness of Anchises' stay in 80–1
   Virgil's modification of Plato's account of metempsychosis 77, 78
Pyrrhus (Neoptolemus), son of Achilles 205

Raphael Sanzio 133
reception of Virgil 6, 7, 25, 46
   and his memorable lines 8, 48
   Ronald Knox and 4–5
Regan, character in *King Lear* 92
reincarnation 77–8, 80, 81, 210
   Anchises' reincarnation partially explained 79
   granted exceptionally 81, 184
   merited by patriots 206
religion 21, 160
   Christian ritual 63
   primitive Roman ritual and taboos 62–3
   and rituals in the *Aeneid* 206–7, 208
   see also under 'Virgil'
res in the plural, Virgil fondness for 56–7
Rhadamantys, judge in the underworld 209, 210
Rhaebus, Mezentius' address to 93, 171
Rhesus, Thracian King 87, 130

rhetoric in the *Aeneid* 160–7
   amplifications 163–5
   rhetorical nature of disputes between characters 160
   stock phrases 166–7
   terse expressions 160, 166–7
Rieu, Émile Victor 234
righteousness, in the *Aeneid* 71, 75
   of the gods 67
   Virgil prophet of 76
Ripheus, Trojan hero 91, 106
Romance, *see also under* 'Euripides'; 'Knox Ronald'; '*Odyssey*' and 'Virgil'
Rome
   birthplace of ceremonial 63
   future greatness of 49, 68
   history of, present in Virgil's mind 49
   primitive religion of 62–3
   representative of civilization 57–9
   walls of 90
Romulus 49, 80
   and Remus 50
Rossetti, Dante Gabriel 6
Rudd, Nial 4
Rutulians 53, 57, 62, 65, 70, 87, 93, 129, 136, 171, 203
   slaughter of 87, 129
Rutulian War, strategy of 148, 149

sacrifices 63
   offered by Aeneas 65–6, 20
   offered by Dido 203–4
   in Homer 67
St Edmund's College 12, 18, 19, 22
   The Edmundian 18, 19, 27 n.18
Salii, priests 50
Salisbury Cathedral 115
Salius, companion of Aeneas 103–4
Salmoneus, son of Aeolus 81
Samians, people of Samos 142, 145
Sarpedon, son of Poseidon, hero in Trojan war 94
Savonarola, Girolamo, Virgil's influence on 47
Saxo Grammaticus 128
scaena, Virgil's use of the word 118
Scaliger, Joseph 4
Scamander, river god 116

scenery in the *Aeneid*
　artificiality of 113, 115
　natural and artificial 113
　pictorial descriptions of 118
　rivers in 116–18
　towers in 113–16
　woods in 119–23
　vignettes 119
　Virgil's love of 113–26
sculpture, the forte of the Greeks 119
Scylla and Charybdis 108
seafaring
　preference of Greek seamen for coastal sailing 142
　realistic description of, in the *Aeneid* 140–7, 139–40
　unrealistic description of, in the *Odyssey* and *Argonautica* 139–40
　Virgil's lack of interest in 131
Selene 207
Sellar, William Young 61, 63 n.1, 180
Sergestus, Trojan friend of Aeneas 49, 106
Sergii, Roman patrician family 49
Setaioli, Aldo 222 n.86
Severn, river 118
Sextus Pompeius 143
Shakespeare 3, 92, 127
　King Lear 92, 138
　Hamlet 128
　The Merchant of Venice 92
　The Tempest 4, 59, 92
　The Winter's Tale 92
Shaw, Bernard 101
shield of Aeneas 51, 70, 133, 136, 147, 197, 215 n.9
　description of 50
Shiletto, Richard 20
Shrewsbury 18
　The Salopian 18, 19, 28 n.19
Sibyl, the 1, 168, 172, 205, 207, 209, 213
　and Aeneas 57, 76, 82, 88, 121, 152, 155
　and Turnus 82, 88
Sicily 67, 109, 142, 144, 145, 157, 194
　Cape Pachynus 108
　Eryx 109, 144, 168
Sidgwick, Arthur 59 n.3, 179, 188 n.3
　the pomposity of his notes 48
Silius Italicus 47, 97

Silvia 107
similes in the *Aeneid* 132–4
　unoriginality of Virgil's 133–4
sin
　mortal 10, 77, 82, 183, 185, 213
　venial 10, 77, 183, 213
Sinclair, John D. 8
Sinon, duplicity of 108
si quis, Virgil's fondness for 171
Sirius 157
Solmsen, Friedrich 208, 221 n.74
sooth-sayers in Dido's sacrifices 69
Sophocles 102
　Philoctetes 102
sortes Biblicae 47
sortes Virgilianae 7, 47, 182
sources of the *Aeneid*
　Homer 128–34
　legends 127, 137
　sack of Troy 128, 156, 163
　Varro 128
Southan, J. E. 233
sow, white 152, 154
Sparta 203, 204
Speaight, Robert 22, 23, 25, 31 n.45, 231, 235, 236
　A Modern Virgilian 236
Spectator, The 8, 48
Spenser, Edmund 129
Statius 8, 47, 97, 175
Stonyhurst 27 n.14, 39
Strophades 141
style of Virgil
　deferred participle 172–3
　epigrams 166
　epithet, proper place of 172, 174
　fondness for certain words 168–72
　frequency of elisions 175–6
　half-lines 165
　oratorical nature of 166
　monosyllable placed after caesura 174
　repetitions 138–9
　rhetoric, *see* 'rhetoric in the *Aeneid*'
　word order 173–4
　see also 'versification'
Styx, river 11, 70, 209
Sulla, Roman general and statesman 54
Summer Fields School 17

Sychaeus, *see under* 'Dido'
Syrtes, shallows on Lybian coast 108, 132

tables, eating of 51, 151, 152
Tablet, The 10, 20, 22, 233, 242
taboos, *see under* 'religion'
Tacitus 37, 47, 160, 166, 173
   gravitas of 61
talis, Virgil's fondness for the word 169–70
Tanith, Carthaginian goddess 207
   associated with image of crescent moon 220 n.69
Tarchon, King of the Tyrrhenians 120
Tartarus 1, 48, 82, 83
   depiction of 114, 117, 185
Tennyson, Alfred 92, 131
   In Memoriam 93
Tertullian 8, 186, 222 n.86
Teucer, Greek hero 105, 144, 145
'The Problem of Dido and Aeneas', *see under* 'Virgil Society'
Theocritus 103, 119, 135
Thera, town, and its inhabitants 145
Thersites, character in the *Iliad* compared to Drances 89
Theseus 184, 208–9, 211, 221 n.75
Thetis 135, 137
'Thomason' 197
Thucydides 148, 202
Tiber 50, 116, 117, 130, 152, 155
Tisiphone, one of the furies 121, 209
Tolumnius, soothsayer 161
Tomi, on the Black Sea 57
'Tomlinsons' 72, 83 n.6
Torrey, Reuben Archer, poor phraseology of 63, 83 n.4
towers, *see under* '*Aeneid*'; 'Italy'; 'Pallanteum' and 'scenery'
tradition
   classical 5, 19
   epic 146, 202
   religious 207
   romantic 99–100
   western 5, 8
transmigration of souls, *see under* 'Plato'
Trinity College Oxford 18, 22, 37, 39, 180, 182, 186, 236
   archives of 37, 40

Gryphon Club at 23, 196
   Knox as chaplain at 5
Triton, Neptune's son 137
Trojans
   a chosen people 67
   as exiles 89, 140
   as homesick exiles 90–1
   intermarriage of, with Latins 109
Troy 21
   burning of the Trojan fleet 51
   lost cause of 89–90
   troiana fortuna 57
   walls of 90
Tucca, Plotius 46, 176
Tullus Hostilius, third King of Rome 50
Turnus
   contrasted with Aeneas 4
   counterpart of Achilles 88
   egoism of 89
   haughtiness of 89
turritus, meaning of 115–16, 198–9, 202
Tyrrhus, shepherd 107, 110

Ufens, river 117
Ukraine, war in 11–12
Ulysses 58, 127, 132, 137, 156
   prototype of *Aeneas* 98
Umbro, warrior priest 117
unus, meaning of 164, 186
   Virgil's fondness for the word 169–70
Utica 70

Valerius Flaccus, 47
Van Eyck, Hubert 1
Van Eyck, Jan 1
Varius Rufus, Lucius 46, 176
Varro, Marcus Terentius 128
Venus 53, 66, 69, 91, 134, 211
   counterpart of Thetis 135
   love for her son 205, 218 n.51, 219 n.56, 220 n.66
   virgo spartana 204
   her visit of, to Aeneas 64, 66
   see also 'Aphrodite'
Vercingetorix, Gallic King 148
versification, peculiarities of Virgil's
   elisions 175–6
   hexameter 6, 47, 49, 174–5
Vergilian Society of America 230, 232

Verres Gaius, magistrate 45
Virgil
   Aeneid, see 'Aeneid'
   Eclogues 1, 45, 98, 124, 175, 218 n.56
      fourth *Eclogue* 8, 9
   Georgics 1, 13n.1, 45, 113, 117, 123, 124
   his accurate prophecies, *see* 'prophecies'
   adapting Homer's account of Odysseus' wanderings 129–30; *see also* 'Homer'
   adapting Homer's battle scenes in the *Iliad* 130–4; *see also* '*Iliad*'
   an *anima naturaliter Christiana* 8, 21
   his appreciation of scenery 113–26; *see also* 'scenery in the *Aeneid*'
   appropriations of 3, 7–8, 47, 182
   his art, *see* 'art of Virgil'
   artistry of 76
   his attitude towards destiny 67, 68; *see also* 'destiny'
   his attitude towards future life, *see* 'eschatology of Virgil'
   his attitude towards Providence 68, 69
   Catholic intimations in 10, 213
   Christian sentiments of 1, 9, 10, 82, 86, 212–14
   as 'the classic of all Europe' 2
   his coining of phrases 166–7
   his conception of *pietas* 10
   compared with earlier Latin poets 74, 83, 128, 129, 132, 138–9
   his debt to Homer 129–34
   his description of armour 146–7
   as the first romantic poet 85
   fond of dramatic episodes 102, 109–10
   his fondness for certain words, 56–7, 167–72
   inconsistency of 153, 155
   his influence on later literature 46–8
   his interest in landscape 6, 113–25
   imperialism or jingoism of 3, 59
   impressionist descriptions by 6, 105–6, 125, 198
   'humanitarianism' of 131
   life of 45–6
   his models in the *Aeneid*, *see* 'models followed by Virgil'
   morality of, *see* 'morality'
   his personification of rivers 116–17; *see also* 'scenery in the *Aeneid*'
   pessimism of 8
   poetic genius of 7
   political outlook of 49–60
   as a *praeparatio evangelica* tradition 10
   his premature death 47
   pseudo-Virgilian poems 45
   pure-mindedness of 98
   reasons for reading 2
   reception of, *see* 'reception of Virgil'
   religious outlook of 61–84
   rhetorical prowess of 45, 47; *see also* 'rhetoric in the *Aeneid*'
   romance and pathos of 85–95; *see also* 'pathos of Virgil'
   his skill in creating characters 105
   his skill in devising plots 109–10
   spelling the name of 5, 48, 232–3
   his style and versification 159–78; *see also* 'style of Virgil'
   uniqueness of his writing 6
   untranslatability of 6, 48
   his use of his sources 127–50; *see also* 'sources of the *Aeneid*'
   his use of parenthesis 79–80
   his views on purgatory 10–11, 76–8
   and western civilization 2
   and women 135
   word order observed by, *see under* 'style of Virgil'
Virgil Society 22, 25, 230–7
   Catholic ethos of 234
   development of 229–34
   lecture by Knox to 22, 235–6
   mission of 236–7
   'The Problem of Dido and Aeneas', a lecture delivered to 22, 241–2
Volscens, leader in the Rutulian army 206
Voltaire 47
Vulcan 50, 51, 66, 117

Waddell, Helen 11–12
Walsingham, Shrine at 230, 231
Wansbrough, Henry, OSB 24, 25
War, as a supernatural agency 72
Waugh Evelyn 17, 20, 22, 23, 180, 190 n.19
   death of 24, 31 n.45

    and the Knox-Eyres correspondence, 20, 31 n.45
    views on Knox's Virgil lectures 25
    views on Knox's *In Three Tongues* 20
weakness, triumph of 87–8
Wells, H. B. 232
West, Neville 231
William the Conqueror 52
Woodruff, John Douglas 231, 232, 233, 235

woods 62, 118, 119–23
    magic of 120
    mystery of 119–22
Woollen, Wilfrid 30 n.41, 214 n.1, 234, 236
Wordsworth, William 113, 138

Xenophon 148
Xerxes, the Great (486 to 465 BC) 147

Zancle (Messina) 145

www.ingramcontent.com/pod-product-compliance
Lightning Source LLC
Chambersburg PA
CBHW071815300426
44116CB00009B/1326